FAMOUS NATHAN

FAMOUS NATHAN

A Family Saga of Coney Island,

the American Dream,

and the Search

for the Perfect Hot Dog

Lloyd Handwerker
and Gil Reavill

FLATIRON
BOOKS
NEW YORK

FAMOUS NATHAN. Copyright © 2016 by Lloyd Handwerker
and Gil Reavill. All rights reserved. Printed in the United
States of America. For information, address Flatiron Books,
175 Fifth Avenue, New York, N.Y. 10010.

All photographs courtesy of Lloyd Handwerker

www.flatironbooks.com

The Library of Congress Cataloging-in-Publication Data is
available upon request.

ISBN 978-1-250-07454-6 (hardcover)
ISBN 978-1-250-07456-0 (e-book)

Our books may be purchased in bulk for promotional,
educational, or business use. Please contact your local
bookseller or the Macmillan Corporate and Premium Sales
Department at (800) 221-7945, extension 5442, or by e-mail
at MacmillanSpecialMarkets@macmillan.com.

First Edition: June 2016

10   9   8   7   6   5   4   3   2   1

To my grandparents, Nathan and Ida
And to the workers

"I don't know how it came to me,
so much common sense."
—Nathan Handwerker

Contents

FAMOUS NATHAN

Prologue

Three, Two, One—Go!

"Give 'em and let 'em eat!" Nathan
Handwerker of Nathan's Famous.

JULY 4TH, 2015, a Saturday. The corner of Surf and Stillwell Avenues, Coney Island, Brooklyn. The world famous Nathan's Famous International Hot Dog–Eating Contest is about to begin.

The Barnum-like voice of George Shea, the event's straw-hatted announcer, booms over the public address system as he paces across the stage. "In the name of all that is holy, I have never seen a better crowd! Ladies and gentlemen, it's the Fourth of July!"

Salt air mixes with the scent of fried food. Hoarse shouts and the screams of seagulls melt into the beat from competing loudspeakers. The Bunnettes, the contest's cheerfully amateur dancers, warm up the crowd with random shakes and shimmies. Near me a twenty-something kid holds up a placard that reads, "Nathan Handwerker is my homeboy." I ask him if he knows who Nathan Handwerker is.

"You mean he's a real person?" he asks.

I wonder how many contest-goers know the story of how Nathan's Famous began, who founded the place, and the family saga behind it, the Jewish immigrant who arrived almost penniless in America, only to go on to establish the iconic hot dog stand that lends its name to today's internationally celebrated event.

"Are you ready?" bellows Shea. "It's go time! Count it down with me! Ten, nine, eight . . ."

On the stage with him are the reigning champion, Joey Chestnut, and his closest competitor, Matt Stonie. Spectators in the tens of thousands cram Coney's streets and beaches. Everyone pushes toward Nathan's Famous. Audience members hoist oversize photographic cutouts of their favorite competitors. Hot dog outfits and Uncle Sam regalia are everywhere.

Every July 4, this small patch of Brooklyn becomes the center of the media universe. As it has every year since 2004, ESPN is broadcasting the contest live. The event pulls in higher ratings than the Major League Baseball games broadcast that day. The millions watching on TV dwarf the number of people in the streets. Yet it seems everyone in the world is here, jostling and pushing.

"Seven, six . . ."

The event has grown enormously in the past few decades, from a folding table set up in an alleyway to . . . this. Whatever this is.

A sporting event? It has to be, since ESPN is here. A spectacle? The incredible number of people present indicates it is so. A joke?

No one seems to take the whole business quite seriously. The end of the world? So say a few old-timers and wet blanket cultural critics.

"Five, four . . ."

The crowd surges forward, eager. The eaters—insiders know to call them "gurgitators"—poise over their piles of hot dogs, ready to wolf them down.

The audience members scream the countdown along with George Shea.

"Three, two, one—go!"

Cheers erupt as the contestants begin their frantic gulping and gorging.

It all makes for slightly surreal entertainment. I think how fast food was pretty much invented here on the corner of Surf and Seaside Walk, with Nathan Handwerker being one of its most visible pioneers. On a summer weekend, in an era when McDonald's wasn't even a gleam in Ray Kroc's eye, Nathan's restaurant sold as many as seventy-five thousand hot dogs. The owner urged on his employees with a constant refrain: "Give 'em and let 'em eat!"

Sammy Fariello, the longtime star counterman at Nathan's Famous, could serve sixty frankfurters in toasted buns in sixty seconds. In 1981, on the occasion of the sixty-fifth anniversary of its founding, Nathan's Famous celebrated the sale (to a Brooklyn cop) of its 565 millionth hot dog.

It wasn't called "fast food" back when Nathan started his Coney Island restaurant in 1916. The phrase wouldn't become popular until the 1950s. In Brooklyn slang, Nathan's Famous was termed a "grab joint," where you could get fed quickly and cheaply. The speed of service is echoed, or perhaps parodied, in the international hot dog–eating contest.

With the crowd packing in tighter by the minute, I can barely glimpse the stage. The Bunnettes hold up scorecards behind each competitor, like ring girls at a big fight. Three minutes into the ten-minute contest, the two leading eaters are neck and neck, having each just swallowed their nineteenth dog.

Nathan Handwerker was my grandfather. He founded Nathan's Famous in 1916. With his wife, my grandmother Ida, he worked hard to build it into one of the most popular restaurants in the world. During the heyday of the early 1950s, the business grossed $3 million annually. In the sixties, Jackie Kennedy ate in the restaurant's tiny dining room. Both Barbra Streisand and Frank Sinatra ordered Nathan's Famous frankfurters flown over when they were performing in London. But the place was never about celebrities. It was democratic through and through.

When I was a child, I would visit my grandfather at the original Coney Island restaurant. I remember following him through the busy back kitchens, feeling self-conscious that the workers were pointing me out as the grandson of the founder. Back then, I had only a general idea that the place was cherished by a lot of New Yorkers and visited by people from all over America and the world.

As I got older, I became more curious. I was eager to know the full story of Nathan and Ida. I also wanted to explore the lives of my father and uncle, Sol and Murray Handwerker, who had worked with Nathan but experienced a bitter sibling rivalry and eventually had a falling out.

Beyond my grandfather's rags-to-riches story, and behind the family disagreements, I knew there was something else worth exploring, something harder to pin down. A mythology surrounded Nathan's Famous. Whenever I would mention the place, people would speak of it with reverence. It seemed to connect them to their childhoods, to summer days on the beach, to a time long past but caught in memory.

"We used to . . ."

"I went with my parents . . ."

"Every summer weekend, we'd visit . . ."

So the stories always started, and they'd spill out with wistful enthusiasm.

"I loved those crinkle-cut potatoes . . ."

"I can still taste . . ."

It became clear to me early on that the story of my family involved something great, a tale of America itself. I studied photography and filmmaking in school, and began speaking with dozens of family members, former employees, patrons, friends, and business associates of my grandparents. I logged over three hundred hours of interviews. I then wove it all together in a documentary and now this book, all in an effort to paint a portrait of my grandfather's legacy.

The complete story has never really been told. A collection of widely circulated legends has developed around Nathan's Famous, most of them the work of various public relations executives as Nathan's business grew and grew. The nostalgia with which people approach Coney Island, their childhoods, the taste of Nathan's hot dogs, make them wish all the tall tales were true.

The Nathan's Famous International Hot Dog–Eating Contest? Organizers called the 2015 event the "99th Annual," but that claim stretches the truth. Sure, there have been plenty of Coney Island eating contests on and off over the years, some of them connected to Nathan's Famous. But the modern version of the event dates only from the early seventies. Though "The Store," as everyone who worked for Nathan called it, started in 1916, the contest is of a fairly recent vintage.

Far be it from me to burst any bubbles. The true story, the bedrock-real tale of Nathan and the fantastic arc of his life, doesn't need any press agent embellishing.

My grandfather died in 1974, when he was eighty-one and I was seventeen, before I could fully know him as an adult. Luckily, my cousin David taped an interview he conducted with my grandfather in 1973. It represents the only testimony we have of Nathan telling his own story. His words, some of which I quote in the following pages, enable us to better understand the man that he was, especially his beginnings in the Jewish shtetlach of eastern Europe and the Lower East Side of New York City.

"There's one Babe Ruth in baseball, there's one Einstein in science, there was one Nathan in the food business," said Al Shalik, one of my grandfather's longtime employees.

His workers were paid well and enjoyed yearly bonuses. Many remained on the job for decades, over fifty years in more than one case. My grandfather wanted his crew to feel as if they were part of a family. There are small details that indicate a close-knit relationship, such as Nathan's practice of pulling an employee's apron string loose when it was time to go home.

By the last pages of this book, I hope you'll have a better grasp of the truth behind the legendary Nathan's Famous. You'll better understand a man—Nathan Handwerker; a restaurant—Nathan's Famous; a place—Coney Island; and an era—the boom years of the last century. You might even find yourself hungry for a hot dog.

The story begins, as a lot of classic American stories do, four thousand miles away, in Europe.

1

Narol

"My father couldn't make a living. We didn't have a lot to eat." Main village street, Narol, Habsburg Galicia, ca. 1900.

IT WAS IN Galicia, Austria-occupied Poland, on June 14, 1892, that Nathan Handwerker had the misfortune to be born.

During the nineteenth century, Poland staggered under bullying assaults from the more powerful nations that surrounded it. The Three Powers—Russia, Germany, and Austria—sliced and diced the country with repeated partitions. The nation of Poland essentially ceased to exist as a sovereign entity.

The Austrian-annexed section of the former Polish-Lithuanian Commonwealth encompassed a hilly, hardscrabble region called

Galicia. The area was so impoverished that "Galician misery" (*bieda galicyjska*) became a proverbial term. Historian Norman Davies nominated nineteenth-century Galicia as "the poorest province in Europe," its population in more desperate straits than that of Ireland at the start of the Great Famine.

Yaakov Handwerker and Reizel Gewissenheit—or Jacob, born in 1852, and Rose, born in 1869—married in 1883, when the bride was just fourteen. Their third-oldest son, Nathan (in Yiddish, Nachum), would eventually take his place among thirteen siblings. The Handwerker name means "craftsman" or "artisan," a catch-all label that included Jacob's chosen profession of shoemaking.

Nathan's first name, family tradition has it, came from a good deed, a mitzvah, once performed by Jacob and Rose when they nursed an invalid named Nachum. His niece later suggested that this act of charity bestowed good luck on Nathan, leading to his success.

Jacob was slightly built, heavily bearded, and religiously observant. There were merchants in the family background. Jacob's uncle bought horses and shipped them to Russia, returning with tobacco for Austria. That was all in the past. No one had the money for horse-trading anymore. Jacob's shoemaking never yielded enough to support the family and for long periods provided nothing at all in the way of wages. Rose took care of the children and house, as well as bringing in a little money selling fruits and vegetables.

Their son Nathan came into the world in the Galician village of Narol, a shtetl of around five hundred people. When he was a week old, his mother brought him to join Jacob, who worked in the larger town of Jarosław. They remained there for three years before moving back to Narol.

Village or town, the family failed to thrive and in fact participated in its share of Galician misery. They were *Ostjuden*, eastern European Jews, and what one of the fathers of Yiddish literature, Mendele Moykher Sforim, called "*kaptsonim*," defined as "Jews without a cent to their name."

"My father couldn't make a living, so he had to go begging from town to town," Nathan said. "One time, in the wintertime, it was about forty below zero, and he came back to us for a couple of days. He never sent any money from the road, or very little, very little. We didn't have a lot to eat."

At the age of six, Nathan apprenticed to his father as a shoemaker. "They put me on the bench to teach me to make the shoes, sweep the floors, take apart old shoes, what's good to use, what's not good to use."

The family possessed a sewing machine, but young Nathan was not allowed to use it. "We paid a dollar a year, to pay it off. My older brother was learning to sew on the machine, and my father was learning too. My father learned to cut forms in any size he wanted. He took measures to make a pair of shoes. I never wanted to learn these things."

Jacob could read Hebrew texts but had no knowledge of math. Rose was illiterate. Apart from minimal training in Hebrew from ages three to six, Nathan would have no formal schooling at all. Poverty and family circumstances robbed the boy of the literacy that was increasingly a birthright for the European middle class.

The Handwerkers dwelled in a series of shtetlach, predominantly Jewish communities attached to larger, more ethnically mixed towns. Both Narol and Jarosław are now in southeastern Poland, near Ukraine, but in the pre-WWI period, they were located within the borders of the Habsburg Empire of Austria-Hungary.

Shtetl living meant that Jews were set apart from and victimized by the Austrians, Germans, Hungarians, Czechs, Slovaks, Ruthenians, Russians, Roma, and Ukrainians who surrounded them. Galicia was also referred to as "Habsburg Poland," and it had a brutal pecking order. Austrians oppressed the Poles. The Poles ganged up on the Ukrainians. Everyone dumped on the Jews.

"The shadow of the Holocaust is long," writes author and shtetl historian Eva Hoffman, "and it extends backward as well as forward." The persecution of Jews during the pre-WWI period, in other words, gave way to the later systematic Nazi campaigns of murder, eradication, and obliteration, the genocide that effectively erased all trace of eastern European shtetlach.

Devoted religious practice represented a common refuge from the rampant discrimination of the culture. The Jews of the "Vistula provinces," between the Vistula River and the Bug, were known to be especially conservative. The Hasidic movement was born in Galicia and Western Ukraine. Jewish society in the area considered Torah-based study to be an honorable lifelong occupation and a paramount reason for any community to exist. Religious scholarship was a value shared by both "black-hat" and "hatless" Jews.

Jacob Handwerker was not alone, penniless and out on the road. There were plenty of others. In many quarters, poverty could be seen as an aspect of piety, especially if it was paired with rigorous application to the manifold mysteries of the Torah.

The Handwerker family always struggled with the bitter effort of wringing a few pennies out of an impoverished land. The most searing memory from Nathan's childhood was one of hunger.

"Once I looked to see a sugar cube sitting on a shelf. Everybody had forgotten about it. It was so covered in coal soot that it looked black. I quick put it into my mouth, anyway, so no one else should eat it," Nathan remembered vividly.

There was hunger and bone-chilling cold. When Nathan was ten, he took a journey with his father and second-oldest brother, Joseph. From Narol, they traveled to nearby Cieszanów and then onward to Jarosław. With produce piled high for the thirty-mile trip to the larger market town, Jacob allowed Nathan to ride in the wagon while he and Joseph walked beside. The temperature fell to below zero.

"They were afraid I should freeze," Nathan said, employing his usual Yiddish-inflected phrasing. "Every few minutes, my father came up to see if I'm not freezing."

Despite or perhaps because of the deadly cold, Nathan fell asleep while perched on the wagon. Jacob roused him and made him walk too. On winter journeys such as this one, the choices were simple. Walk or freeze, stay awake or die.

In the months after that trip, Nathan begged that he be allowed to accompany Jacob on his forays into the world beyond Narol in search of work.

"Take me along," eleven-year-old Nathan pleaded with his father. "I'll be able to get a job."

Jacob took Nathan to Radymno, a town of five thousand souls located just south of Jarosław. Father and son slept that night on benches in the local synagogue. For pillows, they used their boots, footwear that Jacob had made.

"When people came early in the morning to the synagogue, I had to get up," Nathan recalled. "So I said my morning prayers, and then we went around the town to give us to eat. We begged for money to eat. Nobody refused me."

Visiting a Radymno bakery, Jacob made inquiries to the wife of the baker. "Do you have a job for my boy?"

She did indeed have employment for Nathan, his first job

outside the family. The woman loaded up a huge basket with loaves of challah, potato knishes, and kasha knishes, sending him out into the street to sell the goods. The young salesperson had soon hawked his whole inventory to passing townspeople.

When Jacob left for Jarosław, the baker asked Nathan to stay on as a permanent employee. They gave the boy a pallet to sleep on in the kitchen. Every morning, he set forth with a towering basket of baked goods. "*Knischala!*" he called. "*Heys knischala!*" Knishes, hot knishes! For each delivery, he earned an Austrian nickel, the smallest denomination of coin, the culture's equivalent of a penny.

After a week, Nathan turned lonely. He left the bakery without a word of explanation and headed on foot back to Narol. On the road, he had the good luck to run into Max, his best friend from his home village. The two of them frequently played together, ice-skating in the wintertime, heading into the woods, rolling down the hills, picking berries in the summertime.

"Max!" Nathan cried out. "Where were you?"

"I was in Radymno," the boy replied, explaining that he stayed there while he worked on a dairy farm near Jarosław.

"You were in Radymno? I was in Radymno the whole week! If I knew you were there, I would have had someone to talk to, and I wouldn't have left."

The two returned together, Nathan retracing his steps to the town he had just quit. Too ashamed to return to the original bakery, he found a job in another one. "I knew already in the bakery I had a lot to eat," Nathan recalled. Starvation serves as excellent motivation. At age eleven, the future restaurateur probably didn't realize he had stumbled on his path in life.

The new baker had a mother-in-law who was startled at the young hire's appetite. Nathan overheard her talking about him. "The boy is eating up all our bread!" The baker's wife soothed her mother's fears. "Don't worry, he's just a poor boy who's hungry. He'll stop eating soon."

He would stay in Radymno for two years. Bakers keep odd hours, and Nathan went to sleep on a cot in the bakery's kitchen every night at seven in the evening. At midnight, the baker would shake him awake for work.

"The baker gave me a big sifter, about two feet in diameter," Nathan recalled. "He used to put the flour in the shuffle, and I used to mix it. He mixed it up, too, because I had little hands, and I couldn't make such a big batch."

Nathan cut the risen dough into pieces. The baker shaped it and weighed each loaf. His young helper laid out the loaves in three or four lines on a long wooden table for a second rising. "When the dough started to raise up, the baker had the stove heated to put the bread in. He sat in a big chair so he could put his feet up. I had to hand over the loaves, a ten-pound basket at a time, and put the dough on the shovel, the wooden shovel. He shoved them in the oven."

It was an exhausting, repetitive business, and it lasted through the night. Nathan recalled sessions of sleepwalking during his back-and-forth trips with the dough and receiving a rude awakening. "By the time I took the basket, and I came back to the oven, from the table to the oven, I fell asleep. I touched the oven, it's hot, I woke up!"

After baking all night, the mornings were spent in delivery. "We had to put the bread in big ten-pound baskets, twenty or thirty baskets at a time. We had a long wagon that had one wheel in the front and two handles in the back. The handles had a strap to help you push. I pulled the strap on my shoulders, and the baker loaded up the wagon."

Nathan delivered to a baked-goods store located in the railway station in the middle of town. "It was a big walk," he recalled. He was too small to push the wagon up one of the hills. He had to unload, transfer the bread into a basket, and balance the basket on top of his head. Mid-hill, his strength would give out.

"I had small hands, I was eleven years old, I was tired. I remember there was a fence on one side of the road that was about the same height with me. I had to put the basket down to rest a little. I propped it on the fence and held it so it wouldn't turn over."

On the other side of the fence was an encampment of soldiers. He spent a long moment watching them, assessing the muddy misery of army life. The sight impressed itself upon his young mind. Then he struggled to heft the huge basket of bread.

"I put my head under it again and went on."

After two years toiling at the bakery in Radymno, separated from his family in Narol, the now-thirteen-year-old Handwerker son prepared for a visit home. He had just started his bar mitzvah lessons at the local synagogue. The bakery closed for Passover, since the business was not allowed to bake bread during the holy days.

"I'm going home for vacation," the young baker's assistant announced to his employers. But he did not want to return to Narol empty-handed. During his two years of work, he put aside his pay groschen by groschen, penny by penny. At the end of that time, he had amassed twelve Austrian-Hungarian kronen, a little over two U.S. dollars at contemporary exchange rates.

"I took the money that I saved, and I run to the butcher shop in Radymno. I showed them how much money I got. I say, 'I'm going home to Narol. There's not much good meat to eat there.'"

The farmers of Radymno had the reputation of raising the

finest beef cattle in Galicia "They fed their cows with cooked food, nothing raw," Nathan explained. "And that was the best meat in the whole country." The beef was, of course, slaughtered in accordance with Jewish dietary strictures.

Young Nathan asked what he could get for the money he had saved. The butcher put the precious Radymno beef in wrapping paper, and the prodigal son headed home to Narol. To travel quickly, in order that the meat wouldn't spoil, he rode rather than walked. "I paid, like a taxi driver, but instead of taxi, a horse and wagon," he recalled.

Rose Handwerker, Nathan's mother, kept a strict kosher home. "Everything was already kosher, kosher made. They used to heat up bricks, make them hot, burning hot, and with pliers, you take them and the table should be made kosher by that." When Nathan arrived into the bosom of family with his package of kosher meat, he knew that he could place his prize on the household table with perfect assurance.

"So I see the table is clean, so I take the sack, take it up, and take it out and put it on the table, and say to my mother, 'Now you give the children to eat, here.'" Rose was overjoyed to see him, and Nathan's little brothers and sisters were happy to see the miracle of beef appearing before them.

Beyond the heartwarming homecoming, there is a hint here of the future of Nathan Handwerker. Even as a thirteen-year-old boy, he was aware of the importance of quality. He didn't go to any butcher; he went to what he knew was the best butcher in town. He didn't bring his family run-of-the-mill meat; he brought them Radymno beef. The boy in the story would grow up to be a man who was fanatical about ensuring the quality of everything he sold.

There is other prescient evidence, other inklings that fate was shadowing Nathan's path forward. Poland was (and still is) the land of the sausage. The Handwerkers were too poor to include a lot of meat in their diet, and much of the local product was pork based and thus *trayf*. Though the family cupboard might have been a bit bare, nevertheless, the area in which the Handwerkers lived had rich and varied culinary traditions. The ethnic food-ways were intermingled to the degree that even today, dietary historians can't be certain whether classic chicken soup originated as a Jewish dish or a Polish one.

Kraków spread its influence throughout the region and, eventually, throughout the world. A famous dish associated with the city, duck cooked with mushrooms and buckwheat groats, would have been beyond the family budget of a poor shtetl shoemaker. But during his time at the Radymno bakery, Nathan must have turned out baked items also closely linked to Kraków, including jam-filled rolls called *buchts* and a yeasted wheat creation very similar to a bagel but referred to in the area as a "pretzel." In fact, Kraków and thus Galicia has been commonly credited with the origin of the bagel, known originally as the *bajgiel* and traditionally given to women during childbirth.

And sausage? "The intestine is endless" went the old Polish saying, and Poles used pig, sheep, and cow intestines as casings for a dizzying number of kielbasas and wursts, stuffed with smoked, cured, chopped, fermented, minced, or ground meats from all manner of animal and plant product, spiced with all manner of ingredients, including salt, garlic, pepper, milk, caraway, nutmeg, coriander, allspice, marjoram, cumin, juniper, sugar, lemon, bacon, and lard.

Each locality had its specialty. Kraków was associated with a wonderful dry sausage, *Krakowska sucha,* hot smoked, dense, and shot through with such spices as coriander, allspice, cumin, and garlic. "Kielbasa" was merely the Polish word for sausage, and the version most closely linked with Galicia is *Kielbasa lisiecka*. Coarsely ground from lean, heavily salted pork, the cured meat was spiced with pepper and garlic. In a time-honored method, butchers cased the mixture and had the links looped on sticks to be hot smoked over hardwood fires.

The primary ingredient of such Galician sausages was pork, and thus they would represent double negatives for a poor Jewish table like that of the Handwerker family—not kosher in the first place and too expensive in the second. Probably the first sausage that Nathan Handwerker ever ate was a *kishke,* which was not really meat based at all. A cow intestine (*kishke* is the Yiddish word for "guts" or "innards") was stuffed with various mixtures of matzo, flour, and chicken fat. The result was a kind of spiced, tube-shaped matzo ball in a meat casing, often served with gravy.

But there was a local Polish meat sausage that might have stirred an early awakening in the taste buds of the young son of Galicia. The *parówka* was a fat, linked wurst popular throughout Poland. It could be made with pork, but there were kosher, beef-only *parówka,* too. Chicken was often used as a filler. The meat was mildly spiced and finely ground. The *parówka* suspiciously resembles the stubby, all-beef frankfurter that a certain Polish immigrant would later serve up to the Coney Island masses.

Whether or not the *parówka* might be the holy grail first wurst of the future king of the hot dog, it was definitely a commonplace sausage in the Galicia of Nathan Handwerker's youth. It might have provided the boy with a glimpse of the future.

Nathan never returned to the bakery in Radymno. He stayed with his family. Jacob continued his desperate journeys through the countryside, searching for work. The relationship between the father and his third-oldest son took on a chilly, slightly competitive turn. Jacob ridiculed Nathan when he returned from a foray into the outside world having made no money. And in an incident Nathan remembered for his whole life, Jacob promised him new trousers for Passover to replace his single much-mended pair and then failed to produce.

But beyond poverty, there was another age-old enemy stalking Galicia at that time, a malicious presence that would grow until it engulfed the whole of Europe in a nightmare of blood and fire.

The young and vulnerable Nathan Handwerker would make a perfect victim for the beast.

2

To America

"Angels covered me up." The Handwerker family in Galicia.

IN THE YEARS leading up to World War I, anyone who could not foresee the looming conflict was a fool. Anyone who was not a fool looked for ways to get out. Nathan Handwerker sought to escape. He well remembered the soldiers he had seen across the pasture fence as a young boy.

"I didn't want to get killed," he recalled later. "I saw a war was coming. The emperor came to Galicia."

Franz Joseph arrived in the region for the shield-clashing military exercises that the Austrian army held every year. There were other telltale signs. When Austria constructed a railroad that year, Nathan noticed that it did not lead to the market town of Jarosław but directly to the huge military installations at Prysmzl.

All the preparations for war at least temporarily buoyed the Handwerker finances. The soldiers of the underfunded Austrian army had to buy food to augment their meager rations. Rose Handwerker had by that time taken over much of the responsibility for making the family living.

"She was a businesswoman, selling vegetables," Nathan recalled of his mother. "She rented a cellar, a deep cellar without lights, a cellar to go down two floors deep, because the deeper the cellar is, you didn't have to heat it up for the winter."

It turned out that Rose had to go farther and bargain harder to purchase her produce. "The local merchants gave her trouble, so she went to the outskirts. The farmers liked her better there. She spoiled them. She gave them more money in order to be able to buy from them. One farmer had a whole wagon of cabbage. One farmer had carrots. A farmer had radish, horseradish. Potatoes. Chickens. Chickens were tied up at the feet, so she put them in boxes, stacked them, sold them in town. People come up from the army. Everybody's coming to pick up food."

For five years, from the time he left the bakery in Radymno to when he departed for America, Nathan's job was to assist his mother in her produce business. Recalling the period a half century later, he retained sharp memories of those repeated trips down into the rented root cellar.

"Whatever was left over from the day's selling, I had to carry it into the basement overnight. So I used to carry it down in the dark. If I had a sack of potatoes, it would be hard for me to pick it up again, so I had to go down slow, two floors deep and no light."

Nathan managed to keep his wits about him and not act simply as a beast of burden. In July 1906, he noticed that the markets of Jarosław were entirely sold out of potatoes.

"Let me go to Narol," he asked his parents. He knew of a potato farm in his home village. He used to work in the fields there as a child. The wealthy landowner would be sure to have a ready supply.

"I went to this rich farmer—they call him 'the Baron,'" Nathan recalled. "The richest man in the whole neighborhood—not only in the town but around the town, too. I go in, and I ask him in Polish, 'So have you got any potatoes?' He took me to a big warehouse; it went up to the ceiling, and the potatoes it filled up."

Nathan managed to buy 180 pounds of spuds at a penny a pound. He took them back to Jarosław by horse and wagon and made a good profit.

"I was fourteen years old, and this was my first deal that I made for my family. We got about five groschen for a bag of potatoes, five times what I paid. My father and mother made a lot of money."

The incident helped teach the young boy the unchallengeable law of supply and demand. It also demonstrated how the sale of an inexpensive, humble food can yield a small fortune. Although he never received a formal education, Nathan was a quick study. Always watching and listening, he retained the lessons from his years working as a child, ideas and practices he would later bring to his business. From an early age, he realized the value of an experienced worker and that a premium should be placed on reliable business partners.

Though he did not get along well with his father, Nathan took many of his adult values from examples set by his mother. He followed her idea that maintaining relations with loyal suppliers was good business. Rose also taught her son the virtue of looking out for the wider community. In the case of the great Jarosław potato bonanza, his mother made it a policy to sell only a single bag per customer. "My mother says, 'No, give everybody a chance to get some.'"

As Nathan came of age, remaining in Galicia meant dodging *chapper* gangs of forcible recruiters and essentially playing chicken with history. Mounting anti-Semitism plagued the whole area. "The Poles were the biggest Jew haters," Nathan recalled. In the market, a Polish woman once shouted at him, "Jew, go to Palestine!"

Against such bigotry, there were only three bulwarks: religion, the tightly knit Jewish community, and the refuge of family. But faith and family, which had helped preserve shtetl societies for hundreds of years, failed to protect them now. Multiple threats from a collapsed economy, impending war, and ethnic hatreds worked to tear Galicia apart and took their toll on the Handwerkers, as well.

The formerly close-knit family separated. Israel, Nathan's oldest brother, departed for a new life in America. Other Handwerker brothers made exploratory forays into the nearby towns of Lublin and Sandomierz, always working at their father's trade of shoemaking. Nathan proved himself the thrifty one. "I didn't spend too much. When I went out to eat, I used to eat a bowl of soup and one piece of bread. A slice of bread was for three cents. I could eat more, but I wanted to save money."

Joseph Handwerker, Nathan's older brother and the second oldest sibling, traveled to Germany, the first step in his journey to America. He sent word asking his little brother to come join him.

Nathan needed help to decipher the message. "I get a postal card, but I can't read, I can't write. And I couldn't add two and two. I packed up, but I didn't have enough to pay for a railroad ticket to go to Frankfurt."

His sister Anna loaned him going-away money. "I kissed her good-bye and said, 'Don't tell nobody.' I knew she wouldn't."

Nathan told his father he was departing for America, intentionally breaking the news in the synagogue, where he knew Jacob could not cause an argument. He said good-bye with a simple phrase, "*Ich gay avek*" (I'm leaving).

He carried what few clothes he had in a burlap onion bag, because a valise or suitcase would attract the suspicions of the police. He was an eighteen-year-old male, perfect cannon fodder. Nathan made his journey in constant fear of the authorities. At any step along the way, if he had been questioned by the police, he would have been shipped back to Austria and into the army. That would be tantamount to a death sentence, but by some miracle, it never happened.

"On the train, there was a long bench from one end to the other. I was lucky with the policemen when they came to check to see if anybody was crossing the border without papers. I would look down the train car, and when I saw that who was coming was wearing boots, polished boots, when I saw one foot, a polished shoe, I knew it was a policeman." He would bolt from the train and reboard by a different door.

Nathan later remembered disembarking in Frankfurt early in the morning, a stranger in a strange land, admiring the gardens, the fountains, but having only a "penny and a half" left to his name. All he could afford was a soft pretzel. So he bought a pretzel and went to a fountain to fill up on water.

"I slept in a synagogue. I slept on the floor. I couldn't read, I couldn't write. I had nothing. I slept in my shoes."

From the mouths of everyone around him, he heard the same word . . . America. Emigration was like a fever, everywhere in the air. Newspaper ads listed daily departures of passenger ships. His brother Israel, already in New York, wrote to Joseph, encouraging him and Nathan to make the crossing. Behind them lay poverty and war. There was no reason to turn back. The whole Handwerker family was either moving or planning to move.

Nathan was in Germany, but he wanted to be in America. "I was dreaming about it." Joseph Handwerker was restless, too, and soon moved on from Frankfurt to Berlin, and then on to Antwerp, Belgium. Nathan followed, having to cross a series of borders to get there. Guard after guard failed to detect the young Galician refugee.

"Angels covered me up," Nathan said about his journey. "That's the only way I can see it. Four days sitting on the train. Three borders. The German border, Luxembourg, and Belgium. And nobody asked me where I'm going. When I got off the train, I knew they wouldn't send me back. And I bent down and I kissed the sidewalk."

In Antwerp, Nathan applied himself to building up a nest egg for the cross-Atlantic journey. He was tireless, going door to door in the diamond district of the busy Belgium port city to sell his services as a cobbler. "I want to make shoes," he told anyone who would listen. "New shoes, men's and ladies' shoes, and soles and heels. You'll be satisfied."

Scrimping and saving, in half a year he managed to build up a bankroll of several hundred Austro-Hungarian kronen, the gold coins of his countrymen that he could easily change for any other currency. He kept his money in the bank. His brother Joseph was not so frugal. He got swept up in the nightlife of the city, going out almost every night while Nathan stayed home and worked at the cobbler bench.

Both brothers were making more money than they ever could have dreamed back home in Galicia. But only one kept his eye on the prize. "My brother Joe, when he went to a restaurant, he used to eat the biggest piece of fish, the best. He spent money on gambling, on going out, on girls."

After six months in Antwerp, Nathan was ready. He headed off to join the oldest Handwerker brother, Israel, in New York City. A steerage ticket on a passenger ship to America cost him one hundred of his hard-earned kronen. He traded in another thirty kronen for American dollars, spending money for the New World. Nathan thus took his place amid the single greatest wave of emigration in human history.

On Saturday, March 16, 1912, nineteen-year-old Nathan Handwerker boarded the SS *Neckar* in Rotterdam, Netherlands, bound for New York City. (Once again, he had to manage a border crossing to get to his departure port, and once again, angels had covered him up from the hostile eyes of the authorities.)

"I could buy a ticket, I found out, for a certain amount, around a hundred dollars American. I needed twenty-five more dollars for when I arrived at New York, or else immigration wouldn't let me in. I know about this since I talked to people. I had to find out myself where I am and where I'm going."

His brother Joseph cooked Nathan a chicken for the journey, using a lot of garlic, and also bought him oranges and salami. Nathan felt safe enough that he could travel with a valise now, so he packed up all the foodstuffs into the suitcase with his only suit.

SS *Neckar,* one of four Rhine-class steamships running on the Norddeutscher Lloyd line, had four decks and space for almost three thousand passengers: 140 first class, 150 second class, and 2,600 third class. *Neckar* was actually an old cattle ship repurposed for the booming trans-Atlantic passenger trade. At least in the crowded quarters of steerage, the livestock idea fit perfectly.

When Nathan boarded the SS *Neckar,* he quickly realized he was out of his element.

"I didn't understand what they were talking," he recalled, describing his inability to understand the instructions of the ship's crew. "They were taking away my valise with the food and put it in the checking room. A lot of people are going in the same boat, so we had three people to a room, three beds, one on top of another."

He had heard of thieves and pickpockets victimizing passengers on these Atlantic crossings, the poor immigrants arriving in America robbed of what little they had. "So I grabbed the top bed. If the thief is going to rob me, he has to go to the top." He hid his money in his sock and once again slept in his shoes.

Joe's garlic chicken was even then rotting somewhere in the baggage hold of the ship. Nathan never saw his valise again. He eyed the food offered to steerage passengers like him. Not liking the look of the meat, which he immediately judged to come from horse, not cow, he chose the herring instead. For the whole crossing, he survived on that, bread, and potatoes ("They gave us them with the peels").

"The only thing I had to buy was a glass of beer for a nickel. I was afraid to take out a dollar because they shouldn't see I had money. Every morning, I went out to the deck, and I take off my shoes. Because the money I had hidden there smelled, and I aired it out."

At the SS *Neckar*'s steady pace of thirteen and a half knots, it took Nathan twenty-two days to cross the Atlantic. He spent his time perfecting his signature. He did not yet know the Latin alphabet and still had no ability to read or write at all. He had someone write his name for him. Then he carefully learned to imitate the letters, practicing over and over.

Also on the same sea that spring, making the journey at a higher latitude, was the mighty RMS *Titanic*. Aboard were many of the richest and most celebrated people of the age, but also 1,706 steerage passengers who more resembled Nathan Handwerker than Jacob Astor or Benjamin Guggenheim.

Nathan's initial sighting of the American shoreline might very well have been a spray of white light on the horizon. The illuminated wonders of Coney Island's amusement parks could be seen from thirty miles out at sea and were often the first glimpse of the New World for immigrants nearing the end of their exhausting transatlantic journeys.

Neckar arrived in New York Harbor on April 7, 1912, an Easter Sunday, the sixth day of Passover that year. Manhattan was not yet a crowded forest of skyscrapers, but for an immigrant from the countryside of Poland, the view was still impressive. Dominating the New York skyline was the ornate, still-under-construction Woolworth Building—at 792 feet, the tallest structure in the world.

The weather on the day of Nathan's arrival, according to newspaper reports, was "charming," the warmest Easter it had been in forty-two years. President Taft played his first game of golf of the season that weekend. Oarsmen were out on the Harlem River. The holiday crowds "filled Fifth Avenue with color."

Nathan saw none of it. U.S. immigration authorities allowed first- and second-class passengers to disembark when the boat docked that Sunday at a West Side pier. Third-class passengers like Nathan were made to wait until the next day, when they would be ferried to the immigration facility on Ellis Island. Later that afternoon, with the SS *Neckar* still docked and Nathan still on board, the weather turned nasty. What was termed in the press to be "a mini-hurricane" or "a gale" rocked New York Harbor.

Back in Europe, war clouds had continued to build. Russian armies mobilized. Serbian troops laid plans for an autumn offensive that would carve up huge tracts of the Balkans for annexation. War was fast becoming modernized, with the first aerial bombing (of Turkish troops by an Italian dirigible) accomplished that March. The next month in Moscow, the first issue of the underground organ of the Communist Party, *Pravda*, was distributed, only to be immediately confiscated and burned by Tsarist police.

That was the world from which Nathan Handwerker had escaped. He had gotten out just in time. As James Joyce said about his hero Stephen Dedalus (writing during the same period as Nathan's miraculous journey), history was a nightmare from which he was trying to awake. Now at last Nathan had done so. He had arrived in America, the land of his dreams.

His difficulties began almost immediately.

3

Luncheonette Man

"All you have to say is, 'All hot—get 'em while they're hot!'"
Nathan, age twenty, far right.

THE FERRY RIDE from Manhattan's West Side docks to Ellis Island represented a last ordeal in an immigrant journey packed full of such trials. Immigration authorities transferred steerage passengers—so-called because their cramped quarters were often in the ship's stern, where the steering mechanism for the old sailing ships had once been located—to ferries a few hundred at a time. The ferry fleet was made up of small, flat-bottomed crafts designed to be able to negotiate the shallow waters around Ellis.

Facilities on the boats were few and crude. After transatlantic voyages that had lasted three weeks, passenger hygiene failed to maintain a high standard. Ship captains crammed the Ellis ferries full and then idled for hours offshore, waiting for processing backlogs to ease on the island. The decks were crowded. Immigrants often bulked themselves up by wearing their whole wardrobes in layers. Memoirs and oral histories repeatedly cite the stench and misery of the three-mile trip across the harbor.

Although the weather that Monday of Nathan's transit had turned cold, his memory of his trip to Ellis Island was tinged with fondness for the bounty of the new country: "The first nickel I spent on the boat that took me to Ellis Island, I bought a pie for a nickel. A whole pie. And I don't remember what to drink."

From 1901 to 1914, an average of five thousand newcomers a day—and sometimes as many as eight thousand a day—took the same ferry ride to Ellis. Nathan Handwerker arrived near the tail end of America's second great wave of immigration. The first wave, primarily from famine-struck Ireland, came aboard the "coffin ships" of the mid-nineteenth century. The second lasted from the turn of the century to the beginning of the First World War. During this period, a million immigrants a year passed through Ellis, two-thirds of whom shared backgrounds in eastern, central, or southern Europe.

The U.S. Congress initially placed immigration regulation and policy under the purview of the federal Treasury Department, the focus being the potential revenue these aspiring citizens would bring to their adopted homeland. But in 1903, the Bureau of Immigration was reassigned to what was then called the Department of Commerce and Labor. The turn-of-the-century influx of European immigrants gave rise to various concerns. Did the new arrivals bring disease? Would they spread their strange customs and their radical politics? Would immigrants flood the labor market, or would hard-working Americans be forced to support them as public wards?

Ellis Island's immigrant inspection station was conceived at least in part as a dam against the flood. We tend to forget that Ellis could be a place not only of reception but of rejection, too. Overall, only a small number of those processed—around 2 percent—were denied entry and sent home. Still, anxiety over possible deportation remained a common theme in the recollections of many new arrivals. Ellis soon earned the nickname "the Island of Tears."

After the wait offshore—at times hours long and seemingly interminable—the ferries from the West Side docks pulled up to the Ellis Island wharf and discharged their passengers. The inspection station's main building, just over a decade old when Nathan first saw it, was designed to impress. The French Renaissance rock pile represented a formal gateway to America, Emma Lazarus's "golden door," or what another commentary called "the Plymouth Rock of its day." The redbrick façade featured quoins, elaborate corner belvederes, and three arched entrances. The structure's exaggerated profile lent the building distinction even when viewed at a distance, as it so often was, across the water.

Inside, a gauntlet. Medical division staff members from the United States Public Health Service posted themselves along the stairway to the Great Hall on the second floor. They subjected each new arrival to a blazingly fast, six-second medical examination. Shortness of breath while climbing the stairs singled an immigrant out as suffering from lung or heart conditions. The uniformed doctors peeled back eyelids with metal buttonhooks or hairpins, looking for conjunctivitis. Any sign of infectious disease or disability brought out the chalk, and the health inspectors marked the suspect with stigma-like symbols: *G* for goiter, *PG* for pregnancy, *X* for "mental defects."

Immigration inspectors checked for viruses not of the biological but the social kind. Officials demanded answers to such questions as "Are you an anarchist?" or "Are you a polygamist?" With much of Europe engulfed in ideological ferment, the largely WASP establishment of America was perhaps more worried about communism than about conjunctivitis.

A widespread belief exists, spread most prominently by *The Joys of Yiddish* author Leo Rosten, that Ellis Island was where the term "kike" first surfaced. Originally not an ethnic slur at all (that came later), the word was used by personnel on the island to refer to eastern European Jews like Nathan Handwerker. Illiterate newcomers, or at least those not familiar with the Latin alphabet, were directed to sign their names with an *X*. Deeply religious Jewish immigrants refused, seeing this mark as the sign of the Christian cross. Instead, they used a circle, the word for which in Yiddish is *kikel*.

By the time Nathan was asked to sign his entry paperwork, he was ready. He had learned his signature on the voyage over. Illiterate though he was, he was able to sign his name on his entry papers. In the present-day environment of endless bureaucratic red tape and Homeland Security checks, it seems inconceivable, but when Nathan officially entered the United States, official identity forms were not required.

"I had my twenty-five dollars," he said, citing the rumored amount that Ellis Island officials required new arrivals to possess in order not to be declared indigent (the equivalent of $585 today). "I also had a workbook. You couldn't work in Galicia if you had no workbook. But no passport. I didn't need it. They only take the signature when you come in. So I signed. No papers. They didn't ask for anything."

Entering the United States that day, Nathan was two months

shy of his twentieth birthday. He had reached his full adult height, a meager five feet three inches tall. He didn't have the bulk necessary to describe him as a fireplug, but he had a pleasant, open, strong face and a hank of dark hair that hung over the right side of his forehead. The resemblance to a young Pablo Picasso was uncanny. Most important, and probably like Pablo, he had a look of determination in his eye.

The healthy-as-a-horse Nathan survived the Ellis Island medical gauntlet unchalked. "I wasn't afraid," he said.

He wasn't alone, either. After he finished being processed, he descended from the Great Hall to the first floor to meet his brother Israel. Here was the age-old immigrant story, the one who came before paving the way for others. Nathan left Ellis the way he had come, returning to Manhattan with Israel in the same flat-bottomed ferry.

His brother took him to a restaurant for his first meal in his new home. "He says, 'Come with me, we'll eat there; they'll give you a good meal for ten cents.'" Afterward, Israel guided him to the tenement apartment of a Handwerker cousin, the son of his mother's brother. "They have a cot bed in the kitchen, and they pulled it out for me to sleep, so I slept there for two nights."

It was the last day of Passover. Nathan had successfully completed an epic, life-changing passage. His guardian angels had "covered him up" the whole way. Millions of others accomplished similar journeys, to the degree that 40 percent of the people in the United States have an ancestor who passed through Ellis Island. Nathan took his place among a city teeming with immigrants, what was then a metropolis of five million people.

Now, after a meal, after sleep, work.

The new arrival did not allow grass to grow under his feet. Nathan arrived in New York City on a Monday. Tuesday afternoon found him employed at his first job, working for a shoemaker's at First Avenue and Ninth Street. Today, the neighborhood is part of the East Village, but in the early part of the last century, it was still within the precincts of the dense, flavorful, immigrant-heavy area known as the Lower East Side.

Nathan had taken up Jacob's profession, though the mundane details of the job were slightly different. "I was used to work with wooden nails, and here I have to work with stainless-steel nails. But I learned fast."

That small detail of wooden nails measures the gulf between Nathan's former world in Galicia and his new one in Manhattan. In another sense, though, the new boss was the same as the old boss. The shoemaker's trade was eminently familiar to him—the smell of leather, the cobbler's crouch, the endless *tap-tap-tap* hammering. Had Nathan crossed an ocean simply to fall back into a timeworn routine of his youth? Wasn't this a chance for new beginnings?

He finished out the week at the shop but was increasingly restless. "I worked, but I couldn't do it. I didn't want to be a shoemaker."

On Friday, Nathan asked his older brother to help him look for a new job. Israel bought a copy of the *Der Morgen Zshurnal*, the *Jewish Morning Journal*. New York was at that time an incredible newspaper town. There were 112 dailies, weeklies, and monthlies being published, including six in Yiddish, Yiddish-English, or Hebrew. That morning, Israel found Nathan an ad for employment at a luggage factory, across town at Fourteenth Street and Ninth Avenue. Clutching the newspaper with the ad circled, the rookie New Yorker set off into the maze of the city.

North of Fourteenth Street, the grid plan brought a measure

of order to the layout of Manhattan, but the old neighborhoods downtown could be confusing, a welter of crisscrossing streets and logic-defying lost quarters. In the area where Nathan headed through, for example, West Fourth Street actually intersected West Twelfth and headed north to West Thirteenth. He depended on the kindness of strangers to help him find his way.

"I started to walk from downtown and asked, 'Where is this?' And I showed them the paper, the ad in the paper, so people showed me, 'Go this way, that way.' When I got to the factory, it was twelve o'clock, noon. I come upstairs, I see a Jew with a beard."

"What's your trade?" asked the luggage factory boss, speaking Yiddish.

"Shoemaker," answered Nathan.

"Can you sew seams straight? With luggage, fancy leather luggage, you gotta sew seams."

Like job seekers everywhere, Nathan put the best face on his experience. "The best, straight, nothing better."

"I'll give you eight dollars a week," said his new boss.

But since Nathan had arrived at the luggage factory midday on Friday, the place was about to close in observance of the Jewish Sabbath. The workers had already departed. His new employer told him to come back the following Monday at eight o'clock.

"Still, it bothered me to work in the factory," Nathan recalled. "I wanted something else, not to be a shopman."

Both the luggage factory and shoemaker's shop participated in a Yiddish-based, highly communal Jewish culture that dominated whole city neighborhoods and entire industries. At this time, an astonishing 70 percent of America's women's clothing (and 40 percent of its men's) was created in New York. Half the country's garment factories were located there. And three quarters of the workers in the "needle trades" were Jewish.

Jewish immigrants naturally gravitated to jobs where their co-workers came from the same area of the world and often from the same towns as they did. They wanted employment that did not require them to know English, that would allow them to maintain a kosher diet, keep the Sabbath, and observe the high holy days.

Convivial as the fellowship of countrymen might be, the hours were long, and the pay paltry. The term "sweatshop" was born here, referring not only to the stifling atmosphere of the rooms where the work was done but to the fact that employers "sweated" their workers, "in the same manner an animal would be milked or bled," in the words of one history. Social reformer Jacob Riis described typical sweatshop laborers as being "shut in the qualmy rooms . . . the livelong day." It was this claustrophobic, dead-end labor against which Nathan Handwerker rebelled.

Something else spurred him on to seek other occupations. He remembered his experience at the bakery in Galicia. It was hot, strenuous work, but at least he was always guaranteed a meal while employed. No one ever forgets childhood hunger. It was a specter that haunted Nathan as he grew to adulthood.

"I always knew I was going to be in the restaurant business," he said later. "There's always food there. I grew up so poor, and this was a way of guaranteeing that I'd never be hungry."

That Sunday, Nathan had Israel buy him another copy of the *Journal*. This one advertised a job in a luncheonette. He took the newspaper, folded to display the ad, and again asked passersby to help guide him to the address, on Delancey Street near the terminus of the Williamsburg Bridge. When he got there, he realized that the place was closed on Sunday. Nathan couldn't understand. Why advertise in a Sunday-edition newspaper when you were closed that day?

A wasted trip. As he stood in front of the place, a teamster with a horse and wagon pulled up, a deliveryman for Holstein Bakery on Houston Street. He had come to collect the empty cartons from the previous week's deliveries, egg crates that were tossed into a pile after they were empty. The teamster saw Nathan, and the two of them struck up a conversation in Yiddish.

"Why did they advertise if they're not going to be open Sunday?" Nathan asked.

The teamster explained the baffling ins and outs of big-city commerce. If the luncheonette owner advertised for two days, he would receive a cheaper rate. Ads on Sunday were cheaper still. So the owner had taken the ad out for both the Sunday and Monday editions of the newspaper.

"But if you're going to come back Monday," the teamster told him, "get here before six o'clock, and you'll be first."

Nathan was there Monday morning at five. "I got up at four o'clock and walked an hour in the dark. I found the place more easily because I was there the day before. The first time, it took longer because I had to ask people where to go."

He saw the luncheonette boss arrive. Nathan knew enough not to bother him right away; he just made sure the man saw that he was first in line. The boss went in, set the coffee to boil, and came back out to give some to his job seekers.

Then he addressed the eager beaver in English.

"Want to wash dishes?"

Nathan didn't understand the words. "But I said, 'Yes.' I nodded my head for yes."

"Four and a half dollars a week." The boss held up four fingers and crooked another one to indicate half. His name was Max Leventhal, and he was offering low-level employment to a worker who had already secured a position in a luggage factory that offered almost twice the pay.

"I had a job for eight dollars a week," Nathan recalled. "But no food. And it was a factory. I didn't want to be a slave in the factory, breathing dust and everything. Those were my fears. And I always wanted to be in a restaurant. I told myself that I should take the job for four and a half, and maybe I could work up to something else."

Dishwashing—"pearl diving" in a slang formulation just then becoming current in his new homeland. When anyone started at the very bottom of the food service business, it's what they found themselves doing. It wasn't glamorous—in fact, it was the exact opposite of glamorous, but it was a foot in the door.

———

That same Monday, the first reports of a disaster at sea began to filter into New York. The passenger steamship RMS *Carpathia* radioed bulletins to the Cape Race wireless station in Newfoundland, but the transmissions were confused. Initial accounts had *Carpathia* towing the crippled luxury liner RMS *Titanic* into port at Halifax. The Monday-morning headline in *The New York Times* scooped the world:

NEW LINER *TITANIC* HITS AN ICEBERG; SINKING BY
THE BOW AT MIDNIGHT; WOMEN PUT OFF IN LIFE-
BOATS; LAST WIRELESS AT 12:27 AM BLURRED.

No one wanted to believe it. Philip Franklin, a spokesperson for the owners of the ship, had a stalwart message to reporters that morning: "We place absolute confidence in the *Titanic*. We believe that the boat is unsinkable."

By Monday evening in New York, the true scope of the catastrophe became apparent. *Titanic*, the largest ship then afloat, had gone down. An eyewitness report detailed the exact moment the news hit the city.

"The scene on Broadway was awful. Crowds of people were coming out of the theaters, cafés were going full tilt, and autos were whizzing everywhere when the newsboys began to cry, 'Extra! Extra paper! *Titanic* sunk with 1,800 aboard!' Nobody could realize what had happened, and when they did begin to understand, the excitement was almost enough to cause a panic in the theaters. Women began to faint and weep."

In the stretch of days between the sinking and the arrival in New York of the survivors on *Carpathia*, the city became a death-haunted place. There was no way the news could not have reached Nathan, so complete was the grip that the calamity asserted on the public imagination. A new phrase entered the American vernacular: "Women and children first."

It was all anyone talked about. That Thursday, thirty thousand people gathered at Pier 54 on the Hudson River for the 9:00 P.M. docking of *Carpathia*. Almost every cop on the city's force was summoned to duty in the neighborhood, which was cordoned off by ropes hung with ghostly green lanterns. A misty rain and occasional lightning flashes heightened the drama of the scene.

"There was almost complete silence on the pier," wrote an eyewitness. "Women wept, but they wept quietly."

For a transatlantic immigrant who had crossed the same seas just a week previously, the story of RMS *Titanic* must have taken on a tragic weight. Five hundred thirty steerage passengers died when the liner sank. Nathan Handwerker could have been one of them. He could well have left Europe not from Holland but from Cherbourg, France, *Titanic*'s second-to-last port of call. Nathan had to believe that he had just dodged a bullet.

But he was too busy to be spooked. The new hire worked at the luncheonette, a small "store," as he called it, with only four or five other employees. There was a single communal table for customers, mirrored walls, and an L-shaped counter with chairs. Nathan's boss gave him two aprons, both white, one to wear below his waist and another on top.

A hitch arose: he had to be called "Benny," not Nathan. A manager's name was Nathan, and it would have caused too much confusion for there to be two Nathans in the tiny kitchen.

It didn't take long for "Benny" to move up the restaurant food chain. After a single morning at the sink washing dishes, his boss approached. "He comes over [to check his work]. He never had seen anything like it. Clean!"

The boss offered a fresh apron. "Put on the apron, Benny. You're going to be a busboy."

"What should I do?" Nathan asked in Yiddish.

The boss gave him a rag. "If you see a customer leave, you pick up their dishes, bring them to the sink, and wipe the counter." He mimed the actions so that Nathan understood.

The noon rush was upon them. Customers stopped at the counter for sandwiches and frankfurters and then grabbed seats. They were reluctant to return to the counter for their desserts and coffee, in fear they'd lose their place at the table.

"When people get busy, you'll take orders," Nathan the manager told Nathan the new busboy.

"Boss, I can't," Nathan said in Yiddish. "I'm Jewish. I can't speak English."

"One at a time," the manager said, holding up his forefinger so that his busboy could grasp the concept. "One order at a time."

Language impaired or not, the new employee was quick. "I caught on right away what he meant. Small coffee was one cent. A large coffee was three cents. The manager was on the coffee counter. I would hold up one finger or three to get coffee."

In this slow, laborious manner, Nathan Handwerker learned English. He would call out orders before he knew what the words meant. "Milk" became the next vocabulary entry, and then "pie" and "cake." The clientele flung unintelligible phrases at him: "half a coconut pie," "half an apple pie," "a cheesecake." Rush hour in a busy Manhattan luncheonette, a trial by fire. Somehow, Nathan made it through.

On the afternoon of his first day, as the tide of customers ebbed, Nathan's boss came over to take charge of the money the new busboy had collected during lunch. Proud of his honesty, Nathan was exact with the count: "Not a penny short, not a penny over."

The boss was happy. "Go eat, Benny," he said.

Nathan motioned that he needed to be shown how he could take a meal. The manager gave him a small measure of the unbelievable bounty of the New World: three sandwiches, one stuffed with sliced beef, one a cheese sandwich, the third a hamburger. The employees were charged three cents for half a pie and a penny for glass of lemonade. As generous as the staff lunch was, it didn't satisfy the new immigrant's bottomless hunger.

"I could have eaten three times as much, but I was afraid to lose the job," Nathan recalled. Cheese and beef together? His kosher dietary strictures went by the wayside.

On the cook line ahead of Nathan/Benny was the frankfurter man, a veteran who had more seniority. The newcomer worked on one side of the counter, the frankfurter man was on the other. Frankfurters with sauerkraut cost two cents. With a toasted roll added in, the tally went up to three cents. The job of dishing up the sausages would represent a step up the ladder for Nathan.

The next Saturday was payday. Nathan stood last in line to receive his money, four and a half dollars for the week. When his turn came, the owner, Max, gave him five dollars.

"Boss, you gave me too much money," Nathan said, still speaking Yiddish. He displayed his pay.

"I'll give you a raise, but next week, you work on the frankfurters."

Once again, Nathan had to protest, citing his lack of the native tongue.

"You don't have to speak English," the boss said. "All you have to say is, 'All hot, get 'em while they're hot.'"

He made the newly promoted dishwasher say it. "All hot, get 'em while they're hot."

"Griddle frankfurters three cents," the boss said. "Boiled frankfurters two cents with sauerkraut."

Nathan repeated the lines until he had them down cold. The phrases were probably among the first hundred or so words that Nathan learned in English.

When he came into the luncheonette the following Monday, he worked the frankfurter counter. Nathan might not have known it at the time, but it was a match made in heaven. He had been in America all of two weeks.

4

The Tenth Ward

"How long is he going to stay with us? He's eating up the food."
Lower East Side, New York City, ca. 1912.

THE WORLD THAT Nathan stepped into when he came to America—
the early twentieth-century Lower East Side community of Jewish immigrants packed into a teeming, flavorful, overcrowded
ghetto—has long been distorted by nostalgia. The memory of it is
rose colored, but the reality was oftentimes dreadful. Nathan was a
"*greene* Jew," a "greenhorn," as opposed to the "*gelle*," the yellows,
experienced residents who had a few years in the country. His
fellow immigrants both disparaged and embraced such newly
arrived figures as Nathan Handwerker.

The ghetto was crowded with poor Jews, poorer even than the greenhorn from Galicia. The average amount of money brought to America by Russian Jews was eight dollars, and Nathan had three times that. New York City was a shock to the immigrant's system, but it was a shock buffered by traditions, customs, and practices that were instantly recognizable from the eastern European culture left behind. Nathan immersed himself in it as in a cold bath. He lived in a succession of tenement apartments in Brooklyn and on the Lower East Side.

His initial landing place, the apartment of a cousin where he spent his first nights in his adopted homeland, did not last long. He lay awake on his kitchen cot one evening soon after he arrived, listening to a discussion between the host couple. Nathan soon realized they were talking about him.

"How long is he going to stay with us?" asked the wife of his cousin. "He's eating up the food."

Nathan didn't wait. He was too proud to be where he wasn't wanted. He left early the next day, taking his paltry belongings with him.

"I didn't want to eat breakfast with them in the morning," he recalled. "I didn't tell them why."

Such was the extent of New York's well-established Jewish community that a greenhorn like Nathan, even an itinerant one, could survive and even prosper. It was possible for immigrant *Ostjuden* to work, live, and worship in venues that did not demand them to speak English. Whole neighborhoods, congested as they were, offered Nathan safe harbor among fellow countrymen.

The Lower East Side neighborhood was incredibly concentrated. A third of a million Jewish immigrants lived in a forty-block area around Allen, Essex, Canal, and Broome Streets: the

Tenth Ward of New York City. Home to some of the most densely crowded buildings on earth, the neighborhood had a population of 69,944, or approximately 665 people per acre. The language used to describe such dwellings is uncannily reminiscent of descriptions of Old World shtetlach, invoking some of the same words.

"The rooms were damp, filthy, foul, and dark," stated one government sanitary inspector. "The air was unbearable, the filth impossible, the crowded conditions terrible, particularly in those places where the rooms were used as workshops. The life of the children was endangered because of the prevailing contagious diseases, and children died like flies."

One vital difference existed between the Galician misery of the Old World and the Tenth Ward congestion of the new: there were jobs for willing and able employees in America. Nathan himself had three separate offers of employment in his first week in the country. The jobs might have been low paying and grueling, but they represented gainful employment nonetheless.

Common in the neighborhood were positions doing piecework in the garment business, much of the time accomplished in the same apartments in which the workers lived. A garment jobber might subcontract out batches of cut fabric for buttonholes, trim, or simple stitching, collecting the completed pieces from the sweatshop workers to return to the manufacturer. Almost half of New York City's workforce was engaged in clothing production. A pieceworker could earn up to ten dollars a week (compare this to Nathan's weekly wage of $4.50 at the luncheonette). Rent of a tenement apartment was usually around ten or twelve dollars a month.

Pushcarts were another common neighborhood livelihood. At the turn of the century, there were some twenty-five thousand of them on the Lower East Side. Hester Street in particular became something of a movable bazaar, nicknamed *chazermark* or "pig market" for its crowds and fulsome odors.

There were also shadier occupations available to newly arrived immigrants. Jewish gangsters Ben "Bugsy" Siegel and Meyer Lansky began their criminal careers as lowly stickup men on the Lower East Side. Street prostitution, brothels, and white slavery were commonplace enough to cause hand-wringing in the press and action by relief organizations. A survey of a Manhattan magistrate's court in 1908–09 revealed that three-quarters of the women arrested as prostitutes were Jewish.

Many immigrants sought livelihoods in the New World that were simply a natural continuation of what they had done in the old. Polish tailors became sweatshop pieceworkers in their new tenement homes. Former Ukrainian peddlers bought pushcarts and trolled Orchard Street for customers. There had been brothels in Galicia just as there were in the Tenth Ward.

What is today euphemistically called the "hospitality industry"—restaurants and hotels—had its Old World incarnation, too. In the late nineteenth and early twentieth centuries, Jewish entrepreneurs were among the only people licensed to sell alcohol and operate public houses and dining establishments in Poland, Galicia, and the Pale. Since the trade was seen as beneath the dignity of the Polish gentry, it was traditionally left to Jews to satisfy the demand.

Nathan had worked in bakeries in Galicia. His entry into the restaurant business in Manhattan could be seen as carrying on both a personal and a cultural tradition that had its roots in his eastern European past. For Nathan, restaurant work in America was the next step after having sold knishes in his homeland. The Delancey Street luncheonette catered to people just like him, the tenement masses in the densely populated Jewish neighborhoods all around. The language barrier wasn't absolute, since at least a few of the customers were ordering in Yiddish.

At that first food service job, he learned the tricks that would serve him well later, such as the proper way to make lemonade. His boss, the other Nathan, showed him how. "He didn't even have a glass to squeeze out the lemons. I had to squeeze with my hands. With a whole bushel of lemons, I put half a gallon of water in and squeezed them out."

A contemporary board of health might look askance, but at the time, the practice was to put whole lemons into water and to hand-squeeze the citrus to release the essential oils from the skins. This gave the drink a fuller flavor.

Nathan continued the process. "I put another half a gallon of water in to wash all the peels for more juice, added another gallon in with the lemons, then put in four pounds of sugar."

The final and most necessary step was to ensure the sugar melted in the bottom of the four-gallon lemonade pail. "There shouldn't be a lump of sugar at the bottom. My boss had me make lemonade and orangeade. He only had to show me once."

Nathan's Old-Fashioned Lemonade
1 bushel (80–100) lemons, sliced or quartered
3+ gallons water
4 pounds (8 cups) sugar
In a half gallon of the water, hand-squeeze the lemons, making sure to bruise the peels. Add additional half gallon of water. Add four pounds of sugar and the last gallons of water to taste, mixing thoroughly to dissolve the sugar.

Although the ghetto community of the Lower East Side might have tried hard to ignore it, there existed a wider world beyond the Tenth Ward. At the time of Nathan Handwerker's arrival, that wider world found itself in a tumult. The year 1912 was one of those transformative years in the United States, with repeated social upheavals, controversies, and battles roiling the body politic. To a greater or lesser degree, every one of the day's signal issues would impact the life and business of the greenhorn immigrant.

Even as the newcomer made his way as a luncheonette counterman, anti-immigration forces were pushing a bill through Congress that would require each new arrival to pass a literacy test. Such legislation would have denied entry into the United States to the functionally illiterate Nathan Handwerker. Only a veto by President Taft prevented the measure from becoming law.

At the same time that anti-immigration organizations were mobilizing on the political front, progressive initiatives sought to further what today we could call human rights. Just a month after Nathan's arrival, in May 1912, the largest suffragist demonstration in history was held in New York City. Left-leaning free speech protests sprang up across the country, challenging the silencing of labor advocates in San Diego and elsewhere. Both the National Association for the Advancement of Colored People and the Urban League had been founded just a few years earlier.

The *Titanic* disaster continued to cast a pall. The front page of the *New York Times* featured news of the sinking for eighteen straight days. Funerals, memorials, and relief benefits for the doomed ship studded the New York City social calendar. On Sunday, April 21, stage stars George M. Cohan and Eddie Foy gathered together Broadway singers and dancers for a gala benefit, while the following Monday the celebrated Neapolitan tenor Enrico Caruso sang Arthur Sullivan's "The Lost Chord" at the Metropolitan

Opera House. Official inquiries in the United States and in Britain kept alive the contentious issue of who was to blame for the catastrophe.

A popular sentiment of the time was "God went down with *Titanic*," meaning that the randomness of the calamity challenged faith. Commentators extracted various lessons from the wreck, including those that were critical of capitalism, lax maritime regulations, and the hubris of the ship's owners. From pulpits came sermons that linked the sinking to the evils of modern decadence. "The remote cause of this unspeakable disaster," preached the archbishop of Baltimore, "is the excessive pursuit of luxury."

The catastrophe overshadowed the presidential election primary season that year, essentially a three-way race between incumbent Republican Robert Taft, Progressive Theodore Roosevelt, and former Princeton University president (and eventual winner) Woodrow Wilson. From the left came the Socialist candidacy of Eugene V. Debs, orchestrator of the Pullman Strike.

Nathan shared the New York Jewish community with some of the leading historical figures of the day. The pioneer Zionist David Ben-Gurion was there, as was, briefly, Leon Trotsky. Another arrival was the great Yiddish writer Sholem Aleichem, author of the Tevye stories that would later be dramatized on Broadway as *Fiddler on the Roof.*

Passing through the same Lower East Side streets as figures famous and otherwise, living amid noteworthy historical shifts, Nathan pursued his anonymous workaday ways. He lived with relatives, for a period in "a shoemaker's cellar," other times in tenements, always paying no more than a dollar a month in rent. He later remembered the meager weekend fare in his lodgings. "Eggs were $1.40 a dozen [$32 in today's money], so they only gave me one—they only ate one egg for Sunday breakfast."

It didn't matter much what his impoverished home life was like, since he was always working. Nathan negotiated the world of Manhattan luncheonettes with something that approached sure-footed confidence. He seemed to know instinctively when to leave a job and when to stay, when to follow a boss or when to cut himself loose.

Within a month, the restaurant where he originally worked was sold. The new owner, Sam, asked Nathan to stay on. "Sam called me 'Benny,'" Nathan recalled, because of the problem with multiple Nathans working in the same place. "He said to me, 'Benny, I want you to be the manager.' So he made me the manager of the coffee counter, cakes, and pies, in charge of everything. He gave me the keys to the store. I came in at six o'clock to open up the place."

But Nathan's old boss beckoned. Max Leventhal was opening a new luncheonette on Eighteenth Street between Fifth and Sixth, near architect Daniel H. Burnham's Flatiron Building, one of Manhattan's first skyscrapers and surely its most distinctive. The neighborhood was busy, near to the shopping district called Ladies' Mile.

Max came to Nathan with a job offer. "I want you to come work for me. In two weeks, I'm opening a new place."

Nathan jumped. He didn't even ask the salary. "Why? Because I knew if I worked for him, I'll learn the business, because he really knows the business, in and out. And Sam, the new boss, he was a tailor who wanted to try something new. I didn't know how long he was going to last or if he's going to last at all in the business, so I didn't want the surprise."

Max Leventhal's new place would be a franchise in the Busy Bee chain, founded by Maxwell Garfunkel, the Moldavian immi-

grant owner of more than a dozen luncheonettes located throughout lower Manhattan. Innovative for their period, every Max's
Busy Bee worked on the principle of slim profit margins and high
volume, making money a penny at a time. The patrons were office
boys, building workers, struggling young lawyers, businessmen,
and the host of others who did not have much money to spend on
their lunches.

Maxwell Garfunkel had come to the United States at age
thirteen from Chişinău, near Odessa, in 1888. Arriving in New York
with all of fifty cents, Garfunkel toiled and saved. Eight years later,
he had amassed a $7,000 bankroll—the equivalent of $164,000
today. He used the money to open his first restaurant, on Ann
Street in downtown Manhattan. Everything in the joint—coffee,
pies, lemonade, typical luncheonette fare at the time—could be
had for two cents. Max's Busy Bee would not vary its prices for
twenty years.

When Garfunkel retired in 1928, he offered a glimpse of the
life of a hardworking luncheonette man. "For forty years, I've
worked from five o'clock in the morning until eight o'clock at
night. I've never had a real vacation. I am going to retire. I am tired.
Money is not everything. Frankfurters, coffee, lemonade, savings
accounts, seven days a week, little sleep, bustle, shouts, profits,
frankfurters, soft-shell crabs—these are my memories."

In his new job at the Eighteenth Street Busy Bee, and after only
six months in America, Nathan would make $7.50 a week. When a
competing luncheonette on Twenty-First Street offered essentially
to double his salary, he turned it down. "I says, 'Sorry, I'm working,
and I'm not going to give up my job.' Why? Because I didn't know
how long the Twenty-First Street place was going to last in the
business."

During this period, Nathan posed for three photographs of himself at the luncheonette. A bright-eyed but serious twenty-two-year-old man stares fixedly at the camera. In two of the shots, he stands apart from his fellow workers. An accident of the situation? Or is he already separating himself out from the crowd?

On the job, Nathan held various positions, including an early twentieth-century version of an advertising Mad Man. He used to post himself on the sidewalk outside the Busy Bee and loudly hawk its fare.

"So I was standing and working at the lemonade, a penny for a glass of lemonade. I took in fifteen dollars a day." (Which, to stop and think about it, means he sold 1,500 servings! In a ten-hour day, that works out to be more than two sales a minute.) "And I was hollering, 'Lemonade! Lemonade!' And the cops used to come over, trying to stop me."

The former authority-cowed Galician immigrant had learned by then to stand up for himself. He told the police, "Don't tell me, Officer, to stop. Go to the boss and tell him to stop me. If he stops me, I'll be glad to help, to stop hollering."

For two years, the hardworking, full-throated young Nathan followed Max Leventhal around Manhattan, moving from the Eighteenth Street store to another at 99 Spring Street, between Mercer and Broadway. The luncheonette business was a movable feast. But a change was afoot. Awaiting Nathan was an introduction to a fabled realm that would utterly transform his life.

5

Nickel Empire

"I'll give you a dollar and a half a day, but you have to pay if you eat a frankfurter." Feltman's Ocean Pavilion, the original hot dog haven at Coney Island.

THERE MIGHT HAVE been sufficient hours crammed into Nathan's five-in-the-morning-to-eight-at-night workdays, but there weren't enough days in the week. Because of Abrahamic traditions, the restaurant business in Manhattan was a somewhat limited affair. On Saturdays, businesses were either closed or slow because of the Jewish Sabbath, and Sundays were dead because of the Christians. What was a determined young luncheonette counterman to do? Two days of thumb twiddling wasn't an option. He needed to *work*.

Gradually, the whole Handwerker clan emigrated from Europe. Nathan's older sister Anna was one of the early arrivals. Everyone was too busy to see much of each other, but Anna told him tales of a beach town in Brooklyn where she sometimes found part-time employment. It sounded like some fantasy destination, an amusement park similar to, but far outdoing, the famed Prater in Vienna.

He had first visited one memorable Saturday during his first summer in America. Nathan took a younger cousin of his, a girl whose name has been lost to history, for a day at the beach. The journey through the city from Manhattan to the sea was arduous. The train lines stretching from Manhattan all the way to Coney Island were still a couple of years in the future. Nathan and his cousin hopped aboard a subway from Manhattan to downtown Brooklyn. From there, they took a ten-cent streetcar ride along Flatbush Avenue, spending another nickel for a transfer at Prospect Park Circle to a train that ran south on Ocean Parkway.

The famous boulevard, a creation of Central Park designers Frederick Olmsted and Calvert Vaux, cut through the heart of Brooklyn. It was the kind of broad, stately thoroughfare that allowed New York to rival the great capitals of Europe for elegance. As its name implies, Ocean Parkway led Nathan and his cousin straight to the Atlantic.

A small spit of scrubland, sand dunes, and beach, Coney Island served as a barrier island for the mainland, protecting it from the crash of storms. The Lenape tribe named the place Narrioch, meaning "land without shadows," since it faced south and was bathed in sunlight for the entire day. The first settlers from Europe, the Dutch, called it Conyne Eylandt, or Rabbit Island, for the copious number of the long-eared critters that infested the grassy sand dunes. By the time a pair of Galician immigrant cousins showed up in the seaside resort town, it had taken on its modern name.

Nathan was feeling flush. He had five dollars in his pocket, a full week's wages, the equivalent of $120 today. All the amusement rides were a nickel. At Feltman's, the sprawling restaurant and pleasure garden that its founder had developed from lowly push-cart beginnings, frankfurters in a warm bun were sold for a dime.

Nathan sponsored the whole trip. "I was glad to do it. I enjoyed it." He recalled that his cousin "bought a whole stack of Cracker Jacks." The snack—actually Cracker Jack, singular—has been called "the first junk food." Even back then, it was already associated with America's national pastime of baseball, from a well-known mention in the 1908 song "Take Me Out to the Ball Game." Nathan later remembered getting angry and yelling at his young cousin when she flippantly gave boxes of the snack away to passersby, a willful squandering of his hard-earned money.

All told, though, it had been a fine summer outing, one of the first days Nathan had taken off in his new homeland. Back in Manhattan, he began to encounter constant mentions and references to the Brooklyn beach resort that he and his cousin had visited. Max Singer, a Coney Island businessman who owned a small stand on Surf Avenue, made it a habit of dropping by Max's Busy Bee every Thursday. Mr. Singer was romantically interested in Nathan's sister Anna and soon struck up a friendship with her brother Nathan. Eventually, Nathan asked the man about employment, trying to fill his slack time when the Manhattan luncheonette traffic dwindled on the weekends.

"Mr. Singer, could you give me a job in the summertime, Saturday, Sunday? We close the place [Max's Busy Bee] in the afternoon on Saturday. So I can come out and work for you on

Saturday. I could work half a day on Saturday, until one, two o'clock in the morning, and then Sunday a whole day."

His current seventy-five-hour workweek wasn't enough. Nathan wanted more. But Max Singer couldn't do anything for him. He suggested that the eager beaver should go out to Coney Island himself and canvass the many restaurants that were springing up along Surf Avenue, catering to the growing crowds of visitors.

It took him a while, but in the summer of 1914, Nathan finally went out to Coney Island to seek seasonal work in earnest. At first, he struck out. A certain Mr. Kissler, a contact given to him by Singer, was friendly but unable to help. "I'm sorry, I'm filled up," he was told. "But go to this fella, across the street." When that establishment also lacked openings, Nathan would return to Singer. "Can you give me another place to go?" he would ask. He was dogged, unwilling to take no for an answer, unafraid of bothering people again and again.

Finally, Singer said the magic words. "Go to Feltman's."

The restaurant complex first founded by Charles Feltman in the boom years after the Civil War was hard to miss. By the time Nathan visited, it sprawled over a full city block, West Tenth Street from Surf Avenue to the beach. The place hosted a million visitors during the summer season.

Charles Feltman died in 1910, but his business continued to thrive under his family. When Nathan went to the restaurant looking for work, he approached Sam Land, a frankfurter chef at one of the grills. The man was a subcontractor of sorts, working for a percentage of the sales, and he hired out workers on his own.

"Mr. Singer sent me," Nathan told him, not quite an outright lie. "I want to ask if you can give me a job."

"Where are you working now?" asked Land.

"I'm at the Busy Bee in Manhattan."

"What are you doing at the Busy Bee?"

"Everything," Nathan replied. "Selling frankfurters, cutting rolls . . ."

"Are you a good roll cutter?"

"Excellent." That wasn't a lie. He had enough experience to know he was a good roll cutter. After all, how bad can one be at such work? The real skill was speed. On a busy summer's day, Feltman's dished up forty thousand hot dogs to one hundred thousand customers.

"I'll give you a dollar and a half a day," Land told Nathan. "But you have to pay if you eat a frankfurter."

"So I worked," Nathan remembered in his characteristically understated way. His summer workweek stretched to seven days. He returned home from Coney on Sunday at one or two o'clock. In those days before a subway connection, the commute into the city took him at least ninety minutes by trolley car. Monday morning, he had to show up at his regular job at the Busy Bee by 6:00 A.M.

Hard work. Coney Island. Frankfurters. He might not have immediately realized what he had done, but Nathan had put together a winning formula that would propel him to success. There was just one more factor to the algorithm, and it would take him a little while to discover it.

The nickel.

The Coney Island that Nathan first encountered was in the midst of a startling change, transforming from an elitist playground into a truly populist one. In the early years of the twentieth century, what attracted wide interest to the area was not the sea, not amusements, not food. The words "Coney Island" meant one thing: horse racing.

Three tracks—sponsored by the Brighton Beach Racing Association, the Coney Island Jockey Club, and the Brooklyn Jockey Club—catered to a mania for horse flesh and gambling. Racing made Coney famous, with the season stretching from May to October.

Even as it attracted up to forty thousand spectators for a race, the turf was by and large a rich man's game. Diamond Jim Brady, millionaire scion William Kissam Vanderbilt, corrupt attorney Abraham Hummel all ran thoroughbreds. Wealthy Wall Streeters, industrialists, and business magnates lined the shores of Sheepshead Bay with their pleasure boats and summer beach houses. The three tracks each had a different atmosphere. Brighton Beach was known for racing touts and gamblers, Gravesend drew the hoi polloi, while Sheepshead Bay ("America's Ascot") invited the social elite.

Growing hand in hand with the tracks were attractions catering to the adult male: brothels, beer halls, and gambling dens. Located in the so-called Gut District of Coney's West End, these disreputable businesses were mostly wood-framed structures that regularly burned to the ground, only to rise again, phoenixlike, from the ashes. The Gut gave Coney Island its seamy, dangerous reputation.

The horse-racing craze helped Coney Island to grow, with several rail lines servicing the area and Ocean Parkway providing a direct link to downtown Brooklyn. But in the years before Nathan arrived to take up his lowly duties as a Feltman's roll cutter, a wave of moralistic and Progressive fervor swept over the country that proved fatal to the Coney Island tracks—and to the Gut.

Ministers railed against the excesses of gambling. The kind of elite monopolists and robber barons that supported the sport fell prey to Teddy Roosevelt's reforms. In 1908, Albany established regulations against betting at the tracks. Two years later, when the rules were tightened, the law sounded the death knell for Coney Island racing.

The tracks died, but Coney continued its upswing. A surging turn-of-the-century economy put a modicum of disposable income into the pockets of New York's laboring classes. The increasing recognition of the workers' half holiday on Saturday meant more free time for many. The idea of the weekend—opposed to the Sabbath—was slowly being born. In place of the elite horsemen, Coney began to attract the hordes of working day laborers who now found themselves with free time and a small amount of cash to spend on leisure activities.

By the end of the 1800s, the rail lines and roads that had led to the tracks now allowed the further development of a new sort of pleasure ground, one that welcomed and embraced even those with the most limited of means. This would be the cresting tide that would lift Nathan Handwerker to prosperity.

Charles Feltman could serve as his model. The founder of Nathan's new place of employment never got the opportunity to meet the ambitious young roll cutter posted at one of his famous restaurant's grills. But he would have seen glimmers of his own work ethic and drive in the young man's face.

Born in the German district of Hanover in 1841, Feltman came to America at age fourteen. He worked many different jobs, in a coal yard and on a farm, before fate led him to a bakery on Smith Street in South Brooklyn. While he was delivering baked goods, he first encountered the charms of the seaside at Coney Island.

A company brochure from Feltman's credits its founder with having invented the hot dog: "Charles Feltman is widely known to have invented the hot dog at Coney Island in 1867," the pamphlet reads. But the truth is that the hot dog has many fathers. Charles Feltman is undeniably one of them. He never used the term himself, however, preferring other names: frankfurter (after the city of Frankfurt in his native Germany), "dachshund sandwich," or "Coney Island red hot." His creation was specifically a pork sausage lovingly nested in a warm bun.

Others claim precedence—or at least incidence. At the 1904 Louisiana Purchase Exposition in Saint Louis, a Bavarian immigrant named Anton Ludwig Feuchtwanger supposedly handed out gloves for his customers to handle the hot sausages he sold them. When that practice proved too awkward and expensive, Feuchtwanger's wife proposed placing the frankfurter in a bun. He remains prominent in the lore because the name "Feuchtwanger," when connected to sausage, is too hard to resist.

The popularization of the hot dog has also been credited to Harry Stevens, a Brit who innovated concessions at American baseball games in the early twentieth century. On a cold day, when his ice cream sandwiches weren't moving, Stevens instructed his staff to sell "dachshund sandwiches" instead. Ted Dorgan, a cartoonist commemorating the event, did not know how to spell "dachshund," so he called them "hot dogs" instead.

The mythology around the invention of the hot dog may be charming, but the actual facts are elusive. Smallish pork sausages known as *Würstchen* that were similar to the modern hot dog seem to have originated in the area near modern-day Frankfurt in the Middle Ages. "Weiner" is another spelling of Vienna, where a pork-beef variation became popular in the 1700s. "Dog," as applied to sausage, arose from the fact that dogmeat was sometimes used in German sausage making. The first verified use of the term "hot dog," as applied to sausage, cropped up in an 1892 New Jersey newspaper article.

None of this detracts or diminishes from the incredible up-by-the-bootstraps story of Charles Feltman. The years immediately following the Civil War found him hauling a lowly pie wagon around the dunes and "sandy wastes" of Coney Island. The crowds had not yet descended upon the windswept beach, but even then, there were hints of the future. Feltman sold his fare to the horse-racing aficionados and to the swelling numbers of people who came to Coney for the bracing seaside air.

For the first few years, Feltman worked his pushcart. Clams were the big sellers in the neighborhood. The humble bivalves were harvested in seemingly inexhaustible numbers along the shores of Sheepshead Bay, on the leeward side of the island, and to a lesser degree along the ocean shore. It was the clam, a cheap and abundant staple, not frankfurters, that was most closely associated with Coney during the late nineteenth and early twentieth centuries. Grilled clams, clam roasts, and the clambake were common features of a visit to the beach.

Throughout the 1860s, the young Feltman brought pies from Brooklyn bakeries and delivered them to Coney Island businesses. He made the rounds of what was then a ramshackle collection of seaside saloons and hotels. Responding to popular demand, he began to sell seafood to the tourists from his pie wagon. But when the weather turned brisk, customers wanted not cold clams but hot food. How to serve up a hot sandwich from a pushcart?

The mythology surrounding the rise of Charles Feltman records the specific circumstances of what happened next. The pie wagon entrepreneur presented his problem to a wheelwright named Donovan (first name or last is unknown) who had built Feltman's original pushcart. Donovan worked out of a shop at East New York Avenue and Howard Street, on the far eastern edge of Crown Heights in Brooklyn. There he first fabricated an innovation that has lasted to this day, installing in the well of Feltman's cart a charcoal brazier for the sausages and a metal warming box for the rolls.

Thus, in the year 1867—other sources say 1874—came the birth of the hot dog, the frankfurter in a bun, on American shores.

The dream was always to step up from the pushcart to a permanent location. In 1871, Charles Feltman did exactly that, leasing a small tract of land for his first restaurant. Three years later, Feltman purchased land outright, a tract at West Tenth Street that stretched to the sea. In those days, the shoreline was ever changing, and in subsequent years, Coney Island's foremost restaurateur saw his property actually increase in size as sand piled up on the beach.

He took advantage. His Ocean Pavilion sprawled. It would grow to become an incredible assemblage of restaurants, attractions, and gardens, capable of plating eight thousand dinners at a time. Feltman fully recognized that a good businessman had to have a little showman in him. He built a ballroom, a roller coaster, and an outdoor movie theater. Feltman's 1877 carousel was designed by master carver Charles Looff. The *New York Times* reported that he imported "the first Tyrolean yodelers ever heard in this country."

Feltman's employed a thousand workers. In addition to the nine restaurants and seven grills on the premises, there was also a hotel, a bathhouse, a model Swiss village, and a *Deutscher Garten*—a German beer garden—modeled after those in his beloved hometown of Hanover. Feltman's maple garden was famous as a gathering place for high rollers from the seaside horse tracks. The whole Ocean Pavilion complex fully deserved the appellation "pleasure garden."

In 1886, Feltman started his own bakery on Classon Avenue in Brooklyn's Bedford-Stuyvesant neighborhood. As that prospered, he erected a massive building at Sixth Avenue and Tenth Street near Prospect Park to house his thriving business. Ocean Parkway, the main stem leading directly to Coney, was just a few blocks away. Feltman could bake his own rolls for the dachshund sandwiches he sold in the thousands. The record was forty thousand Coney Island red hots sold in a single day. Be that as it may, the most celebrated dish at Feltman's Ocean Pavilion was not the frankfurter but the "shore dinner" of clams, oysters, lobster, and fish.

When Nathan became a Feltman's roll cutter, he found it difficult to economically justify his weekend job. To take the trolley for two days, coming and going, cost him sixty cents and an hour and a half of his time. He made six dollars for the two days of work, so the commute cut into his wages. So did lunch. It was a bothersome fact of life that Nathan had to eat. With the advent of World War I, the price of Feltman's frankfurters had just been raised from a nickel to a dime.

"One frankfurter wasn't enough, and if I buy two frankfurters, it would cost me twenty cents for lunch," Nathan recalled. "I had to buy a glass of beer for five cents, so all in all, that's a quarter."

In Europe that June, what was then called the Great War finally kicked off in earnest. Self-involved, isolationist America had little idea hostilities were about to break out. Thousands of clueless American tourists were caught unawares, their tour of the Continent rudely interrupted by cannon fire. The little shoemaker's son from Galicia had proved prescient.

Nathan may have been too distracted to give his former homeland much thought. Between the Busy Bee in Manhattan and Feltman's in Coney Island, his seven-days-a-week schedule was brutal. To cut expenses, he would sometimes sleep on the floor in one of Feltman's kitchens. When the Sea Beach line connecting Manhattan and Brooklyn opened on June 22, 1915, the commute to Coney got quicker and cheaper, ten cents each way. Nathan was promoted to a waiter's position, and his wage gradually increased to the point he was making twelve dollars for the weekend, double compared to when he'd started.

"So I was in good shape," he said. "I was able to save a few dollars." Specifically, he put away $2.50 a week, a princely $130 per year—in buying power, the modern equivalent of about $3,000.

There were cruel bumps along the road. A bank failed, and Nathan lost the money he had deposited. It was a crushing blow for the newly arrived immigrant, a hard-earned $150 gone without recourse. During those perilous economic times, banks failed with regularity. In 1913, forty-six collapsed in the United States, with total assets of $13.8 million. In December of that same year, President Wilson signed the Owens-Glass Act, a measure that created the Federal Reserve System and was designed to quell the financial panics that led to bank failures. But the legislation was too late to help Nathan Handwerker

He had to pick himself up and start all over again. After the setback, he simply continued with his program of long workdays and the painstaking, week-by-week putting away of a few dollars. He didn't go out much. He lived a frugal life. The whole routine was difficult. Somehow he kept his spirits up under the strain. Nathan didn't broadcast the news, but inside, he nurtured a secret dream.

The Store

"I'll be there seven days a week, and I'm making five cents a frankfurter." Nathan's Famous, ca. 1920, looking south on Seaside Walk.

HUMANS HAD BEEN plundering the fat of Coney's land for a long time. Even before the coming of the Europeans, the Lenape and Carnarsie tribes mined Coney Island's shores for oyster shells to turn into strings of seawan, or wampum currency. In the modern era, one political boss after another milked the place as a cash cow.

The more things changed, though, the more they remained the same. Coney Island, as Nathan encountered it in 1914, was in the process of shedding one nickname, "Sodom by the Sea," in favor of another, "America's Playground." Coney Island could have been pried out of the hands of private interests and developed into a people's park. Instead, it was sliced and diced like a hog at a rendering plant.

Real reform was a few years down the line. The boardwalk was piecemeal: a section in front of Steeplechase Park, another farther to the east, all privately owned. A continuous oceanfront public promenade was as of yet just a proposal of a few progressives. Access to the ocean was still a hit-or-miss proposition, with large sections of the beach controlled and fenced off by private bathhouses, hotels, and beer gardens (including Feltman's).

The legality of all this was murky. Property titles along the beach were notoriously tangled, a state of affairs that allowed moneyed interests to elbow aside local leaseholders.

But in the early years of the twentieth century, a magical transformation happened. Somehow, despite pressures from all sides, Coney Island was in the process of stumbling into its golden age.

"It is blatant, it is cheap, it is the apotheosis of ridiculous, but it is something more," author, screenwriter, and New York bon vivant Reginald Wright Kauffman wrote of Coney Island in 1909. "It is like Niagara Falls or the Grand Canyon or Yellowstone Park. It is a national playground and not to have seen it is not to have seen your own country."

That summer of 1909, twenty million fun-seekers trekked to Coney Island. Among them was Sigmund Freud, on his first and only visit to the United States. The good doctor labeled America "a mistake, a giant mistake," but claimed that Coney Island was the only thing about the country that interested him.

Credit for this has to be given to the growth of the American amusement park, which swept up the area in a sort of riot of the imagination.

The country's first roller coaster opened at Coney Island in 1884, a gravity-powered prototype that hit a kiddie-ride speed of six miles an hour. A year later, Sea Lion Park became the first enclosed amusement park in the country. With its sole popular attraction, the Water Chute, it lasted only until 1902. Other larger, more sophisticated establishments soon took its place.

Chief among them, the holy trinity of Coney's golden age, the Big Three: Steeplechase Park, Luna Park, and Dreamland.

They came on in quick order. Brilliant entrepreneur George Tilyou founded Steeplechase in 1897, spending the next years constantly enlarging and refining its attractions. Luna Park opened in 1903, taking over and enlarging the footprint of the original Sea Lion Park (and, earlier, the site of the famed Elephant Hotel). A year later, the last and arguably trippiest of the Big Three, Dreamland, completed the classic Coney Island trifecta. Together, they formed a million-lightbulb "Electric Eden," the brilliantly garish phantasmagoria that newly arriving European immigrants could glimpse from far out at sea.

By 1914, in his post cutting rolls and waiting tables at Feltman's, Nathan was square in the middle of the action. Dreamland burned in spring 1911, but Luna Park ("The Heart of Coney Island") faced Feltman's on Surf Avenue. Just past the amusement park loomed the 125-foot Iron Tower, imported from Philadelphia's Centennial International Exhibition of 1876 and equipped with steam elevators. Seven blocks to the west was George Tilyou's new, updated Steeplechase, easily reached by that alleyway of broken dreams, the busy, attraction-packed lane called the Bowery.

Working at Feltman's was like living at a three-ring circus.

Across the street at Luna Park, actual premature infants inhabited a collection of baby incubators. Igorrote tribespeople from the Philippines were put on display like show animals. Freaks, geeks, and daredevils drew crowds at the sideshows of the Bowery.

Some of the booths in the Bowery's "Little Cairo" section offered erotic dancers, tame by modern standards, daring for the day. In fact, sex was the secret allure that permeated the whole area. Coney Island was to some extent extraterritorial, a free-fire zone where the rules and restrictive customs of society were loosened. The genders mixed. A visitor to Steeplechase, for example, might be thrown against a stranger of the opposite sex in the Barrel of Fun, the Human Pool Table, or the Whirlpool. Coney Island was promiscuous in a way even the overcrowded streets of Manhattan's Lower East Side were not.

Beyond the parks lay the sparkling Atlantic. Doctors had only recently begun touting the health benefits of ocean bathing. Women's bathing suits covered torsos and extremities with a vengeance, but because they dared to show bodily forms, they were considered risqué. Men's topless bathing remained taboo. Even children were swaddled within an inch of their lives. Yet the sensuality of bathing with thousands of strangers remained.

Build it, and they will come. The number of visitors to Coney Island rose each season, from tens of thousands in the 1870s to the early twentieth century when on summer weekends the daily crowds routinely topped one hundred thousand. Every year, Feltman's served more than a million customers, pumping out its shore dinners and dachshund sandwiches by the thousands.

More than a physical reality, Coney Island began to develop a dream reality, too. What was once a deserted, sandy wasteland now situated itself in the world's imagination like an intoxicating mirage. Postcards documenting seaside visits poured out in streams, and then rivers, and then floods. Coney Island became the most postcarded venue in the world and, even to this day, in history. On a single day in September 1906, two hundred thousand postcards were mailed from the resort town.

Yes, Coney Island was a head-turning kind of place, and Nathan's head spun along with everyone else's. But where others saw mere amusement, Nathan focused on opportunity. He saw the millions funneling through gates of Culver Terminal and the nearby Sea Beach line. A thought naturally occurred: a few pennies, nickels, and dimes from each one of those visitors could add up to something big. The two ends of the retail spectrum are volume and exclusivity. Coney had the one to such a degree that it didn't need the other.

Through his job as a Feltman's waiter, a few of those nickels and dimes had already found their way into the pocket of Nathan Handwerker. Bank failures notwithstanding, in two seasons at Coney Island, 1914 and 1915, and during four years while working at Manhattan luncheonettes, Nathan had managed to save $300.

In the summer of 1916, he took a rare day off. A coworker at the Busy Bee named Sam (again, last name lost to history) ran the waffle-and-ice-cream concession at the luncheonette. The two men spoke of going into business for themselves. That day, Nathan suggested a scouting trip.

"Sam, let's go out to Coney Island."

Saturday. Nathan still worked at Feltman's. He should have been in a waiter's apron that day. His bosses could have found him out. But it was easy to remain anonymous amid the numberless throng along Surf Avenue. The season was just beginning. He and Sam joined the vast parade of humanity. The first rental property they looked at was a barbershop.

"They asked $150 [per month] for the place, for just a piece of counter," Nathan recalled. "So I'm hesitating. I didn't like it. There's nothing there—no water, no sinks, nothing, no sewer."

While Sam remained behind, negotiating with the barbershop's owners, Nathan returned to the bustle of the street to look around. He stood in the middle of the block between Stillwell Avenue and Fifteenth Street. Looking up and down the block, he noticed a building on the south side of Surf Avenue that stood out from a small lane then called Seaside Walk.

The lane would soon be renamed after a local bottler of soda water, Philip Schweickert Sr. At some point during the succeeding years, the *c* was dropped, and the street sign became "Schweikerts Walk." (The good news is that you have a small slice of Coney Island named after you—the bad news is that the New York City Department of Transportation is going to forever misspell your name.) Even in the mid-1920s, the lane was still sometimes referred to by its original appellation of Seaside Walk.

The counter offered for lease was tiny, just five feet long on Surf and another eight feet deep on Schweikerts. Nathan noticed that some structures on the street seemed to disappear amid the crowds of people. But he could see the little corner building from the middle of the block.

He returned to the barbershop and summoned his erstwhile partner. "See that place? There's a corner there. Let's go and see."

A man dozed inside the store's cramped interior. Sam approached him, and the two of them spoke German, of which Nathan understood a little. The proprietor wanted $300 for a lease on the premises.

ach
spe-
on a

ring
ence
un-

g to
for a

ting

me,

off,

t to

and
ome
ss as
at 97
. The

oney.
the

ord."

than said.

it?" Sam responded, doubtful.

partner, I'll take you. And if you don't want

signed the contract for the tiny counter
weikerts. The landlord accepted $150 from

pire was born. Like a lot of great empires, it
from the start.

d to the Surf Avenue location as "the store."
nan's Famous" then. It wasn't called any-
guys, Nathan and Sam, selling frankfurters
ade and orangeade going for a nickel.
what would become an empire was literally
ore had no real foundation. Nathan laid
directly on the dun-colored Coney Island
placed planks over them. Proper concrete
s in the future.
ng Coney Island's main stem was certainly
s flocked to the amusements, vaudeville
es along Surf and the Bowery. Feltman's,
of Nathan's new store, hosted over two mil-
r.
't add up. Nathan and Sam took in a grand
n their first weekend, Saturday through
gh to keep the place afloat. The competi-
could look over to the nearby intersection

of Surf and Stillwell and count four restaurants, one on
corner, including an outlet of the popular Nedick's chain. It
cialized in frankfurters, which sold for ten cents and came
toasted bun.

"Sam, let's make them a nickel," Nathan suggested, refer
to the store's own dime frankfurters. He had years of experi
at Manhattan luncheonettes, moving five-cent dogs in the
dreds per day. Why not at Coney?

"Nathan, I'm afraid," Sam responded. "They're goin
put us out of business. You'll be the only one selling them
nickel."

Nathan silently cursed. He sensed his partner was ge
cold feet all around.

"My fiancée gave me an argument," Sam said. "She aske
'Why did you get a place?'"

"Well, what do you want to do?" Nathan asked.

"Pay me off."

Nathan didn't have to think too long. "Okay, I'll pay yo
$150. Good enough?"

Sam agreed. "But you have to bring the money. You
bring on Thursday the money."

Nathan had exhausted his savings on his half of the leas
purchasing equipment and inventory. How was he going to
up with $150 in four days? He reached out for a loan to his b
Max's Busy Bee, who had just opened up another restaurant
Spring, a cafeteria-style eatery next door to the luncheonette
loan was late in coming.

"So, Thursday, no money," Nathan recalled. "Friday, no m
Saturday, still." He was in danger of losing his investment i
little Surf Avenue storefront.

Sam came to him that weekend. "You didn't keep your v

But the next day, the loan came through, and the buyout was settled. Nathan no longer had a partner. He was the sole leaseholder of a thin slice of Coney Island commercial real estate, a store that so far had failed to pay for itself.

Seventy percent of new start-up restaurants fail, a ratio that has held constant over the years. Nathan was desperate to succeed. "When I came to this country, I had nothing," he said, looking back at this period. "I knew that if I didn't really work hard and do something, I couldn't survive."

His first idea was to expand his product line. He knew of a store on Broome Street in Manhattan, a block south of the Busy Bee, that sold malteds, candy, and cigarettes. The place had a machine for sale, used and cheap, a mixer for making malted milkshakes. He bought the rig and then went farther downtown to Delancey Street, where he knew of a firm called I. Lefkowitz & Son, a syrup manufacturer.

Nathan had in mind to create the finest malted in New York. He purchased a half gallon of chocolate syrup and a half gallon of vanilla, the latter to "open up the flavor of the malted." Enlisting his older brother Joseph, he lugged the machine and the stock of ingredients out to Brooklyn and the little cubbyhole store on Surf Avenue.

"Three cents for a malted, five cents for a malted with ice cream, six cents for a little ice before the machine mixes it up. I had the best malted to buy."

He wasn't finished. In Coney, he bought another "little machine," one that would grind a whole pineapple to make juice. "Two cents for a pineapple juice. Fresh made, like the orangeade and lemonade."

It didn't matter. Nothing did the trick. He was still selling frankfurters for a dime and still grossing no more than sixty or seventy dollars on summer weekends, not enough to keep him in business.

There were other difficulties. Joseph Handwerker had been working as a peddler, and Nathan wanted to give his brother a leg up. He brought him out to the struggling Coney Island store.

"'Come, want to help me?' I says to him. 'Come on.' I didn't tell him anything. I didn't promise to make him a partner. I thought that I'll see how it works out."

He first gave Joseph the deceptively simple job of making lemonade, something that, by that time, Nathan had been doing nearly every day for four years. Joseph might not have yet grasped the fact that in Nathan Handwerker's world, there was a right way and wrong way of doing everything—at least, everything within the microcosm of a luncheonette.

"I told him what to do to make lemonade. I tell him how to make it, and he makes it another way. The way he makes it, the sugar wouldn't melt. Because if you put the lemon and the sugar in together, the sugar gets hardened up. First you got to put the lemon, then half water, then sugar, then spoon, mix it. Four gallons a night to make."

How hard could it be? But perhaps the issue was a younger brother telling an older brother what to do. A disagreement ensued, escalating into a full-blown argument, with the two siblings yelling at each other. The passersby on Surf Avenue might have thought it was just one more Coney Island sideshow. The quarrel culminated in Joseph cursing Nathan out and spitting in his face.

"He cursed me the devil to my mother in Yiddish," Nathan recalled. Since the two were brothers, it was an odd oath. "I say to him, 'Why are you cursing your own mother?'"

The first experiment in Handwerker nepotism ended in disaster.

"I didn't say nothing to him after that," Nathan recalled. "At night, I paid him off. And I says, 'Joe, I'm sorry. I didn't want to fight with you. Business is business, and I can't do it. You're not for me. I told you what to do, you didn't do the right thing, you didn't listen to me, and you're not for me.' I didn't hire him anymore."

Nathan was a tough boss from the start. At the young age of twenty-four, he had already developed an uncompromising management style. Business was business, as he said, and in business dealings, he would forever be a hard soul. Early poverty in Galicia had broken many people, but with Nathan, it seemed hardship had only tempered his steel.

There were two elements for success in business. There was toughness on the one hand and on the other a taste for calculated risk. Joseph Handwerker was content to work a pushcart. ("If you want to be a peddler, be a peddler," Nathan said when showing his older brother the door.) On a scale of daring, perhaps opening a store on Coney was not extreme, but within the context of Nathan's hard-scrabbling, dog-eat-dog immigrant world, it was a gamble.

As was his next move, lowering the price of his signature product to a nickel. He had proposed this plan to his first partner, Sam. Now, with no partner to object, Nathan forged ahead. Frankfurters would be five cents instead of ten, and two cents for lemonade.

Sam had originally objected to the idea out of fear that the Coney Island bosses wouldn't welcome a threat to the status quo. Nathan himself remembered worrying about the boldness of his new business plan: "I was afraid of the politicians trying to close me out for underselling everybody. But I took a chance. I didn't give up."

Were his fears justified? Would there be interference from Coney Island bigwigs, angry over competition for such powerful establishments as Feltman's? Ever since its beginnings in the nineteenth century, the resort town had always been rife with cronyism. The audacious newcomer with his tiny five feet of storefront would be underpricing the big boys. Nathan didn't know how such a move would go down in the tightly knit business community around him. He had learned during his childhood in Galicia to fear the arbitrary moves of those in authority. The notorious Habsburg bureaucracy had taught him well.

But as he waited for the other shoe to drop, it never did. "Nobody ever bothered me about it," Nathan said later.

No one interfered, and there's some question if anyone in power even noticed the little store on the corner of Surf Avenue and Schweikerts Walk. Who did notice—in droves—were the working people who came on holiday to Coney Island. Many of them were common laborers, visitors who had to count their pennies and well knew the difference between a dime and a nickel. They recognized a bargain when they saw one.

The first weekend Nathan dropped the price of a hot dog, he more than quadrupled his business. He took in $260 as opposed to the $50 or $60 he had been grossing before. He had discovered a price point, as modern business schools would term it, and he had done so instinctively, without a day's worth of education and indeed without even being able to read or write.

He was on his way. Nathan didn't need to be told twice, and he didn't hesitate, either, but plunged in with both feet. It was another business lesson he grasped intuitively. Recognize a win when one comes along.

"I go to my boss on Spring Street," he recalled. "I say to him, 'I'll give you a week's notice until you get somebody.' Instead of going to Coney just for the weekend, I'll be there seven days a week, and I'm making five cents a frankfurter."

7

Ida

"I liked her very much. So I hired her."
Nathan and Ida Handwerker, ca. 1920.

THAT SUMMER, WHILE Nathan was getting his first tantalizing taste of success in America, the war that would have killed him had he stayed in Europe cranked up to an unbelievable level of ferocity. Russia's celebrated June Advance of 1916 rolled over Nathan's home province of Galicia, one of the most lethal offensives in the history of warfare, with an incredible 1.6 million casualties.

It took another full year, but the United States entered the conflict in April 1917, the country dragged kicking and screaming into a war it had done its level best to ignore. Turning a blind eye didn't work, and in May, the Selective Service Act, passed the previous December, was enacted. The same monster that licked its lips in Galicia now reared its head in America, with modern-day *chappers* reaching out for recruits.

War fever gripped New York City. A ubiquitous stern-faced Uncle Sam, in J. M. Flagg's celebrated "I Want You" poster, jabbed his recruitment finger at passersby. Boarding the subway in Union Square, Nathan would have witnessed the surreal vision of a battleship afloat in the middle of the city. The navy erected a full-scale wooden mock-up of a vessel in the park, christening it USS *Recruit*. The government used the ship for enlistment and training.

Nathan experienced an uncomfortable sense of déjà vu. "I came from Europe to America for one reason—because from Europe I heard that a young man didn't have to go in the army in America." The new draft laws changed the rules.

But Nathan sidestepped them. The young immigrant, long enough in his new country not to be labeled a greenhorn, remained ineligible for the draft. The United States had entered the war on the side of the Allies (the UK, France, and Russia) against the Central Powers (Germany and Austria-Hungary). Since Nathan hailed from Austria-Hungary, he was considered an "enemy alien" and unsuitable as cannon fodder. He had not yet taken out "first papers," the initial step toward United States citizenship. He was safe.

As the world turned its fond gaze to violence, Nathan Handwerker found romance.

In modern parlance, he had no life. Nathan was spending all his time at the store, often sleeping overnight on a straw mattress or on the big burlap sacks full of potatoes. He installed a bell on the counter, so that if someone wanted a frankfurter at three or four in the morning, say, they could ring the bell and wake him up.

What he didn't have was a cash register. "I had a sugar box from a hundred pounds of sugar; it came in five-pound packages, twenty to a box. I turned over the box, and I put in all the money I made during the day. I had a little bag, a sleeping bag. And I slept next to the box."

Predictably, whatever social life Nathan had came through work. His sister Anna, the Handwerker sibling who had first introduced him to Coney Island, tried her hand at a business just down the block on Surf Avenue. She and a friend of hers, Ida Greenwald, had a small concession stand.

Nathan visited and could tell immediately that the two women weren't making any money. He refrained from criticizing because Anna's business partner was attractive. He asked Ida to come work for his store. In Nathan's world, such an invitation was tantamount to courtship. Anna Singer, who didn't seem to begrudge her brother poaching her partner, always said that Nathan offered Ida "big money" to make the switch.

"I liked her very much, so I hired her. She worked so fast, serving frankfurters and drinks and giving change." It was love. His new employee proved a speedy worker who could peel a fifty-pound bag of onions in under an hour. Nothing could have proven a more certain path to Nathan's heart.

In summer of 1918, sleeping in the store, he had a dream that he would become engaged to Ida. "I got dressed, and there was a fruit stand across the street. I says to myself, 'I'll buy a pear for her, a pear for me.'"

But his dream lover refused his humble offering. "Give it to your sister; she needs it better."

Nathan could be direct enough in business, but he was shy in love. Too nervous to come right out and pop the question, he asked Anna to speak for him. "I need you to go up and tell Ida that I want to get an engagement. If you do it, if you come back, if she'll accept it, I'll give you fifty dollars." Nathan watched as Anna went to Ida. He saw the two women talk and then shake hands. Anna came back to him.

"What did she say?"

"She said she's going to ask her father and mother."

"She agreed?"

"If she asks her father and mother," Anna said, wise to the ways of the world, "that means she agrees."

"When we make the engagement," Nathan said, "you get the fifty dollars."

On July 13, 1918, Nathan and Ida formally got engaged. They set October 26 for the wedding. In addition to the reward payment to his sister, Nathan also had to find someone to cover for him at the store during the engagement celebration. The process of getting hitched was proving to be an expensive proposition.

A summer Saturday in the middle of the busy season. He and Ida planned to go into Manhattan for the party. By that time, Nathan had a nephew working for him, another Joe Handwerker, Israel's son, named after Nathan's brother Joseph. Joe put on a formal jacket, naturally assuming he'd be invited to the festivities.

"Who's going to stay here?" Nathan asked. "We can't close; it's a hot day, it's July 13. How can I close the place?"

Joe sensed an opportunity. "Give me the fifty dollars you were going to give Anna."

Nathan hesitated.

"You gotta pay cash," Joe added.

What could Nathan do? A man has to celebrate one of the

most important events of his life. He dipped into the sugar box and counted out five thousand pennies for his nephew Joe. He had to dig even deeper for Ida's ring—$650 for a diamond solitaire, $10,000 in today's money. Then he went and got engaged.

That same summer of 1918, U.S. Marine casualties mounted in the vicious hand-to-hand combat of the Battle of Belleau Wood along the Marne River in France. In Russia, Bolshevik radicals lined the czar and his family up against a wall in a basement room and executed them. The disconnect between the bloody chaos in Europe and the chattering, laughing crowds at Coney Island had to be unsettling.

In Luna Park's War of the Worlds building (shaped like a massive battleship), paying customers watched the model boat navies of Germany, England, and Spain maneuver on a pretend sea. The armadas attacked New York Harbor, only to be repulsed by the heroic Admiral George Dewey and the American fleet. Until the caskets started coming home from France, the Luna Park show was the closest the war came to the homeland.

All during this period, Nathan's business had been growing in leaps and bounds or, more to the point in his case, foot by foot. Almost as soon as he leased the small store on Surf and Schweikerts, he had begun expanding.

"I bought a saw and made a bundle of wood and carried it in the subway. I had hammer and nails. I made an extension to my counter. Two feet more, because I didn't have enough room for an icebox. I needed to put more than one can of milk there. I needed two cans. I had to buy two cans, and each can was forty quarts."

The store lacked refrigeration. Keeping his food cold was a constant issue. A health inspector came by the store and demanded Nathan dump one of his cans of milk because it had not been stored at the proper temperature. He needed ice cream for his malteds. It was a common engineering problem that the totally un-schooled Nathan would solve in a simple but ingenious manner.

"I had no freezers, no refrigerators. So what could I do? I took some barrels, fifty-gallon barrels for sugar. I got them when they were selling sugar in a fruit stand nearby when they were making jelly apples."

Nathan cut the wooden sugar barrels in half and drilled a hole in the bottom. "I put a faucet in to drain the water out. Then I put a layer of ice, and a layer of frankfurters, a layer of ice, and a layer of frankfurters."

The cracked ice came in waxed, thirty-pound boxes, and the store would go through a whole box on busy summer Sundays. "If I didn't sell all the frankfurters, I used to take them out of the barrels every day, let the ice melt, and take the frankfurters out, and put more ice in, the same way, a layer of ice, a layer of frankfurters. I never lost a frankfurter, never got green, never got spoiled."

The hot dogs kept selling. Nathan kept the same limited menu, offering frankfurters, malteds, ice cream sodas, lemonade, orangeade, pineapple juice. He resisted adding new items. The walls of the storefront served as a bill-of-fare billboard. All the drinks sold for three cents except root beer, which was a nickel. An ice cream cone cost five cents, a malted milk five cents also.

The most expensive item was an ice cream soda that went for eight cents. In an early example of what would become a common practice touting the quality of the food, Nathan posted a sign offering a reward to anyone who could prove that the milkshake wasn't made from good Borden's ice cream.

He also made it a practice of shouting out his wares, as he had when he was hawking lemonade on a Manhattan street corner. Now that the products he was selling were his own, he put his lungs into it. "You could hear me for twenty blocks."

The menu stayed small, but the store kept enlarging. Nathan displaced a couple of neighboring businesses on what had now been renamed Schweikerts Walk, a shoeshine stand and a cigar store. "I kept on making two feet more, five feet more, stretching it out. Another piece of store, another piece of store."

The place was small, and for the whole first season, it was anonymous.

At the end of the summer, a woman approached the store. "Who is the boss?" she asked.

Nathan didn't want to tell her. He was standing in front, on Surf Avenue, hawking frankfurters. Questions were never good. Questions slowed him down. They implied a problem with customers or the intrusion of authority.

His workers, Ida and his nephew Joe among them, knew enough to stay silent, but the woman was persistent. "Why don't you want to tell me? What are you afraid of? I must know who the boss is."

The woman seemed almost ready for a fight. Nathan turned to her. "Ma'am, why do you want to see the boss? I'm the boss."

"I'm sending people to you, and they can't find you. You haven't got a name on your place. Why don't you put a name on so we can be able to find you? I know your stuff is very good. When I send my friends from the Bronx, they come here and can't find you."

"Lady, this is the end of the year. Labor Day is going to be here soon, and I'll be closing up the place for the winter."

By the following summer season, he told himself, *when I open up, I'll have signs.* "Next year," he promised the pestering woman, "I'll open up with a name."

As annoying as the nudge was, she had a point. Nathan started to think about a name for his store. *I've worked for Max's Busy Bee.*

But if I put Nathan Handwerker on, "Handwerker" would be hard to remember. It would take a hundred years to know how to find the store if it was called Handwerker's. So why can't I do the same thing like Max's Busy Bee in Manhattan?

Nathan's. Not "Nathan's Famous"—that addition would come along in a few years. "I put on Nathan's, and I paid three and a half dollars for the sign."

The Coney Island sign painter of choice in those days was Harry Wildman, who came to America from Austria in 1875. He designed the green Nathan's logo, complete with elaborate curlicues and serifs. Wildman's iconic work has survived, with a few modifications, to this day. As he had done with numerous signs and ads around Coney, he painted the broadly stylized lettering on oilcloth. Finally, the store had a name.

In later days, when the press agents took over publicity for the business, they deemed the true origin story too banal. A more romantic legend got cooked up, linking the naming of the business to a song that was popular at the time. The new story presented Nathan at the store, mulling thoughtfully over what he might call his new establishment. From a nearby café, a gramophone record played Sophie Tucker singing the chorus of a song, "Nathan, Nathan, Why You Waitin'?"

According to this version of events, while trying to come up with a name for his business, Nathan overheard Sophie, the "Red-Hot Mama," belting it out. He said to himself, *Wait a minute—my name is Nathan, so why don't I just call the place "Nathan's"?*

Naturally, in the way of all press-agent confections, the tale got mangled over time. "Nathan, Nathan, Why You Waitin'?" wasn't a Sophie Tucker's song—at least, she never recorded it. It was actually another chanteuse, Rhoda Bernard, who first put out a novelty number called "Nat'an (For What Are You Waitin', Nat'an?)." Comedian and singer Fanny Brice came along afterward with a reply song called "Oy, How I Hate that Fellow Nathan."

The lyrics of the Rhoda Bernard original offer a charming glimpse into romance, circa 1916.

> *Nat'an, Nat'an, Nat'an, tell me for what are you*
> *   waitin', Nat'an?*
> *You said we'd marry in June, my dear*
> *You told me the month, but you didn't say what year*
> *My whole family, they keep asking me, "Nu? When?"*
> *And I don't know what to tell them*
> *Nat'an, Nat'an, Nat'an*
> *I'm sick and tired of waitin' Nat'an*
> *Every minute seems like ages*
> *I should live to see to see the day*
> *That you make heavy wages*
> *Nat'an, Nat'an, what are you waitin' for?*

Labor Day came and went. The summer crowds dwindled and then disappeared entirely. But a funny thing happened on the way to Nathan closing up shop for the season. Day by day, he continued selling frankfurters. He kept telling himself that the next weekend would be the last, that finally it would no longer make economic sense to keep the little store open.

Coney Island was a summer resort town, but it was increasingly becoming a year-round residential neighborhood. The area was populous enough—and hungry enough—that there were customers even in the harshest weather. The store became the little hot dog stand that could.

Winter conditions at the store challenged all the employees. "My nose used to turn like a popsicle," recalled one veteran worker, adding that he once suffered a frostbitten ear from working in the cold. The store kept a fire in an ash can behind the counter. No matter how low the temperature fell, Nathan continued to exhort his troops.

"Sell!" he would call out. "Give 'em! Sell 'em!"

It was as though the new entrepreneur was walking a tightrope, knowing all the time that any minute he would fall off. But he never did. The store would never close from the day it first opened.

Nathan himself did take a rare weekend day off that fall—Saturday, October 26, 1918, when Nathan stopped keeping Ida waiting and they celebrated their marriage vows with an elaborate wedding. But once again, history would poke its ugly snout into Nathan's life in a disagreeable way. A specter of death more deadly than even the carnage on the battlefields of Europe cast a pall over a day that should have been sunny clear through.

———

"So I made a wedding. I hired a woman, a cook. I went to a butcher and bought fifty chickens. I bought fish, forty or fifty dollars' worth. I bought a big sack of flour, a whole box of eggs, a big box. Then I went down to the baker and paid him for a day's work. He used to bake all kinds of cake. Honeycake, spongecake, and cookies. I paid him forty dollars for the whole thing. And I bought a whole case of oranges for the wedding."

Here was Nathan declaring his new prosperity, spending what would have been, for him, only a few years before, an exorbitant sum—$1,700 in today's money—on his big day.

Only one thing was wrong. "Everyone was sick," Nathan remembered. "They had a fever."

A contagion stalked humankind at that time, one of the deadliest in history. The H1N1 influenza virus would wind up killing untold numbers of people. Fifty to a hundred million victims fell, a toll that is staggering both in its extent and its inexactitude. All told, 3 to 5 percent of the world's population died. In a perverse change from the usual, the young and healthy perished in greater numbers than did infants, the elderly, or the infirm.

The troop mobilizations allowed the contagion to spread quickly. "I saw hundreds of young stalwart men in uniform coming into the wards of the hospital," stated one U.S. Army doctor that fall. "Every bed was full, yet others crowded in. The faces wore a bluish cast; a cough brought up the bloodstained sputum. In the morning, the dead bodies are stacked about the morgue like cordwood."

On the Tuesday before Nathan and Ida's wedding, a record 869 New Yorkers died of influenza or the resulting pneumonia in a single twenty-four-hour period.

Nathan had invited three hundred guests to the nuptial celebration—members of the extended family, a few friends, fellow worshippers at their synagogue, and business associates—pretty much everyone he and Ida knew in New York.

Only 125 showed up. Like the rest of the public, Nathan couldn't quite grasp the true scope of what was happening. To maintain wartime morale, the horrific extent of the pandemic was suppressed in news reports. No one outside of public health officials and those in government knew that millions were dying. To Nathan, the event remained a private annoyance as much as a public tragedy.

The big day was a big bust. There was a lot of food left over.

After the wedding, the officiating rabbi approached Nathan. "Mr. Handwerker, what should I do with all this food? Where do you want to take it?"

"Give it to whoever you want," Nathan responded. He described his feelings: "I was sick and tired and disappointed."

The following day, Sunday, he and Ida were back at work in the Coney Island store.

8

The Frank

"Nothing went across that counter unless it was A-1 quality." The hot corner at Nathan's Famous, scene of the fastest action.

AT THE END of May in 1919, just in time for the summer season, there came a development that made Nathan Handwerker's fortune.

Success follows a certain pattern. The willingness to work hard is demanded, and with his seven-day workweeks and twenty-hour workdays, Nathan certainly qualified in that respect. But there are plenty of examples of hard workers who labor in obscurity and remain mired in borderline poverty. Industry is a necessary but not sufficient quality for achievement. An additional element is needed—something ineffable, random, and hard to pin down. Call it luck, or label it being in the right place at the right time.

The same angels that had covered him up during his journey to America now watched over Nathan in Coney Island. On May 29, 1919, West End Depot formally opened at Stillwell and Surf Avenues. The depot served as a combined terminal for almost all the transit lines coming in from Brooklyn and Manhattan. Trains had long arrived at nearby Culver Terminal, but this was different. Coney Island was now a nickel subway ride away from the five and a half million souls who lived in New York City, including the teeming neighborhoods of the Lower East Side.

And a hundred feet down Surf Avenue to the west of the depot was Nathan's store.

The crowds spilling from the trains came straight out of Emma Lazarus's poem: "Give me your tired, your poor, your huddled masses yearning to breathe free, the wretched refuse of your teeming shore." Whereas in the decades before, Coney had been a playground of the upper and middle classes, now more and more it became the province of the people, the Nickel Empire. The huddled masses endured the rocking, clanking, claustrophobic subway ride from the city. They emerged from the West End Depot yearning for . . . a frankfurter.

The train lines funneled thousands of potential customers every day directly past the store. The truism about the three most important factors in real estate—location, location, location—was true in spades for the fledgling frankfurter salesman. A restaurant like Nathan's lived and died by sales volume, and in the early years, volume depended in large part on foot traffic.

Subway riders left the depot and turned right—west—in order

to reach Steeplechase Park. Straight ahead toward the beach were the sideshow attractions of the Bowery. Both paths led directly past Nathan's Famous. A left out of the depot and a stroll of only a couple of blocks would put the hungry visitors at Feltman's, with its sit-down restaurants, pleasure gardens, and ten-cent frankfurters. But why take the trouble when Nathan's nickel dog was right in front of one's nose? Who needed Tyrolean yodelers?

Nathan's, Coney Island, and the hot dog were elements of a massive cultural shift happening in America at the time. In the United States, newly arrived immigrants were gaining access to a standard of living that would have elevated them to the middle class in their homelands. The labor and reform movements contributed to a vast, ongoing democratization of society. The economy screamed into overdrive, racing ahead toward the ditch plunge of the Great Depression.

Jazz music, the automobile, and radio all emphasized the increased velocity of day-to-day life. F. Scott Fitzgerald wrote of Jay Gatsby's riotous nouveau riche mansion on Long Island. A new kind of "fast woman" debuted, the flapper, hinting at a broad transformation in gender relations and sexual mores. Prohibition—the Eighteenth Amendment was ratified in January 1919—should have put a brake on things but only served to heighten the newfound sense of speed, illicitness, and danger.

Everything else was becoming faster—why not food? No one used the term "fast food" back then, but in practice, what Nathan Handwerker was doing on Surf Avenue represented a sign of the future. He had refined the quick-paced serving process to a science. Feltman's was a beer garden stroll. By comparison, a visit to Nathan's was a sprint.

With the new egalitarian atmosphere of places like Coney Island came a worry about lowering standards, a coarsening of the values of American life. Racial, religious, and ethnic biases played a part in this. In the nightmares of the WASP establishment, the whole country was slowly turning into a vast version of Manhattan's Tenth Ward.

Oddly enough, the hot dog became an element of the wider suspicions about rampant changes affecting society. The sausage—lowly, homely, often containing (gasp!) garlic—was deemed of suspect provenance, just like many of its consumers. Who knew where the population of the Lower East Side came from, and who knew where the ingredients of the hot dog came from? Trash people ate trash food.

It didn't help that lack of manufacturing standards and lax food inspection meant that sausages were oftentimes made from unhealthy, decayed, if not downright poisonous components. Lingering in the public imagination was the common German practice of incorporating dogmeat into sausage recipes. Horsemeat was another widely rumored ingredient. Meat-packers added sawdust and fillers to their products, regularly adulterating the links with formaldehyde and other toxic preservatives.

Upton Sinclair's popular 1906 novel, *The Jungle*, painted a horrific picture of meat production. The filth, sludge, and scraps from the slaughterhouse floor, Sinclair reported, were swept up to provide filler for sausages. The book had a hugely negative impact on meat sales in general and sausage sales in particular, helping spur passage of the Federal Meat Inspection Act and the Pure Food and Drug Act.

"I aimed at the public's heart," stated Sinclair, "and by accident I hit it in the stomach." In the aftermath of *The Jungle*, sausages suffered from an unhealthful reputation. "Laws are like sausages: it's better not to see them being made" became a popular saying at the time. Like a lot of famous quotes, the source of that one is in dispute. It's widely misattributed to German chancellor Otto von Bismarck, but no one has been able to pin down a source conclusively.

Hot dogs aren't really even the subject of the law-and-sausages metaphor. Legislatures, so his parallel goes, are like meat grinders. Given the low approval ratings of politicians, perhaps sausages were getting the worst of the comparison. In a sense, the hot dog was reborn with the onset of the Progressive Era. A food that had become suspect now needed a rigorous reform of government in order to become palatable again.

Nathan opened his store a full decade after publication of *The Jungle*. He worked hard to combat any unsavory associations the public might have with the product he sold. He explained to worried customers that there was a law in New York State, stipulating that if horsemeat was used in a food, a sign had to be posted saying so. "No horsemeat!" Nathan pledged.

Displaying the beginnings of a true Coney Island sense of showmanship, he hired a half dozen hospital orderlies, dressed them in white lab coats and stethoscopes, and then posed them at his counters, wolfing down frankfurters. Another sign went up over his counter: "If Doctors Eat Here It Must Be Good!" The idea was that if even physicians ate at Nathan's Famous, it just had to be safe and healthful. Just because the store's dogs were cheap at a nickel, they were good for you and were never, ever made from inferior ingredients.

Nathan distinguished his product in another way, too. The Nathan's frankfurter was all beef, made from quality cuts, brisket ends, beef cheeks, and sirloin scraps. Down the way on Surf Avenue, Feltman's dachshund sandwich was made with a pork sausage. Nathan sold a frankfurter that was billed as "kosher-style," meaning that while it hadn't undergone the rigorous, rabbi-monitored production of a true kosher dog, it was still all beef, never pork. In the public mind—even in the non-Jewish public mind—"kosher" was always associated with "quality."

Another prime element to the Nathan's Famous frankfurter was its casing, made from sheep intestines imported from Switzerland. The casing served to concentrate the juices inside the sausage and lend it extra flavor. But there was also a delightful tactile aspect to using natural casing. A distinctive *snap!* came with the first bite. The sound itself became a signature of the store's hot dogs just as much as their all-beef filling.

Sticking with natural casing became a point of pride with Nathan, especially after frankfurters made without casings began dominating the market. The skinless hot dog first appeared in Chicago in 1922, courtesy of an innovator named Erwin O. Freund. Working out of Chicago's Union Stock Yard—the same sprawling abattoir infamous from Sinclair's *The Jungle*—Freund made an enormous fortune from the development of an artificial casing that could replace animal intestines in the production of sausages.

The skinless hot dog is not really skinless in that it begins its life encased in an artificial casing of cellulose. The casing is created in a chemical process similar to that in the manufacturing of rayon fabric. Freund accidentally discovered that when his artificial casing was stripped away from the sausage, the meat filling retained its shape. The skinless hot dog was born.

The new product might have turned out a little less flavorful, a little less succulent, since there was no casing to contain the natural juices. Gone was the satisfying snap. Manufacturers deemed the trade-off in ease of manufacture and shipping worth it. They were freed from their reliance on the variable supply chains for pig, sheep, and cow intestines.

Gone also was the tie-off at the end of a natural sausage. Every skinless dog resembled every other skinless dog. A standardized shape was easier to package, transport, and display. Once again, as was the case with the modern tomato, say, a certain amount of flavor and distinction was sacrificed to the dictates of manufacture and distribution. Machines require products to be identical.

A description of the process of making hot dogs details the modern-day approach, which uses a sort of thick meat soup for filler. "The emulsion is pumped and fed into a stuffer," according to an industry trade group. "Shirred strands of cellulose casings are mechanically positioned on the stuffing horn. As the emulsion flows through the horn into the casing, the filled strands are linked into hot dogs of exact size."

The cellulose casings, the description continues, are then removed from the hot dogs by an automatic peeler. In most high-volume sausage factories, the whole affair proceeds assembly line–style, contained within the confines of a single gigantic machine. It's efficient, highly sanitary, and closely controlled.

Nathan preferred a more traditional style of frankfurter. He remained fanatic about the purity of his product and vigilant about quality control. In an effort to provide only the freshest food, the store kept a meticulous log that tracked sales against weather conditions, so that frankfurters and everything else could be ordered on an as-needed basis. Nathan wore a lot of hats in his business, including that of a meteorologist. Working off his store logs, he could predict approximately how many hot dogs the store would move on a rainy Sunday in July, for example, as opposed to a sunny one.

The law-and-sausage comparison naturally leads to another aspect of the hot dog's reputation—its link to democratic ideals.

It's a food of the people. Frankfurter consumption really took off after a watershed public event, the 1893 world's fair in Chicago. This was one of America's first truly democratic spectacles, with millions of people attending. It was like a coming-out party for the country's masses, and the hot dog was there.

At world's fairs and at the beach, portability was a major reason for the popularity of the frankfurter-and-bun combination. Essentially, consumers were offered a food—the dog—that came included with an edible plate—the bun. No utensils required. Portability helped at the ball park, too, further associating the hot dog with the great American pastime.

Frankfurter as a name for sausage came into the American idiom at the end of the nineteenth century, off popular wursts identified with Frankfurt, Germany. "Frankfurter Würstchen" has been a legally protected appellation since 1860, while the all-beef version, Frankfurter Rindswürste, came into being three decades later. Gref-Völsings, a successful Frankfurt butcher shop founded by Karl Gref and Wilhelmine Völsing, created the rindswurst in response to requests from Jewish customers for a kosher dog.

Hot dogs were "road food," meaning food consumed or purchased on the road. The automobile and Nathan's grew up together. The mash-up between car culture and American foodways only become more pronounced with time. Nathan's Famous never needed a drive-up window, because Surf Avenue would function as one.

"Most of the food that Americans hold so dear," stated celebrity chef Alton Brown, "things like hamburgers and hot dogs, were road food, but even before they were road food, they were peasant food."

Peasant food. It seems fitting that Nathan, a peasant from the shtetl, was responsible for popularizing the hot dog in such a major way.

For much of its history, Nathan's sold a frankfurter made by the same manufacturer, a Williamsburg, Brooklyn–based company that eventually assumed the name Hygrade Provision. Nathan knew a representative of the business from his days at Feltman's.

"He used to give me a Christmas present when I was working on the frankfurters," Nathan recalled. "Every year, he gave me fifty cents at Christmas."

It was the beginning of a beautiful friendship. The founder of Hygrade, Samuel Slotkin, born in Minsk, Russia, in 1885, was a gentleman cut of the same cloth as Nathan. "Mr. Slotkin's first loyalty was always to the quality frankfurter, and he used to order a side dish of them even when dining in nightclubs and fancy restaurants" read the man's *New York Times* obituary. "Early in his career he frowned on mixing meats in frankfurters and developed an all-beef frankfurter."

Of the skinless frank, Slotkin was wholly dismissive. "It has no use," he said. "All the use leaks out."

At first, Hygrade didn't want to deliver on the weekend. "They didn't want to come the first year, because if they have to make frankfurters to sell on Sunday, and if it's going to rain, they'll be stuck with the returns."

Nathan made a deal with the company to accept all the frankfurters the firm delivered, keeping them fresh in his non-patented ice-in-a-barrel refrigeration system. "Hygrade made the best frankfurter in the world and sold it to the best frankfurter salesman in the world," said company rep Paul Berlly.

All the same, Nathan didn't hesitate to send back a whole shipment of product if they didn't measure up to his high standards. In those days, the supplier delivered the frankfurters in huge wooden barrels. When an order came in, Nathan would pounce, performing his idiosyncratic kind of taste test.

Pry open a barrel of franks, squish and squeeze, bite off an end, chomp-chomp, spew. Repeat.

"We were getting a load of franks in," said a longtime Nathan's employee named Jimmy Bologna, recalling his first day on the job. "Out of nowhere, I see this old man in the kitchen. Who is this guy? He's just taking franks, and he's squishing them and putting on a scale. He takes a bite off the ends—chomp chomp—spitting out the remains in a little cup. Then he's opening up another box. And I'm just about ready to grab him, because I figured he's got to be a nut. There's a nut walking into my store! A nut! I'm going to get in trouble."

Just in time, a coworker named Johnny Poa stopped Jimmy before he could make a fool of himself. "No, no, no! That's Nathan!" Poa explained that the boss was checking the quality of the hot dogs in the new shipment.

"How do you check on frankfurters by biting them and spitting them?"

"His taste buds are his only mechanism," Poa said solemnly.

What was Nathan doing? There were several elements that sampling a "naked" (that is, without condiments) frankfurter might detect. One was relative texture of the casing, which had to be neither too tough nor too tender. The spice mixture that flavored the meat had to be just right. Another element was the amount of water in the meat filling. Ice was a natural ingredient in sausage preparation, used to cool down the product during the manufacturing process. The blades used to emulsify the meat into a smooth consistency heated up the filler, so ice was added to counteract the effect. Too much ice, though, led to watery dogs, which could result in annoying and even dangerous spatter when the franks were grilled.

Also vital was the exact fat-to-lean makeup of the meat.

"He had to get a certain percentage of fat," recalled Murray Handwerker about his father's franks. "He could tell when you cooked it that the fat ran out. Nothing wrong with it—fat is fat. But he knew that they were not putting in the proper proportions if the fat ran out on the griddle."

When the menu options at Nathan's Famous finally increased, the store maintained the same fierce approach to quality control. Hamburgers were introduced the second season after the store opened. Nathan hired butchers to grind the beef fresh on the premises. Crinkle-cut french fries—always referred to as "potato chips" in the early days—became big sellers. Nathan adhered to the principle that only quality ingredients make for quality food.

Said Hy Brown, a longtime manager at the store: "If he saw a batch of potatoes, he didn't care if it was ten thousand pounds of potatoes there, if they had black spots on it, he would put two, three, four, five people to take every spot out."

Photographic evidence indicates that those early franks from Nathan's little resembled the soft, thin, skinless hot dogs prevalent in the current era. They were plumper and juicier and featured a delightful curve that poked out of the bun to give a promise of goodness. The little hand-tied knots at both ends of all the sausages were clearly visible. In size and shape, they appeared more like what we would recognize today as a kielbasa or a bratwurst.

On special busy summer holidays, such as the Fourth of July or Memorial Day, Nathan would actually increase the size of his franks. He'd order larger ones from his suppliers at Hygrade, going to six links to the pound instead of the usual seven. His theory was that the numberless customers on such busy days would remember the larger servings and become faithful repeat visitors to the store.

9

The Family (1)

"I always want to have all the Handwerkers together." Family portrait *(clockwise from left)*: Murray, Ida, Nathan, Leah, and Sol.

BY 1925, THE business had come to be called Nathan's Famous. Harry Wildman, the sign painter, now joined in the business by his son Lester, created a billboard atop the store. In a demonstration of permanency, the builders fabricated their creation out of wood, not oilcloth.

On the tail-end swoosh that ran off the terminal *n* in the

name, Wildman added the phrase, "Famous frankfurter and soft drink stand." Later the tag would be reduced to the simple modifier, "Famous." Word had gotten out. People came from all over to visit Coney Island. Among the resort town's attractions was the busy frankfurter stand on Surf Avenue.

An excursion to Coney often went like this: Visitors exited the subway terminal and immediately headed to Nathan's Famous to buy a hot dog. They then continued on to the beach, perhaps sampling the demotic delights of the Bowery or Steeplechase Park along the way. When they left the beach at the end of the day, they visited Nathan's Famous once again for a second frankfurter. The store caught them coming and going.

For Nathan and Ida Handwerker, the business was family and the family was business. The line between the two entities blurred. They worked sixteen-, eighteen-, twenty-hour days, both of them on their feet much of the time, fierce in their determination to make the fledgling enterprise succeed. On the busy three-day holiday weekends in the summer, Nathan often never went home.

The work took its toll not only on his person but on his clothing. He always wore a traditional luncheonette uniform of white duck, sometimes—if important visitors were expected or if circumstances warranted—topped off with a black bow tie. Slaving over the stove was hell on fabric. Burn holes and grease stains were constants.

"He always wore his cuffs out, he ran around so much," noted veteran Nathan's Famous employee Jay Cohen.

The damage extended even to his shoes.

Pat Auletta was a prominent Coney Island businessman and community figure who as a boy in the 1920s worked at the shoeshine stand in his father's barbershop. He recalled Nathan as a genial enough customer whose sturdy leather wing tips were a mess.

"It was a great challenge to give him a shine because he always had all this grease on his shoes, from the frankfurters and whatever else came off the grills," Auletta remembered. Any shoe polish the boy applied would simply smear. Nathan would be too busy exchanging pleasantries with Auletta's father and the other customers to notice what was going on at ankle level.

"Every time he came in, I tried and tried to get that grease off his shoes," Auletta said. "Someone suggested to me, 'Why don't you try a match and burn it off?' So I did just that. He was talking to the barbers, so he had no idea what I was doing. The shoes went up in flame. I almost burned his whole leg, and I burned my fingers smothering out the fire."

Such were the hazards of life for a dedicated frankfurter man. On rare occasions, Nathan would head over to Loew's Shore Theatre, directly across Surf Avenue from the store, and slip into the darkened interior for a nap. Otherwise, he seemed to be always busy, always working, always watching. He was, very simply, always at the store.

Nathan had a strict, almost obsessive hands-on approach to running his business. Vigilance was his byword. Though he eventually expanded the premises to include upstairs offices, he always remained very visible presence "on the floor," in both the kitchen and the counter area.

Longtime employees referred to his habitual cigar as a mark of his presence. They'd smell the smoke and know that he was around. He would step into various nooks and recesses at the store. Workers would look up to be surprised to see the diminutive owner staring out at them, monitoring their movements.

"You never knew," said one of his longtime employees. "You turned around and he was right behind you. He was quiet."

"I trust myself and the stove," Nathan said. "I don't trust anybody else."

After leaving to have dinner at home with his wife, Nathan would at times return to the store later without warning. "I hate to see the manager walking around with a clean apron," he would announce, checking the workers for signs they had been hard at it.

One young manager was aware of these late-evening sneak attacks, and while Nathan was absent, he would take off his apron and stomp on it to make it dirty. Nathan must have gotten wind of the trick, since he confronted the kid.

"I got to ask you a question," Nathan said. "You're always working by the steam table. On the steam table, we've got barbecue gravy, which is red, and the roast beef gravy, which is brown. But you never have barbecue gravy or roast beef gravy on your apron. You have footprints."

Nathan started to laugh, and because the guilty party was a good worker, he wrote the whole thing off as youthful high jinks. But the kid learned he'd have to get up pretty early in the morning to slip one past the boss.

During his last rounds at night, Nathan would often check the store's waste cans. He uncovered discarded frankfurters, pieces of meat that had been cut off along with the fat, half-empty bottles discarded with a portion of their contents unused. The next morning, he would confront this or that employee.

"I found too many french fries; what went wrong?" Or "I found some extra hamburgers; they shouldn't be there." If he found anything amiss, Hy Brown recalls "the roof coming off the next day," with the boss checking everything back to the source to figure out what might have happened. Nathan made it clear he was in the business of selling food, not throwing it away. He eventually had the insides of the waste cans painted white, so he could more easily ascertain their contents.

"He really resented wasting food," recalled his grandson Steve

Handwerker. "It's not an idiosyncrasy; it's a valid concern, not just on financial terms but as a moral issue. Because he grew up in a time when he had no food."

The contents of the garbage pails represented the terminal end of the store's supply chain. Nathan paid strict attention to the opposite end, too, keeping close tabs on the wholesalers who delivered the food he served to his customers. Believing firmly that the sweetest potatoes came from Maine, he made excursions to the state himself, actually surveying the farm fields where the crop was being grown. It was almost as if he were replaying an experience of his youth, when he'd purchased a supply of potatoes from the Baron and returned with them in triumph to the spud-less Jarosław marketplace.

Eventually, he settled on a specific region—in the fertile valleys below the slopes of Maine's Mount Katahdin—where he found the best-tasting potatoes. He didn't buy them by the bushel, either, or even by the truckload. If he liked what he saw, Nathan would buy out a farm's entire crop. He had them shipped south via railroad and stored in warehouses. Eventually, it would take fourteen railway cars to transport a season's worth of potatoes.

His vigilance didn't end with these out-of-state trips. Nathan noticed that soaking potatoes in water leached some of the starch out of them, leaving behind the more concentrated sugars that made the tubers taste extra sweet. He instituted the water soak as part of the preparation process. Word got around about the matchless potato fries Nathan was serving. The man was simply not content to sell the normal, everyday fries that every other Coney Island outlet dished up. His had to be not ordinary but extraordinary. He went the extra mile—all the way to Maine—to make it happen.

Today, almost every french fry sold in the country is frozen first and then cooked. The average fast-food outlet never sees a real potato, one that does not arrive in the kitchen already cut and frozen. Frozen products provide ease of distribution, preparation, and storage. As with the roast chicken of Woody Allen's mother, the modern french fry has been "put through the deflavorizer." Current-day consumers might not be able to detect the difference between fresh and frozen.

But for Nathan, freshness mattered.

The same level of care went into every menu item. Nathan was always extremely cautious about adding new offerings beyond the frankfurters and fries that were his staples. An early entry to debut was a roast beef sandwich, added to the bill of fare soon after he and Ida were married.

"I cooked a piece of roast beef at home," Nathan remembered. "I brought it into the store and put it on the griddle. I'd cut it on a board beside the griddle. Five cents a sandwich."

Hamburgers were freshly made. Suppliers delivered beef hindquarters on hooks in the alleyway beside the store. Employees rolled them into a butcher section of the kitchen, where they would cut the meat and blend it. The ground beef went into a hand-cranked patty machine, which flattened the burgers and placed each one on its square of waxed paper. The top round of the beef hindquarters became the meat for the store's roast beef sandwiches.

As an all-cash business, much of it in coins, Nathan's Famous had serious money-handling concerns. In the beginning, Nathan could not afford cash registers. Countermen tossed the pennies, nickels, and dimes they received into open cigar boxes on the floor below them. Eventually, the workers adopted the kind of canvas aprons that newspaper vendors used, with three separate pockets for nickels, dimes, and quarters.

In the very early days of the business, Nathan would summon friends and family members to help tally the money, in festive communal sessions over beer and food. Counting the coins, packing them into paper money rolls, keeping track of the receipts—it all amounted to a major challenge for the new business. Paper currency was easier. Nathan simply placed it into a paper bag and walked it to the bank.

In any enterprise that deals in cash, employee theft is an obvious concern. The store was a sieve with money constantly tumbling through it. There were plenty of opportunities for workers to pluck a few dollars here and there. Even when Nathan finally installed cash registers, they failed to fully solve the problem.

Nathan's son Sol would later provide an interesting analysis of the situation. "You're in a conflicted position," he said. "You want to catch people who are stealing, but sometimes the people who are stealing are your best workers. You didn't always want to catch them because you didn't want to fire them because they were so good. What they were bringing into the business with their effective work was more important than what they were taking."

Over the years, several employees were let go because they were caught red-handed. In one case, a worker was caught hot-footed. Someone alerted Nathan that a certain counterman was slipping coins into his footwear. The boss resorted to a perfect strategy to expose the theft, spilling hot water on the guy's shoes and then insisting that he come to the office to change into a pair of dry socks. The shoes came off, and the coins were revealed. The guilty party had a milk can full of change in his locker.

One father-and-son team was caught in a short-sale scam. The son, working the counter, kept under-ringing every sale. If a customer ordered forty cents' worth of food, the son rang up twenty cents. Whoever worked the registers always needed a lot of change.

When the coins ran short, the practice was to holler "Nickels out!" or "Dimes out!" The father, a little higher up in the store's hierarchy, would head back into the kitchen where the coin rolls were kept. When he returned with the rolls of nickels and dimes, he'd skim off whatever amount his son had under-rung.

The two were caught and fired.

The pilfering wasn't limited to money. Employees were once caught discarding full five-gallon cans of oil into the store's garbage cans. The thieves would return at night, retrieve the cans from the garbage, and head home with a free month's worth of cooking oil.

In response to these situations—and perhaps because of a paranoid element in his personality—Nathan developed what could be termed a Panopticon philosophy of management. He did his best to be all-seeing, all-knowing.

Directly behind the store's frankfurter griddle stood a large root beer barrel, and Nathan would post himself atop a box beside the barrel. This gave him a view down the "drink side" of the counter in one direction and, in the other direction, the frankfurter and french fry stations. From time to time, Nathan would shout out from his post, calling attention to some situation or directing his employees to address a problem. Atop his box, he was like the ringmaster of his own commercial circus.

"He watched whether the men at the counter were handling the food right," remembered Nathan's son Sol. "It was very important to him that they looked clean, that they kept their equipment clean, and they scraped the griddles properly to keep them clean. He was concerned that the food was cooked properly—not overcooked, not undercooked. He was always watching how the men were preparing the food."

He wasn't just watching his workers, either. "He would stand next to the root beer barrel looking at the griddle and looking at the customers," Sol said. "He could tell from the customers' faces how they felt. He could see if they were having fun or were annoyed. He wanted to find out which way they were. He could always tell if something was wrong. His sixth sense about that was always amazing."

Nathan didn't limit his domain to the store's interior, but extended it to the sidewalks and streets outside. In late-night incognito visits, he would don a disguise—a slouch hat that came down over his eyes, perhaps a raincoat or sweater, at rare times a wig—and mingle with the customers. He'd eavesdrop, on the prowl for their comments, compiling a personal sort of pre-Yelp Yelp.

"It's the spirit of a successful business that gave him pleasure, in terms of satisfying the customers," said Sol. "If they were happy, he was happy. And that's what he always tried to achieve."

The hands-on boss never thought menial tasks were beneath him. He would often patrol for litter. Nathan's obsession with cleanliness reached into all corners of the property. The other thoroughfares of Coney were stained dark with dirt, grease, and the tramp of millions of pairs of human feet, to the degree that area sidewalks often appeared black.

"When you came to Nathan's, it was clean," recalled one veteran employee. "You had light-gray sidewalks."

As the volume of sales mounted, the store's physical plant took a tremendous beating. Grease, sand, and salt combined to make cleaning a constant daily—or, as the business began to stay open round the clock, nightly—chore. When the portable steam-vapor Jenny washers came on the market, Nathan was an early adopter. Employees later marveled that the trash facilities at the back of the store were so well-scrubbed that the room never smelled of garbage.

Busy as he was with his constant attendance at the store, in the mid-1920s Nathan found time to complete the final steps to U.S. citizenship. Normally, applicants had to possess the ability to understand, speak, read, and write basic English. In that era, the literacy requirement was often waived, especially for immigrants who had been established in the country for a period.

Nathan tried to learn, anyway. He hired tutors to visit him at home and expand his rudimentary understanding of the English language. He progressed to the point where he could pretend to read a newspaper, becoming a lifelong skimmer, at least, of New York *Daily News*, a picture-heavy publication founded in 1919. But he could never claim to be literate. On the rare occasions that Nathan ventured out to a restaurant not his own, Ida would always have to read the menu to him.

"He didn't read English," his son Murray recalled. "He used to look at the *Daily News* for the pictures. Reading English was a whole different level."

Nathan's literacy cram course turned out to be effective enough. On March 12, 1925, thirteen years almost to the month after his arrival in America, Nathan Handwerker took the oath and became an American citizen. Ida soon followed.

Throughout the teens and the early twenties, members of the Handwerker family had been crossing from Europe to America, coming over in ones and twos. It was as though Nathan was importing his workforce. Soon eight of the thirteen sons and daughters were in New York: Israel, Joseph, Dora, Nathan, Anna, Helen, Lena, and Phillip. In Yiddish, the names were Yisrool, Yuske, Dinele, Nachum, Elke, Chaya, Leah, and Hervel. The only Handwerker sibling never to live in America was the fifth brother, Shmuel, whose brain had been damaged in a street brawl and who later died in a European mental hospital.

In the successive waves of Handwerker immigration, the matriarch of the family tragically didn't survive the transatlantic voyage. Rose Handwerker died in February 1926 aboard SS *Zeeland*, the ship that was carrying her to America to join the rest of the family. She had left Jarosław a month before, traveling with Jacob and her four youngest children, Golde, Yitte, Moishe, and Herschel (in the United States, they would be known as Goldie, Yetta, Morris, and Harry).

The family headed for Antwerp, the same debarkation port from which Nathan had left for New York over a decade before. But at the dock, doctors employed by the shipping line deemed Jacob Handwerker too unhealthy to sail, quarantining him because of an eye infection.

The family was separated. Rose continued on board with her children but was "very much agitated from grief" over being separated from her husband, according to an account of her death printed in a Yiddish newspaper. After eating dinner one Friday evening, she simply "sat down and died," as her daughter Anna Singer phrased it later. Rose was still fairly young, fifty-seven years old, but her hard life in Galicia had taken its toll.

Nathan always felt close to his mother. He didn't get along as well with Jacob but was devoted to Rose. She encouraged him in his first forays into commerce, when the two of them banded together to sell fruits and vegetables in the markets of Narol. Her forlorn death, hundreds of miles away at sea, affected him greatly. Nathan afterward always felt the loss. He felt he never was able to say a proper good-bye to the woman who had meant so much to him.

A situation arose after Rose's death. The children huddled

around the lifeless body of their mother, unwilling to allow au
thorities to take her away. The policy on board the ship was to perform an ocean burial. This was a fairly common practice whenever
immigrants crowded into steerage class died. It saved the cost of
having to preserve the body until the ship reached landfall.

Anna recalled the family in America receiving a telegram
from the ship urgently requesting $125, in order that Rose Hand-
werker's remains would be duly transported to New York. Nathan
and the other Handwerker siblings in New York pooled their re-
sources and wired the requested funds. ("We sent them right
away a bundle of money," Anna recalled.)

The arrival of the ship into port in New York made for a tear-
ful scene. All of Rose's surviving children were present on the
dock. Rose was eventually buried in the family plot in Mount
Lebanon Cemetery, Queens. Jacob, still heavily bearded and limited in his speech to Hebrew and Yiddish, finally accomplished
the crossing on a later ship.

Jacob's presence in the New World provided a symbolic
reminder of the Old. Nathan and Jacob never seemed a good fit,
always seeming to butt heads. Jacob remained an extremely religious figure and because of his adherence to dietary rules would
not eat in his children's homes, only drinking water. He never got
to taste the source of his son's success, a Nathan's Famous frankfurter.

Abroad in the fast-moving world of New York City, the shtetl
patriarch could be childishly naïve. At one point, Jacob was taken
in by a scam that would have never fooled his savvier son, buying
"jewels" on the street that proved to be fake. He lived to the ripe
age of eighty-five, marrying twice more before passing away in
1937.

The stop-and-start nature of the family's immigration led to some unlikely pairings. Some of the younger cousins had never met their relatives. The result was striking, even among the unsettled standards of Manhattan's Tenth Ward.

Joe Handwerker, the son of Nathan's brother Israel, first encountered his aunt Goldie when he was already a young man of eighteen. She was Nathan's much younger sister and was around the same age as Joe. The two met, fell in love, and married, with Nathan's nephew thereby becoming his brother-in-law. Rosie, Joe's sister and one of Nathan's nieces, would marry her uncle Morris Handwerker.

It was young Joe Handwerker who would prove integral to the future of the business. In 1920, Nathan's twelve-year-old nephew had begun to work for his uncle and future brother-in-law. It was the boy's first job. He signed on for the summer season, working seven days a week, twelve to fourteen hours a day, for nine dollars a week. At that point, Nathan's was not yet Nathan's Famous.

Over the next two decades, Joe became much more than a relative twice over. He would eventually rise to serve as Nathan's right-hand man. Among all the Handwerkers who worked at the store, Joe was the one who would stay the longest and have the biggest impact. All the other family members left, some after short stints, some after many years. A few started businesses of their own. Phil had a candy store and a bar and grill. Morris opened a restaurant-bar called H&H.

Because of his mother's untimely death, Nathan never got to say good-bye to her, and Rose would never get to say hello to her new grandchildren. In March 1920, Nathan and Ida had welcomed their daughter, Leah, into the world. Sixteen months later, Murray came along and, after a lag of four years, a second son, Sol. (The family never used middle names.)

As oldest son, Murray was the obvious future head of the family and heir to the business empire. But he lived in the shadow of a praise-withholding father and grew up always trying to prove himself. Sol developed into the family's Hamlet, prone to introspection and rebellion against the authority figures of his father and brother.

A daughter and two sons. The perfect nuclear family. They lived right in Coney or, a little later on, a few miles east in Brighton Beach, always near the store. Even after his children were born, Nathan continued to spend long hours at work. Ida did, too. She would hold a baby in her arms, turning frankfurters on the griddle. She had merely added a second shift to her long workday, taking care of the family as well as taking care of business at Nathan's Famous.

Ida and Nathan would bring the children into the store, keeping one eye on them as they went about their duties. Oftentimes, Leah, Sol, and Murray would find themselves relegated to a makeshift playpen, as Ida plopped them down into the crib-like, three-by-three wooden bins in which the store's hot dog buns were kept. The roll crate became the children's second home.

"I observed a lot of things going on around me," Sol remembered about his earliest days. "There was a lot of commotion, a lot of action, a lot of men working in the kitchen. I remember in particular there were a lot of Chinese men and some black workers, too. The employees were some of my best friends. They were always taking care of me and watching over me. I used to wander around in the kitchen and watch them cutting the potatoes."

The process the store used to create its popular crinkle-cut fries fascinated the young Sol: the fat, yellow-gold spuds coming out of the electric peeling drum and fed, one by one, into the manual cutter. "One of the workers would throw a potato into this machine and with one hand bring down the blade of the crinkle cutter. He kept doing that all day long. I thought it was the most difficult job in the world."

Leah, Murray, and Sol might not have realized it at first, but the new family had a dynamic that was different from most other households. The children were in competition, jostling for attention, vying not just with each other but with the family business. The store dominated the time, focus, and energy of their parents. Al Shalik, a longtime Nathan's employee, put it this way: "Murray and Sol had another brother, and that other brother was Nathan's Famous."

Leah probably suffered the most being that she was the oldest and being a girl. She was born during a time when her parents were working the hardest at establishing their business. She was never going to have an identity connected to the business. It was a symptom of the "delicate flower" gender bias of the period. Females, even the oldest child in the family, were not considered next in line to run such an establishment as Nathan's Famous. Though her mother worked there, the atmosphere of the store was probably considered too rough-and-tumble for a girl, especially when Leah grew to adolescence.

As kids, however, the Handwerker children had a perfect knee-high view of the goings-on in the store. "I used to walk around behind the counter," Sol remembered. "I watched what the men were doing. I used to watch the customers—that was kind of fun. And I used to watch my father. As an employer, my father was a very, very tough man. He was a perfectionist. He was very demanding of his people. If they didn't do the right thing, he let them know in no uncertain terms."

For all of that, Leah, Murray, and Sol enjoyed pleasant, happy childhoods throughout the 1920s and 1930s. When away from the store, Nathan relaxed to a degree that wasn't possible while on the job. Surprisingly, given his domineering ways with his employees, he did not serve as the family disciplinarian. Ida did.

"Although at work [Nathan] sometimes appeared to be a tough man, he really wasn't," said his youngest son. "He was a really soft man. It was my mother who was the tough one. She was the one who'd get angry at me."

Ida's method of punishment wasn't the paddle, the belt, or even the raised hand. "She wouldn't hit me as much as pinch me. She used to like pinching, and it hurt."

The grown-ups were busy with work, but they also devoted themselves to the wider Handwerker family. Monthly get-togethers of the dozen brothers and sisters who had by then emigrated from Poland to America were marked by equal measures of joking and bickering. Nieces, nephews, and cousins took the opportunity to play. The meetings featured raffle contests and dinners, and the group named itself the Jacob and Rose Handwerker Family Circle.

Nathan took the time to attend every family circle meeting. "He was very family-oriented," his nephew Sidney Handwerker recalled. "They had all grown up together as children in Europe."

The family circle's first item of business was always the funding, design, and arrangements for the family burial plot. Endless amounts of time seemed to go into the planning of every detail. But there was also time for socializing, playing cards, squabbling.

"They loved each other, but they fought all the time," remembered Sidney. As he recalled them, the poker games at the get-togethers were marked by a lot of second-guessing. "Why didn't you raise your hand with three aces?" one of the brothers would cry out to another.

"They were some nice people there but they just couldn't get along," said Jack Dreitzer, who married into the family and worked at Nathan's Famous from the twenties onward. Dreitzer remembered Handwerker siblings in stark terms. "Each brother hated the other. Each one was jealous of the other. Each one was envious of the fact that he had one cigar and the other had two. They couldn't get along together. They used to fight like cats and dogs."

An increasingly visible presence at family gatherings, and at the store, was Nathan's nephew and brother-in-law, Joe Handwerker. A small fireplug of a guy with a Jackie Mason accent, he was fast becoming a favorite of Nathan's. He could match his uncle's outbursts of volcanic temper. The family circle meetings featured a raffle. For some reason, the prize was almost always won by Ida. The one time Joe won, the prize for that month enraged him: a bun warmer. He had seen enough of bun warming at work to last him a lifetime. He threw the offending device to the floor and stomped on it.

Gradually, Nathan rose to take his position as first among equals in the family. This was the decade of the Roaring Twenties, when America's prospects appeared limitless. The country boomed, Coney Island boomed along with it, and Nathan's Famous boomed in turn. As Nathan put it, the twenties were a time of getting "larger, every year a little bigger."

At the time, there was stiff competition in Coney, with over two hundred restaurants offering fare in the neighborhood.

One way Nathan sought to address his need for workers was by hiring family members. Nepotism wasn't at all a negative concept around Nathan's Famous. It came to represent a foundational principle of the business. Part of the incentive was to guard against employee theft. The idea was that while relatives might steal from you, they would be marginally less larcenous than strangers. But of course the motivation also stemmed from love, generosity, and simple familial feeling.

"I always want to have all the Handwerkers together," Nathan said. "I want to create a business where all the Handwerkers can work together as a big family."

The founder of the store cherished a vision for it. Nathan thought a great deal about his grandchildren and great-grandchildren. He hoped that the business would go on forever in the family, so he surrounded himself with successive circles of relatives.

Closest to him was the core of his wife and children. Then came the wider spectrum of Handwerker relations, Joe Handwerker most prominent among them, as well as Ida's sisters and their spouses. Sisters-in-law, brothers, brothers-in-law, nephews, cousins all found their way onto the payroll. The idea was to have the business serve as a coalescing force, bringing the whole clan together.

Practice often ran counter to theory. Yes, Nathan wanted his relatives around him. At the same time, he could judge them unworthy of his patronage. A relative could be fired as easily as a stranger.

"He didn't like a lot of the people in the family," recalled his grandson Steve. "Even though he always said he wanted to have a family business, he really didn't. He saw them as lazy, as nonindustrious, or trying to get away with something."

"My name is on that sign," Nathan said. "So whoever is going to be here and on the job is going to do it right or they're not going to be here. I don't reject them as a family member, but I might reject them as employees working for my business."

As the company grew, its manpower demands began to

outstrip even the abundant supply of Handwerker blood relations. Nathan was forced to widen his circle. He did so by creating
another sort of family, a fiercely loyal group of workers who would
go a long way toward making Nathan's Famous the phenomenon
it was.

10

The Family (2)

"You have to be crazy to work here."
Nathan's second family—his workers—
in action.

A JOB AT Nathan's Famous meant long hours in conditions that were oftentimes so busy that employees did not have a chance to catch their breath. It was not easy work. Many were called, but few lasted past a few hours. One notable incident came during a summer rush. Six workers were in the kitchen doing nothing but toasting rolls for twelve hours straight. A number of them quit.

When it came time to hire new workers, Nathan was convinced

he possessed a foolproof, almost mystical sixth sense about who would make the grade and who would wash out.

"How can you know?" asked one longtime worker after Nathan had correctly predicted a newcomer wouldn't last.

"I look at the back of the neck," Nathan answered. "I can tell right away if they aren't going to make it."

What specific qualities he found via his neck checks Nathan never revealed, but he did demonstrate a knack for hiring loyal employees, demon workers who could stand the punishment.

A nice, well-dressed young man once approached Nathan. "Excuse me, who do I see for a job?"

"Are you crazy?" the boss asked him.

"Why, no," said the applicant. "I'm a college man."

"You can't work here," Nathan told him, raising his voice. "You have to be crazy to work here. Get out!"

The poor fellow ran.

"You sometimes see a help-wanted sign that reads, 'We're Looking for Friendly People,'" said veteran Nathan's Famous manager Jay Cohen. "Nathan didn't look for friendly people. He looked for people that were like horses."

By the standards of the day, Nathan paid good wages, always well above minimum wage. He was generous with bonuses and personal no-interest loans. Some of his senior workers felt comfortable enough to refer to Nathan as "Pop." His "horses" stayed with him for decades, with a number of employees putting in more than a half century at the store. Even workers who openly despised the boss's brusque methods still stayed on for extended periods.

Jack Dreitzer was a longtime counterman, one of the first non-blood relations that Nathan ever hired. Married to Ida's sister, he signed on to the store in the twenties, when he was still a teenager. "They used to call me the oldest youngest man in the place."

Dreitzer started at the store in 1928, when street frontage of the counter was about thirty feet all told. "We used to work twelve hours a day. I started for 25 cents an hour, and for that 25 cents I really had to produce. I was just out of public school, making $3 a day. If I worked seven days in the summer, I made $21 a week. I was Coney Island's wealthiest fellow at that time. I dressed beautifully."

Even at a young age, Dreitzer was a bruiser. He grew into his job, boasting that he once served 9,100 hamburgers in the course of a single twelve-hour shift. He became celebrated for his take-no-prisoners style of interacting with the public.

"Man, we used to get some mean people over there in Coney," Dreitzer remembered. "Meeee-an. I'm talking mean."

Dreitzer did not suffer fools gladly. "Of course, I wasn't going to let nobody come over to me and say, 'Hey, you Jew bastard, give me a hamburger.' Nahhh! When they did that to me, I used to say, 'Come here, I want to talk to you.' Then I'd reach over the counter, put my left hand behind his head, and I'd belt him with my right hand."

Two or three times a shift, Dreitzer felt himself compelled to confront the people who made remarks about his Jewish background. "They had to lock me up at least once a month," he recalled. "People used to press charges."

Dreitzer was surly not only with the clientele. He back-talked the man in charge, too. Nathan once criticized him for having a dirty griddle. In response, Dreitzer threw an aluminum tray at his boss, winging it across the store.

"If he didn't duck, he'd've got hit in the head," Dreitzer recalled. "I said, 'Now ya gonna get the hell outta here? Get inside!' Of course, I had no right to do that, but you know, how much can you take?"

The store was a prank-filled environment, and Dreitzer played a few mean-spirited practical jokes. Once catching a rat by its tail, he dangled the squirming creature in front of Ida's face. She fainted. Ida was Dreitzer's sister-in-law, so he felt the stunt was all in good fun.

Veteran manager Hy Brown believed that Nathan put up with a certain amount of insubordination from Dreitzer simply because the man was so good at his job. "He was a fast worker, an efficient worker, but he was very nasty," Brown remembered. "Nathan didn't care much about what you thought about him. If you brought the money in and got the merchandise out, you were a Nathan's man."

The situation became more difficult when the store went to a twenty-four-hour day in the summer. This was where Joe Handwerker, Nathan's nephew who worked with Dreitzer from the twenties on, came into his own. As night manager, Joe kept the store on an even keel when the crazies emerged out of the post-midnight furnace of New York City. The bar crowd could be incredibly unpleasant. But they spent money freely, too.

Arguments, shouting matches, outright fisticuffs were common enough in a venue that was open all night, attracting crowds of the unruly after the city's clubs, theaters, and drinking establishments emptied out in the wee hours. The night shift was busy, exhausting, surreal. Most of the customers were simply tired and hungry. But some people didn't wait for the full moon to turn ugly.

"We'd do more business from twelve o'clock midnight until daylight than you can imagine," said Joe. "When the bars and grills closed, when the movie houses closed, there were twenty people deep at the counters. I thought they were going to push the place into the ocean. That's how busy we were."

In such a hectic atmosphere, a kind of undeclared war existed between customers and workers. Dreitzer was often in the middle of it. "People would throw a ketchup bottle at him or something, and he'd go over the counter," recalled manager Hy Brown. "When that happened, I had to get there first. You'd have to really push him out of the way to get him inside."

The cross fire flew both ways. Jack Dreitzer remembered a prank he would pull on anyone on the other side of the counter who might annoy him.

"We had big glass coolers for the grape, orange, and pineapple drinks; we used to have to put big ice pieces in them all the time. I'd have to run inside the kitchen, [chip off] ice pieces, and bring them out to the coolers. It was very hard. When I see a customer I didn't like, like she's in a white dress or something, saying, 'Gimme a drink, gimme a drink, gimme a drink!' I'd dump the ice pieces into the grape drink cooler."

The resulting splash would inevitably drench the troublemaker. Oops.

"Oh, excuse me!" Dreitzer would say, the soul of innocence.

There were variations on the prank, whereby a drink would be served with a certain amount of enthusiasm, slamming it down on the counter so it would splash onto the target. Dreitzer always sardonically fake-apologized. "Oh, I'm sorry," he'd say.

Dreitzer was known to swat customers, other employees, anyone who angered him with a hot spatula. "Or he'd jab you with a fork," recalled Jay Cohen. "He was a terrible man." For decades, the store served food on ceramic plates, and another Dreitzer trick was to put mustard on the bottom of the plate so customers would get an unpleasant surprise with dinner.

The show would not end there. Whenever angry customers would demand to see the manager, Dreitzer would refer them to another longtime Nathan's worker, Ruben Epstein. The exchange would often go something like this:

Angry customer (pointing at Dreitzer): "I want that man fired!"

Epstein to Dreitzer: "Okay, so you don't come out here no more."

It was all a joke. Dreitzer might remove himself from the front area for a few minutes to assuage the customer. Of course, the subterfuge worked in the other direction, too. Whenever Epstein's customers demanded to see the manager, he would always refer them to Dreitzer, who'd put them off in the same way.

Management refused to put a stop to the shenanigans, because Dreitzer, Epstein, and others were such valuable workers. "It wasn't a matter of being a good employee and being nice to the customers," Cohen said. "It was a matter of how fast you could serve them and how fast you could take the money in."

Nathan had a peculiar, half-paternal, half-adversarial relationship with such long-term employees as Dreitzer, who told a story that he thought summed up his dealings with his boss. One week, he caught his thumb as the cash register drawer banged shut, turning his thumbnail black and blue. A few days later, he made the exact same mistake.

"So I yelled," Dreitzer recalled. "I says, 'Goddamn it, the second time in the same damn place.'"

Nathan was nearby, as he always seemed to be. "Come in the office," he directed his counterman, who was at the moment writhing in pain. "Come inside."

Dreitzer tried to object. "I gotta go out. You know, it's busy. Nobody else can handle it out there."

Nathan persisted. He took Dreitzer into the office and made him put his throbbing thumb in a glass of ice water. "Sit down and stay there."

As Dreitzer soaked, Nathan brought up the real reason he had taken the counterman off the line. "What do you mean, you're sick and tired of this goddamn place?"

Dreitzer was confused. "Who said that? I didn't say that. What, are you deaf? You heard what I said? I said, 'Second time in the same damn place'—second time on the same finger."

Nathan nodded, satisfied. "Oh, I thought you said you're sick and tired of this goddamn place." He would not stand to hear his beloved store bad-mouthed.

"He insisted that I take care of my finger before I went out," Dreitzer recalled. "In other words, he did try to take care of us when some emergency arose."

Nathan often took the core workers out after their grueling twelve-hour shifts. They might go bowling and then hit the S&H diner for breakfast.

"There was eight of us working," Dreitzer said of the morning routine. "When we finished [the shift] at four o'clock in the morning, we'd take the floorboards out and wash them in the alley. We put the shutters up. Almost every morning, Nathan used to bring us to a restaurant on Stillwell Avenue: Gerry Monetti, Sammy and Patsy Augustine, Ruben Epstein, and Mike Barkel. We'd bet who could eat the most. Whatever we ate, Nathan paid for. It's what he did."

Dreitzer remembers his boss not blinking an eye when he ordered and consumed eight double hamburgers.

An early hire rivaling Dreitzer for endurance and length of service was a cook named Sinta Low, who served as the store's kitchen manager. An immigrant from Taiwan, he resembled

Nathan in his diligent, uncomplaining work ethic. His name was always collapsed simply into Sinta around the store, but his realm was the kitchen, and he rarely ventured out front. His dream, never realized, was to become a New York City policeman.

"He ran that kitchen like a czar," said Charles Schneck, the personnel manager of Nathan's Famous. "He even chased executives out of the kitchen. As long as he was there, the kitchen ran like clockwork."

Short and compact like his boss, Sinta possessed deceptive strength. One of the most difficult feats around the store was to manage the huge, ice-filled drink tubs, weighing easily a hundred pounds when full. They needed to be set in place so the countermen could serve the various flavored drinks.

These were the same glass tanks that Dreitzer used to splash customers, and the hulking counterman was the obvious man for the job of lifting them. "I'll put it on the dolly, and we'll move it over," he said, squaring off with one of the tubs one day.

Dreitzer tried to heft the tank, but failed to budge it. Sinta happened to be nearby, on one of his rare forays out of the kitchen.

"One minute," the cook said to Dreitzer. He walked over and lifted the tub into place with a single movement, "like it was nothing," according to one bystander. Other onlookers burst out laughing, so odd was the incongruity of the short-statured cook out-lifting the heavyweight counterman.

Sinta often brought groups of store employees into Manhattan's Chinatown, early in the morning after long days at work. Their favorite place was always a Shanghai restaurant at 32 Mott Street, where the teacups could be filled with either whiskey or tea, depending on the wishes of the customer. Sinta knew the cooks there, who would serve him and his friends huge predawn meals.

Another stalwart employee, Ruben "Eppy" Epstein, was, in

the words of a coworker, "like a machine with one speed. He didn't work fast. He didn't work slow. He worked steady." For years, Eppy was the stalwart at the store's hamburger station. It was probably Epstein who most indulged in the Nathan's Famous tradition of vocalizing while at work. He would stand at his station and call out phrases in his heavy Yiddish accent, coming off like a cross between a cantor and a carnival barker.

"I have hamburgers, hamburgers! *Gildena vera!* A pound of meat and a bushel of onions, I have hamburgers, the best, the best!" The Yiddish phrase meant "golden goods," or, in context, "tasty items."

"All night long, he'd be going like that," said coworker Hy Brown. "Everybody was laughing, but the hamburgers were going out like lightning."

"Oh, we used to sing," recalled Jack Dreitzer. "They used to hear us up on Stillwell Avenue, on the platform of the train station. They knew we were there before they came down from the platform. We used to have different chants. 'With a pickle in the middle and an onion on the top. All hot. All hot.' You had to sing or say something to try and call the people, hustle them up."

The burger station employed a fiendish strategy to entice customers. The countermen cooked chopped onions, sautéing them in the juices drained off from the hamburger grill. The smell would drift across the street and into the subway terminal. When potential customers got off at the station, they were like Pavlov's dogs, already salivating at the aroma of onions au jus cooking at Nathan's.

Hamburgers were all well and good, but it was at the store's frankfurter griddle where the real action went down. Cooking and serving the dogs represented a complicated kind of choreographed ballet. The sixteen-foot-long griddle was fabricated out of three-quarter-inch steel specifically for Nathan's Famous. The store used regular carbon steel, not stainless, which was becoming the norm in other commercial kitchens. The cooking surface was more difficult to keep clean, but the trade-off was a more easily controlled heat.

In the early days, the dogs came in from Hygrade in wooden casks, six hundred per barrel. The movement of the franks across the griddles was as tightly managed as any quiche in the oven of a French chef.

The hot dogs came in from the supplier linked together. "Each end of each frankfurter was tied off," recalled former manager Hy Brown. "So we got them in big strings, and we had men that did nothing all day but separating the frankfurters."

Cutting apart the long ropes of hot dogs was long an entry-level job at the store. The sausages went through several steps as they headed for the griddle. After they were cut from the linked strings, the individual franks were transferred to a box that held precisely six hundred hot dogs. From the box, the dogs were placed on wooden paddle boards, each with twenty-six frankfurters (no more, no less) lined up on them. Such exact counts were at the heart of Nathan's inventory control.

The paddles were carried to the grill in metal boxes. The sausages, which had been smoke-cured at the factory but were as of yet unheated, were slid off the boards directly onto the griddle, at the back of long ranks of more fully cooked dogs. The griddle could fit sixteen franks in a line. Each counterman working the griddle moved his line of frankfurters forward and turned them, so by the time they got to the front, they would be ready to serve.

The ranks of wieners advanced in columns. The counterman could check the status of a particular frankfurter by sight. When they were done, the casing might split once. Two or three ruptures of the outer skin meant the sausage was well done, ready to be served up to customers who requested theirs that way.

Cooking times were adjusted to suit the demand. The griddle had several gas burners positioned beneath it. If business was lax, the ranks of frankfurters naturally moved forward more slowly. The slow movement meant franks spent more time on the griddle, so the heat had to be turned down. During those periods, the griddle might have every other burner turned on.

At busy times, on the other hand, the frankfurters progressed across the griddle quickly. Every burner blasted at full force. If demand peaked beyond busy to frantic, the franks were preheated in the kitchen. They came out on their paddles already partially cooked. Their double-time march across the sizzling hot griddle was accomplished in minutes flat.

When the frankfurter griddle operated at top efficiency, it had eight people working on it. There were three sellers, or countermen, who interacted with the public, served the hot dogs and made change. The fastest worker earned the prime post, at the corner of the store next to the alley. There were other sellers spaced across each section of griddle and, to oversee it all, a cook.

"The cook used to take the franks, pile the grill, and turn them over," remembered manager Hy Brown. "He would know how the frankfurters came out, medium or well done."

The whole ballet depended on the number of customers. More demand, a hotter grill. Sparser crowds, a cooler one.

"Put up the fire," came the call. "Shut the fire! Up the fire! Down the fire!"

One oddity of Nathan's practice at the store was that while he would often taste-test the grilled franks—and even bite into the unheated ones, straight off the delivery truck—he usually preferred to eat them boiled. He would skin the casing off and consume them without the bun, but with mustard. For the whole of his adult life, while he was at the store, Nathan ate at least two franks a day, sometimes more.

While the griddles in the front of the store were devoted to the frankfurters and hamburgers, the four six-foot grills back in the kitchen were primarily used to toast rolls. It was a point of pride to Nathan that no hot dog or hamburger was ever served on a roll that wasn't toasted. Serving anything at all on an untoasted roll represented a cardinal sin, earning the miscreant a tongue-lashing at best and a pink slip at worst.

Field's bakery originally supplied the buns, baked in a steamy oven, so that the texture turned out a little chewy. Later on, Nathan alternated between Field's and Sabrett. He would play the companies off each other in order to get the best price and the best quality. The classic Nathan's hot dog was a water-baked Field's roll with a Hygrade frankfurter with mustard. That's the combination for which the store was best known.

At times, it seemed that Nathan enlarged his conception of family to include not only blood relatives, not only loyal workers, but his customer base, as well. Nathan and his workers often got to know customers by name. He had a natural affection for those hungry hordes who were pushing their nickels, dimes, and quarters across his counters. They were, after all, the people who were making his fortune.

Nathan blew up one time when he realized employees were eating into the store's limited inventory of Drake's raisin cakes. He knew that certain customers preferred them, and he ordered thirty or forty for a week's supply. He didn't make a great deal of profit over such a paltry sale. He was simply interested in taking care of his loyal raisin cake clientele.

In 1933, on the first day that legal alcohol sales could resume with the repeal of the Volstead Act, Nathan threw something of a party for his customers. He obtained one of the first post-Prohibition permits to sell beer. He made a deal with Kings Brewery, the major local supplier, just cranking up legal production again on Pulaski Street in Brooklyn. As a promotion marking the fact that Nathan's Famous would now be offering beer, Nathan took over Anna Singer's custard stand across Schweikerts Walk and gave out free mugs of beer.

Nathan's sons remember the day well. "It was extraordinary, the mobs that showed up," Sol said. "I was standing there watching all of this."

Murray Handwerker, who was twelve years old at the time, recalled, "People lined up from Stillwell down Surf Avenue, down Schweikerts Walk, down to the boardwalk, and under the boardwalk."

Of course, all the mugs containing that free beer had the logo of Nathan's Famous emblazoned on them. The customers were encouraged to take them home as souvenirs, so the stunt had promotional value.

As Prohibition staggered to an end, the country was deeply mired in the Great Depression. In 1933, the worst year of the economic crisis, four thousand banks failed across the United States. Eight million members of the labor force—one out of every four—were out of work. Thirty-two thousand businesses went bankrupt. Included in that number, Coney Island's Luna Park, which filed for bankruptcy, closed, reopened, and then continued a long slide toward its demise.

Likewise, Feltman's Ocean Pavilion, just a few blocks east of the store, experienced a steady decline. Its relatively formal dining rooms, where you could not enter without a jacket and which featured white tablecloths, were out of step with the increasingly populist times.

"Visitors to Coney Island could barely afford the subway ride, let alone a sit-down meal at Feltman's," writes Coney Island historian Jeffrey Stanton.

But expense wasn't the only issue. Speed of service was another. The pace of modern life picked up as the automobile, the telephone, and the radio became more prevalent and popular. Feltman's tony Ocean Pavilion was never a grab joint the way Nathan's Famous was. At some unheralded point in the 1930s, Nathan surpassed his former place of employment, on the way up as the other was on its way down. Rising anti-German sentiment contributed to Feltman's demise.

During the dark economic climate, Nathan's Famous remained a symbol of hope, a downscale one, perhaps, but durable. The famously recognizable billboards that loomed over Surf Avenue stayed brightly lit at night. Nathan's business flourished during the Roaring Twenties. Now in the depressed thirties, the store not only survived, it prospered. It was uncanny. As Nathan watched the rest of the country and then the rest of the world go down the tubes, he remained buoyant.

"My business started to get doubled up during the Depression, twice as big, bigger and bigger and bigger every year."

It turned out the nickel dog was recession proof. Five cents in 1933 had the buying power of ninety cents in today's economy. It was still a stretch, but many of the offerings at other restaurants were out of reach for the impoverished populace.

Nathan's son Sol, who witnessed it all as a young boy, paints a heartbreaking picture. "They would come down with families, and the family would share one hot dog with some french fries. They couldn't go to a regular restaurant, which of course was much higher in price. But they could go to Nathan's. So in a sense, it helped people by encouraging them to come and eat good food at a very, very low price."

Throughout the decade, in bad times and in worse times, the fundamental formula never changed. The holy trinity of Nathan's success—speed of service, quality of food, and low price—had become a religion. Even as the price of his supplies rose, Nathan doggedly maintained the nickel frankfurter. It amounted almost to a superstition with him. The five-cent dog had made him rich. Futzing with the price might lead to problems. It would take a major catastrophe of worldwide proportions to move him away from his magic number.

11

The Count

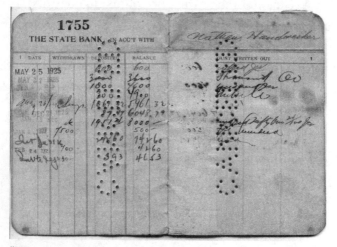

"It was just a single restaurant, but the place was run with procedures that rivaled IBM." Nathan's 1925 bank ledger.

BACK IN 1917, the year after Nathan opened the store, Kenneth F. Sutherland Jr. got himself named the district leader of local Brooklyn Democrats. The son of a machine boss from nearby Gravesend, Sutherland gradually rose in the party ranks to wield nearly as much influence as his father. Familiarly addressed as "Senator" after he served a stint as a state congressman, he became Nathan's longtime political ally.

Sutherland's other nickname was "Little Corporal," a nod to both his stature and his Napoleonic tendencies. He enjoyed the kind of power and reach that could make someone a governor of the state. Coney Island had always followed the "big man" model of politics. The crescent of sandy seaside wasteland had been a prize fought after by a lot of competing interests, and the battles had been close and bitter ever since the dawn of the nineteenth century. Land grabs, graft, and backroom deals were the norm.

Twentieth-century bosses couldn't possibly compete with the corruption of the legendary John Y. McKane, the post–Civil War overlord of Coney Island who once publicly made the forthright claim that "houses of prostitution are a necessity" in any seaside resort. One of McKane's henchmen was Kenneth F. Sutherland Sr., a.k.a. "the Czar of Coney Island," who served a stretch in Sing Sing for election fraud. He died in 1910 after being "horribly mangled" in a subway accident.

The son inherited the sins of the father. By the 1930s, Kenny Sutherland Jr. had Coney Island firmly in his grip. Nathan was right there beside him. The immigrant from Habsburg Galicia well understood the big-man style of power. He formed an easy association with Sutherland, becoming, according to one observer, "as close as cousins." The two of them essentially came up together, the one using successive terms as state assemblyman and senator to cement his power, the other witnessing his business succeed beyond his wildest dreams.

Food was Nathan's passport to influence. He joined the Coney Island Chamber of Commerce, eventually serving as president. Courtesy of his good friend Max Kamiel, Nathan also became an initiate in the mysteries of Freemasonry. When the political powers of the Sixteenth District flocked together, Nathan always catered the event.

Every year, the political elites of the area went away for a weeklong Catskills retreat. The so-called Monroe Boys (named after Monroe, New York, where they sometimes gathered), also referred to as the "summer group," included insiders and old-timers: councilmen, the borough president, judges, and congressional representatives and their minions from all over Brooklyn, but especially from Coney Island. Backs were slapped, hands were glad-handed, and backroom deals were hammered out.

"They were all there, the biggest of the big, and they would really let their hair down," remembered summer group member Pat Auletta, father of writer Ken Auletta and lifelong Coney Island resident (he was one of a series of people to claim the title of "mayor of Coney Island").

The annual retreat centered around eating, drinking, and playing cards. The big shots were inveterate practical jokers. Disdaining the mundane idea of giving a hot foot, they would ignite a whole fire underneath the bed of a napping fellow Monroe Boy. They once had one of their group, a Brooklyn judge, falsely arrested and put in jail, supposedly for stealing a car.

Every year for the event, Nathan would supply hot dogs, hamburgers, and perhaps a side of beef. He would shuttle back and forth from the store to the Catskills retreat, bringing supplies for the hungry politicos. The obvious success of his business and its geographic centrality in the Coney Island landscape—the store was hard to miss with its huge, busy billboards blaring out above Surf Avenue—established Nathan Handwerker's local bona fides.

Eventually, courtesy of his achievements and his participation in such insider rituals as the summer group retreat, Nathan took his place as an integral member of the Brooklyn establishment. In contemporary political parlance, he was a job creator. The store had become a major local employer, "the General Motors of Coney Island," in the words of one insider.

Back when he started out, Nathan had worried about interference from local power brokers for daring to offer a nickel frankfurter. He came to understood that in America as in Europe, good connections made for good business. The Jewish immigrant, a perennial outsider, had arrived at last, if only as a caterer.

His association with Sutherland paid off in concrete ways. With the rise of car culture in America, Nathan's Famous depended less on foot traffic and more and more on customers who arrived by automobile. Lack of parking was a perpetual concern. Plus there was the pesky problem of a pair of fire hydrants along the curb. They interfered with the vehicles that piled up two or three deep during busy periods.

Might it be possible to have the hydrants moved farther down Surf Avenue? And while you are at it, could the bus stop in front of the store please be placed somewhere else? That would give Nathan's Famous clear street frontage to work with. An expensive proposition, digging up the water lines and relocating the fireplugs. And people always screamed when their bus stop was displaced. But Kenny Sutherland got it all done for his good friend Nathan.

Favors flowed the other way, too. Pat Auletta said that Sutherland was definitely an authority figure for Nathan. "If Kenny Sutherland told him to jump off the Empire State Building, I think Nathan would have done just that," Auletta recalled.

Sutherland might have been at the apex of the Coney Island food chain, but he still couldn't be everywhere at once. He relied on the local constabulary as the physical expression of his power. True to form, the big man granted Nathan's Famous the incredible benefit of having its very own cops.

Veteran manager Jay Cohen: "Nathan's being located as it was, and as many people that visited the place in the summer months, it required a lot of police to cover the area for crime, for pickpockets, and things of that sort."

Friendly police officers were valuable for what they could do—crime suppression, traffic control, breaking up fights—but also for what they would not do—write parking tickets.

"If a car was double-parked, the driver ran across the street and picked up three hot dogs, a bag of french fries, and a soda," Cohen said. "He'd go back to his car and eat. As management, we did not want him to be harassed by the police writing him up with summonses."

Courtesy of Nathan's good standing with the powers that be, two police officers were assigned to the sidewalks in front of the store at all times. Each cop worked an eight-hour shift, and there were three shifts per day. Joe Handwerker usually handled the greasing of palms, allowing Nathan to stay out of the fray.

"At the end of the week, every one of those men—which makes six tours, because there's two men each—would get two dollars per day as their tip to make sure that they stayed on the premises," Jay Cohen said. "If the management had trouble with a rowdy customer, a policeman would step in. Of course, he would take your side, because after all, in his own way, he was on your payroll."

The baksheesh didn't stop with the beat cops. The mounted police would also receive what Cohen referred to as "our two-dollar-a-day retainer." At the end of every season, the lieutenants and captains at the local precinct house also got their due. Emissaries from the store would visit and introduce themselves. Envelopes changed hands. Whenever a new police chief took office, Joe Handwerker made a pilgrimage with a paper bag full of money.

"It was a known fact that Nathan's was good people to the police department," Cohen said.

Good in more ways than one. Eventually, Nathan actually created a second break room at the store, next to the employees' break room but reserved for the exclusive use of the police. The employees' dining room also saw a lot of blue uniforms.

"They knew that they could come in the back door and eat," Cohen said. "There was many a day when the employees' dining room had twenty to thirty policemen eating there. Eighty percent of them never paid. That's the way Nathan ran the business."

At times, the cops caused problems instead of heading them off. "At four o'clock in the morning, we had to stop selling beer," recalled Hy Brown. "We had to turn off the spigots on a Friday night at four and on Saturday night at three. We had a lot of drunken cops there, all off duty."

Brown remembered one cop practically assaulting him during an early-morning confrontation. "He took a scissors and cut off my tie. He wanted beer, but we had turned off the air inside, so we couldn't draw beer outside."

The demanding cop took out his service pistol and laid it atop the counter. What could Hy Brown do? "I gave him beer."

Arguments and fistfights, yes. But because of the highly visible presence of the police on the block, the store was never robbed. Except once.

Nathan had gotten his hands on a $1,000 bill that someone came to him to cash. He knew the holder of the bill, a local resident, and the holder knew that Nathan's Famous was an all-cash business. The bank wouldn't take such a large denomination, so Nathan was the next best bet.

A circulating thousand-dollar bill was a very rare thing. To collectors, they were worth more than face value. Their official use would soon be suspended, since electronic banking transfers were becoming the norm, and such big bills were being used primarily by organized crime.

The particular bill in question was a Federal Reserve Note from a 1934 issue that featured a portrait of President Grover Cleveland. Nathan decided to hold on to his prize. He had it framed and posted it behind the french fry station, where the store had various signs of all sorts on the wall.

"$1,000—we will present this bill to anyone who can prove that we don't use pure Mazola cooking oil for our fries." Placed above bubbling vats of hot oil, the sign was visible but not reachable by the public.

At 3:00 A.M. on a night in 1939, a trio of thieves decided to claim the bill without proving anything at all, yea or nay, about the store's use of pure corn oil.

"Three guys started an argument," recalled Nathan's son Murray, a teenager at the time. "One of them drew the attention of the workers. The other two jumped over the counter and ripped the sign off the wall. They had a car waiting for them. The three ran out to their car, and off they went."

A thousand dollars, gone in a puff of getaway car exhaust.

Except . . .

Nathan notified police of the theft. Authorities caught the IQ-challenged culprits in New Jersey when they tried to pass the bill. Collected along with it was the sign from the french fry station's back wall. To everyone's surprise except Nathan's, the bill proved to be counterfeit.

Before he would agree to cash it, Nathan of course had gone to the bank and checked out the validity of the bill himself.

"They told him, 'No, it's a counterfeit.' They wanted to take it away from him, they wanted to condemn it and withdraw it from the market," Murray recalled. "But they knew he wasn't going to pass it off to someone else, so they gave him the bill."

Nathan had told no one about the counterfeit. He did not pony up the cash for the holder who had offered it to him but simply posted the bill as if it were real. A couple of lessons can be gleaned here. One is that Nathan always held his cards extremely close to his chest. Another is that he had the kind of pull in the neighborhood that a bank would allow him to keep a thousand-dollar bill that by law should have been confiscated and destroyed.

Reality is like sculpting clay in a PR agent's hands. Perhaps Murray's version of the story was shaped by publicity ace Morty Matz. Jack Dreitzer always claimed that he was the one who found the fake $1,000 bill, discarded on a sidewalk in Coney Island. "I turned it over and it was an ad for a French brassiere company," Dreitzer said.

Mazola continued as the store's brand of choice. Around that time, Nathan's Famous, the number-one consumer of cooking oil in the New York metropolitan area, developed a novel delivery system for its prized ingredient. Nathan installed a five-thousand-gallon tank atop the store. Originally, it contained simple sugar syrup that was delivered via copper pipes to the drink vats. Converted to a tank for corn oil, it was connected to a system of gravity-fed tubing that distributed the precious liquid to the voracious deep fryers down below.

As much as the frankfurter was the star of Nathan's Famous, the potatoes were celebrated also. Deep-fried to a golden brown, they were sold in small cellophane bags, the store's logo printed on the side. A serving usually came with small, extra-crispy leftover pieces that were, to some, the best part of the meal.

The production process of the crinkle-cut fries rivaled the

complicated ballet of frankfurters on the grill. The crispy potatoes were so popular that it took ten fryolators to keep up with demand. (Two smaller fryolators were reserved for other menu items.) Each one of the deep-frying appliances was drained and filtered in the early hours of the morning, tended by a four-man cleanup and rotation crew trained to keep the oil pristine.

"We rotated the oil from left to right as we filled the frylators, and we filtered them at night," explained Hy Brown. "We used the same procedure, and we started over fresh with the fryolators on the left. That was the secret of the crispy, crunchy potatoes that we had."

Filter devices cleaned impurities from the cooking oil. Oil from the first fryolator was filtered and transferred to the second, the second to the third, and so on. After the used liquid had been cycled through all ten cookers, the crew transferred it to huge barrels that would later be picked up by waste oil companies.

The fresh potatoes went through a two-step frying process. They were peeled, cut, and cooked at 325 degrees until soft, all processes that occurred in the back kitchen. Workers brought the once-cooked fries to the counter in "wires," as the large, round metal frying baskets were called. The temperature in the front fryolators was held at 375 degrees, and the fries were finished off there. Whenever the oil started to "cream up"—display a frothy surface— that meant it was dead and could no longer be used.

"Once a fryolator got creamy, it was no good anymore because it would soak the product with oil," said Brown. "It had to be pretty clear oil for us to cook with it."

Tanker trucks filled with corn oil pulled up in the alley beside the store twice a week, pumping their contents up to the huge reservoir on the roof. The big Mazola tank would be joined later by the celebrated hot dog clock—with a huge, six-foot-wide dial

that sported a pair of wieners for hands—as high-visibility beacons for Nathan's Famous of that period.

Nathan's semiofficial police force patrolled the sidewalks on the
block, and Nathan made certain that other members of New
York's Finest felt welcome inside, too. But there was another layer
of regulation that kept the business on track. In-house policing
proved every bit as essential to success as beat cops and friendships
with Coney Island's power elite.

Business and management practices that Nathan put in place
addressed problems of employee theft, yes, but also issues of inventory, production, and sales. Homegrown yet sophisticated, or-
ganic yet rigorous, a system gradually came to control all aspects
of cooking, serving, supplying, and managing the menu items
for which customers eagerly lined up.

When Nathan started his company, his approach to record
keeping was crude in the extreme. He remained functionally illiterate. In the course of constantly working with sums of money,
however, his facility with numbers gradually developed. Early
workers recall him scribbling business records on a back wall of
the store's kitchen, always using a stubby pencil. At the end of the
year, he would paint over the numbers and start over, keeping a
fresh set of records for the new year. The accounting geniuses at a
top firm like PricewaterhouseCoopers might not approve, but it
worked for Nathan.

At least at first. As sales volume swelled, Nathan's Famous
was on its way to becoming the busiest restaurant in America. The
task of managing all aspects of the business became more difficult.
Nathan struggled fiercely to keep up. All the rules he instituted

flowed directly from his no-nonsense personality. The store became a mirror of the man. His personal obsessions about cleanliness, quality, and service played out in the day-to-day functioning
of the store.

"It was just a single restaurant," said Charles Schneck, "but the
place was run with procedures that rivaled IBM."

Prominent among those procedures was the Count.

"Everything at Nathan's was counted," said former Nathan's
manager Sidney Handwerker. "The frankfurters, the rolls, the
french fry bags, everything." Nathan knew to the dog the number
his supplier delivered. He recorded how many he had left at the
end of the day. He compared the tally with the amount in the till.

"We used to count frankfurters every day," recalled Hy Brown.
"We knew how many frankfurters we started the day with. We
knew how many frankfurters we finished with. Any frankfurters
that were broken were put in a separate box. Any frankfurters that
were given out free—for employees to eat, or the police, or anybody
else who was involved with free frankfurters—we had to put a chip
in the register to account for it. The next day when the tallies were
finished, they were always pretty close to the amount of money we
took in for frankfurters."

As a method of inventory control, it was pretty basic. But it
worked because Nathan had an iron hand. His illiteracy took
nothing away from his business acumen.

Former Nathan's Famous accountant Aaron Eliach recalled
showing Nathan a financial statement he had prepared. "I was
very proud of myself," he said, believing he had done excellent
work.

Nathan examined the spreadsheet. "You're $10,000 off in the
inventory."

"How would he know that?" Eliach remembered asking himself. "I didn't think he knew anything about accounting. But I went through my numbers, and sure enough, he was right."

Eliach realized that his client basically kept track of the store's whole business in his head. "Whenever I discussed numbers with him, he knew exactly what I was talking about. He knew everything that was happening. I mean, the inventory wasn't a small inventory. Ten thousand dollars wasn't a major part of it, because we had inventory in cold storage and in warehouses. This was just numbers, so $10,000 wasn't a material amount. How he knew it, I will never figure it out."

"He felt nothing should interfere with business," said Hy Brown. "Business was business. He could be the kindest, nicest guy away from the store, but in the store, he didn't want anybody to think that he was letting down his guard."

There was another aspect of the Count, just as vital but more troublesome. As owners of other cash businesses know, and all drug dealers come to learn, handling the money can be a much bigger headache than inventory. Banks would not take loose change. Every penny, nickel, dime, and quarter had to be packed into paper sleeves.

The money taken in at the store was in a very literal sense filthy lucre. Coins and bills both were slimed with grease, salt, sand, and sweat. The currency was often crumpled.

With paper money, the job was to count out a hundred one-dollar bills and secure them with a currency wrapper. "You had to take the greasy bills out of a box," Nathan's nephew Sidney Handwerker recalled. "To try to flatten them, we used to sit on them."

Sidney remembered an incident where one of the bills he was sitting on stuck to his behind and threw off his count. "I wrapped up the hundred, and then the next one I put underneath my leg had 101 bills in it," he said.

Nathan double-checked the kid's work and saw that the count was off. "Go back on the sandwich station," Nathan commanded. "You can't count anymore." All because a dollar bill had stuck to the bottom of young Sidney's pants.

Eventually, the money counting operations were transferred to a small room at the back of the store, located beneath the stairs to the second floor. It was what passed for a vault on the premises, where the proceeds from the day's business wound up. The door was made of metal for security purposes.

Rolling the coins, in particular, was tedious work. Count, roll, count, roll, for hours on end. Nathan's oldest son, Murray, was often placed on counting duty. "In those days before the machines, you counted with two fingers," he said. "You spread out the coins—twenty, forty, sixty, eighty. Ten dollars of quarters or nickels. It all had to be packed."

Tallying the avalanche of coins from the weekend took all of Monday. At every step along the way, there were opportunities for employees to skim. One cleaning person was caught pocketing the coins he salvaged when he took up the store's floorboards for a steam wash.

How to handle the immense amount of cash bedeviled Nathan for years. The old method of cigar boxes placed beneath the counter was replaced by a fancier system that used suction to vacuum paper currency away from where it was collected, transferring it to central collection boxes. But coin counting remained a thorn in the side of the business. It would not be fully mechanized until the postwar years—and even then, the modernizing process would cause friction between Nathan and his sons.

12

Growing Up Coney

"That was my whole life, lower Brooklyn." Murray Handwerker, lower right, with sister Leah and Aunt Lily.

DURING THE 1920s and '30s, Nathan and his family lived in a series of rented apartments, always fairly close to the store. In 1925, they moved in at 2890 W. Twenty-First Street, just off Mermaid Avenue, and then relocated three blocks east to Mermaid Avenue and Seventeenth Street. From 1935 on, the family lived in a three-bedroom apartment at 1119 Ocean Parkway in Brighton Beach, across the street from Washington Cemetery. Coney Island was a brisk walk or a short bus ride away.

The residential neighborhoods in the area were overwhelmingly Jewish, with dollops of Irish folded in. Life transpired in a circumscribed, almost provincial environment, embracing such traditional New York City activities as bouncing a Spaldeen against the steps of the front stoop, but with the added charm of having a beach and amusement parks nearby.

"I never went to Queens or Manhattan," remembered Murray Handwerker. "I lived and grew up in Coney Island. The beach, the boardwalk. The boardwalk was built from Sea Gate to Ocean Parkway. I used to walk the boardwalk from the store to Brighton Beach Avenue. That was my whole life, lower Brooklyn."

Murray was four years older than his younger brother, Sol, so he was the first of the boys to sample the joys of Coney Island. There was something heady, almost intoxicating, about having the freak shows of the Bowery and the attractions of Steeplechase right nearby.

"That was part of my growing up at Nathan's—I had to stay out from under their feet," Murray said. "They would tell me to please go on the boardwalk, because I was in the way. There were a lot of people moving around there during busy times, especially in the summer on the weekends."

So Murray dove into the streets, lanes, and alleys of the amusement zone. "Drive Your Own Car!" promised a sign on one ride. What eight-year-old could pass up such an unbelievable opportunity? He'd trek past the food booths and candy shops, sampling the wares. He liked to watch people fish off Steeplechase Pier, hauling in their catches and gutting them in front of the goggle-eyed kid.

Murray sometimes went down to Luna Park to look at the premature infants in the incubators. Dr. Martin A. Couney pioneered what he termed "baby hatcheries" in the United States. When hospitals had refused to take such an untested idea on, Couney had turned to amusement parks for sponsorship. First inaugurated in 1903 at Coney Island's Dreamland amusement park, the whole hospital was re-created at Luna Park after a 1911 fire flattened Dreamland for good.

By the time Murray visited, the attraction had been in place for so long that there were "graduates" who had grown up and were working in the neighborhood. They came together at the amusement park for well-publicized reunions. Two of the male graduates had become doctors themselves.

Many of the Coney Island attractions were off limits for underage customers like Murray. Barkers called out the attractions of Magdalena, a hoochie-coochie dancer who set herself up in a booth just across Stillwell Avenue from Nathan's Famous. There was an amusement called the Dark Ride, a tunnel-of-love arrangement that featured a spooky apparition that appeared suddenly out of the gloom. The famed Cyclone roller coaster was also too adult for such a young kid, who could only stand and watch as the cars screamed past.

Murray became adept at mastering the rides that he could go on. Because the nearby Steeplechase Park was totally enclosed, Nathan and Ida liked for him to spend his time there, believing he couldn't get in too much trouble. The Steeplechase Ride ran in a circuit around the whole park, harking back to the days when horse racing was Coney's main attraction. Murray soon learned to mount up immediately behind the heavier-weight customers. The ride was partially gravity controlled, and the heftier riders would increase the speed on the downhill portions of the track.

There were a few unforeseen dangers in the resort town. Murray once experimented with a sharp-bladed clipper on the counter of a Bowery tobacco store where his father purchased cigars. Patrons used the knifelike arrangement to slice off the ends of their stogies. "I put my finger in there, and it clipped off the end," Murray recalled. "I was scared, really scared and bleeding. They came and put bandages on and everything, but I learned to mind my own business."

One of the boy's local favorites was a scooter ride located on the Bowery just a block to the south of Nathan's Famous. The price was five cents for a five-minute turn, and one day in the late twenties, Murray could not resist the scooter's draw. At age eight, he was allowed to wander alone while his father and mother slaved at the store. He had a nickel burning a hole in his pocket.

Round and round went little Murray on the scooter track. At the end of five minutes, a carny worker approached the riders.

"Do you want to go again?" he asked Murray.

"Yeah, sure, I want to go again," said the boy.

So the carny took Murray's admission ticket and punched it for another ride. At the end of five minutes, the ride jockey came around again, asking if Murray wanted another turn.

"I kept saying, yes, yes. I must have been on fourteen or fifteen times." He might have been a little uncertain about the concept. *Do you want to go again?* Yes, of course I want to go again! When the ride finally cleared and Murray had to get off, he still had the nickel in his pocket, but he didn't have what he owed—five cents times fifteen.

"What do you mean?" demanded the carny. "You gotta pay! You rode fifteen times!"

Murray started crying. He could almost see his parents' store, just a few steps away on Surf Avenue.

"I'm going to call the police!" threatened the carny. He wouldn't let Murray leave the property until the weeping boy paid for the punch ticket that he had in his hand. His parents eventually had to come rescue him.

These were different times, perhaps better times, a period when a young child could be trusted to wander alone with a certainty of safety—even in the hugger-mugger of Coney Island. Most locals recognized Murray. The carny at the scooter ride was an exception.

"On the Bowery, there were always hundreds of people," Murray said. "I wasn't afraid of anyone stealing or kidnapping me. First of all, I knew the right people. And whether it was at a candy store or the rides, they usually knew me, too. They knew I was Nathan's son."

The scion of Coney Island royalty, in other words.

Child labor laws did not extend to the owner's relatives, an exclusion designed to protect family businesses like Nathan's Famous. Life as a son of Nathan Handwerker wasn't always a day at the beach. Murray and Sol eventually graduated out of their roll crate playpen to take on a succession of positions at the store.

Murray went first, employed in 1931 at age ten. He immediately came to an understanding that his father at home was a very different person from his father at work. "If I did something wrong or I piled too many frankfurters on a board so some fell off, or the rolls that I was supposed to separate weren't done right, I caught hell. He was a very tough taskmaster."

Initially, the boys weren't allowed to use knives or operate the machinery in the kitchen. But as Murray grew older, he was tasked with transferring potatoes from the huge drum peeler to the cutter, which was hand operated.

"One time, when I came in and was helping, one potato got away," Murray said, recalling a significant memory of his youth. "I'm working up top, so I didn't see it fall onto the floor."

His father, ever vigilant, came by. "Look at what you're doing," Nathan said to Murray, pointing at the runaway tuber. "Look at what you got there. You got the potato—you think that's not my money? This is a profit you make that you're losing there."

In later life, Murray always remembered being schooled over a lost potato. "After that, I was very careful to keep track of where the potatoes were going," he said. "That's the kind of stuff you watched when you were working at the store."

Small hands were good at rolling coins, so naturally helping out at that job fell to the sons. Murray recalled spending long days in the stuffy little counting room under the stairs. In those days before the war, the store had no air-conditioning, and the fan did little more than move the hot summer air around.

"I'm sitting there, I hear a big commotion going on the kitchen," Murray said. It was his father's voice in an argument with one of the workers. "Excited and screaming, under the pressure of the day's business in the kitchen. So I closed my shop up. I couldn't leave the door open with all that money in the counting room."

He ventured out into the kitchen to find his father dressing down an employee. Murray confronted him. "Dad, what are you so excited about? You'll have a heart attack before you can control yourself."

Nathan turned on his son, pronouncing a line that Murray said he would never forget.

"I don't *have* heart attacks," Nathan said. "I *give* heart attacks."

Nathan's hard-crust exterior at work concealed a soft core. Both Sol and Murray witnessed their father's random acts of kindness throughout their time at the store. Nathan had an informal, unannounced policy of never turning away a hungry person who could not pay. But he verged on phobic about keeping his charity anonymous.

Jay Cohen, a longtime manager, recalled the boss directing him to provide a meal for this or that penniless individual. "Then he would run upstairs and hide so he couldn't be thanked," Cohen said.

"I never saw my father refuse anyone that was hungry," said Nathan's son Sol. "It was something that impressed me and something I never forgot."

For Nathan Handwerker, virtue was its own reward. He was an active contributor to numerous local charities, but his donations were often made anonymously. He didn't play favorites. When a local Catholic congregation didn't have the funds to paint its church, Our Lady of Solace on Seventeenth Street, the priest made the rounds of Coney Island businesses with a request for a contribution. The job amounted to some seven hundred dollars.

"Make sure the father has everything he needs," Nathan told his trusted aide-de-camp, Joe Handwerker. "But make sure no one finds out about it."

Nathan demonstrated a similar shyness when the time came to give out year-end bonuses to his managers, head cook, and other core employees. The bonuses represented a practice that distinguished Nathan's Famous from practically every other business on Coney Island.

Manager Jay Cohen: "He would never, never stick around to give you the Christmas bonus, okay? He just never did it. He knew that there was twenty thousand, thirty thousand dollars allotted to the employees, but he never was around to give it to you. Why was that? It's hard for me to fathom. Maybe he didn't want to be in that position to be seen as a nice guy. Was that it?"

Nathan would deflect any thanks extended to him by his employees, usually invoking the same line. "I can go out and go shopping every day for the rest of my life, and I still couldn't spend what I have."

If Nathan was hard on the outside and soft on the inside, his wife mixed warmth and toughness all the way through. Ida had a friendly, open face matched with a reserved personality. Her children could testify to her uncompromising approach to discipline and had the pinch marks to prove it. She hated pretense and could be quick with a deflating remark whenever she encountered it.

"My mother usually pooh-poohed people," remembers her son Sol. "She was never overly impressed with so-called important folks. She was very—what's the word? Self-effacing?"

"Grandma was a very feminine figure," testified her grandson Steve Handwerker. "People generally don't see her that way because she's a very strong, large woman. But she was a very soft-spoken, very humble person who was just a master in the kitchen. I mean, there wasn't anything she couldn't do in the kitchen, there wasn't anything she couldn't make."

"Ida, she was fun," said her nephew Sidney Handwerker. "She used to wear jewelry that was imitation, not real jewels. She used to say, 'On me, they think it's real.' But she had one pin, a locket, that Nathan had bought her. 'This is real,' she said. She was a regular person. Down to earth, very down to earth."

For her whole life, Ida took the public bus to work. Nathan loved his wife's dedication, which matched his own. Their shared bywords of thrift and industry permeated the store's whole atmosphere.

"Before we had the big tanks of oil upstairs, we used to open up two-and-a-half-gallon cans of Mazola oil," said manager Hy Brown. "Nathan would look in to see if you completely drained the cans. If he'd see any oil left, he'd say, 'You know how many eggs my wife could cook with this oil here?' "

Supposedly, that was the source of Nathan's use of pure corn oil at the store—because Ida favored it at home. "If it was good enough for my wife to cook with," he would say, "it's good enough for my customers to have."

Over the years, a persistent myth emerged regarding Ida's vital contribution to the success of the business. She possessed a "secret recipe" for the spices that went into the Nathan's Famous frankfurter. Ida was the one, in other words, who helped make Coney Island's bestselling hot dog delicious. Some accounts had it that the formula was passed down from her grandmother.

The story filtered into press reports only after Nathan's Famous began to employ advertising and public relations firms, a sure sign that it was a bit of created mythology. The concept of an old family recipe served to warm the aura surrounding the business. It was the kind of homey detail that Americans loved.

Years later, another successful chain restaurant, Kentucky Fried Chicken, would also invoke an "Original Recipe" of "secret spices" from its grandfatherly founder, "Colonel" Harland Sanders. KFC owner John Y. Brown Jr. later identified the ruse as a "brilliant marketing ploy."

Ida's secret spices. The story was compelling. Was it true?

Steve Handwerker, Murray's son and Nathan and Ida's grandson, certainly believed the story to be fact.

"There's no myth. Grandma Ida, she's the greatest cook that I've ever experienced in my life. Whatever she made was just incredible. And she has a tongue, a sense of taste: she could tell you anything and everything that's going on with that food. She came up with the formula for the hot dog. She tasted maybe one hundred different possibilities, and she came up with the right blend of different spices and the meat and how it should be done, how it should be added, and how it should be mixed. It was all Grandma Ida and of course Grandpa."

Steve is adamant about this particular origin story. Ida herself, he says, told him the tale. "We went down to the butcher's to pick out only the best meat that would go into the hot dog," Ida told Steve. "They didn't know about spices at all, these butchers." For the spicing, Ida went to different places, tasting samples.

"No, I don't like this," Ida told the spice makers in Steve's account. "It needs more this and this."

"It was all trial and error," Steve said. "She told me this. She experimented with a different spice and meat, the texture, the consistency, the casing, everything. All her. And him. They worked as a team."

Steve's father, Murray, also came down on the side of Ida. "My mother developed the spice formula," he said. "She worked with the manufacturer of the frankfurter. He had spices in, but Mom and Pop didn't like the mix. My mother is the one who put the ingredients together and turned it over to the manufacturer. He had to sign an agreement that he would not use it in any other product. Only for Nathan's."

Can we take these solemn testimonies with a grain of salt—and perhaps with a dash of garlic? Steve Handwerker was always an unabashed partisan of both Nathan and Ida, with whom he spent a lot of time in his youth. Murray demonstrated a real passion for any public relations effort that enhanced the mythology of Nathan's Famous. For him, the story of Ida's secret spice recipe might have been too good not to be true.

"Is it true?" Ida's other son Sol asked, and then he answered the question himself. "I don't think so. There was no such thing as a secret recipe, I'm sorry to say. They tried different ingredients with the manufacturers, different spices until they got something that they were satisfied with. When Nathan and Ida said that this is what they liked, that was it."

Here's Paul Berlly, a representative of Hygrade, Nathan's longtime frankfurter supplier: "I knew Ida very well. She never said anything about the secret spices, but they gave a recipe to us, what they wanted in a frankfurter. Of course, I hate to say this, but Nathan never made a frankfurter. Hygrade made the frankfurter. And we used the spices to our discretion. We made it just a little different, a tiny bit different from the ordinary spices we would use in our process."

Steve has a succinct reply to Berlly. "Bullshit," he said. "It was all Grandma. She gave [Hygrade] the formula that they ultimately used. They tried to imitate it. And there were issues about that, because [Nathan and Ida] didn't want to see Hygrade stealing the formula. Hygrade had the formula because she gave it to them. The company stole it from Grandma."

Other arguments against Ida's secret recipe exist. Many Handwerker grandchildren have said they never heard the story from their grandparents. Nor did veteran employees remember Nathan telling them about Ida's role in formulating the spices. It appears to be just one more durable bit of public relations mythology.

Just what was the Nathan's Famous formula for its delicious frankfurters? Secret or not, passed down from Ida's grandmother or not, the recipe comprised eighteen different ingredients. Included were specifications on the type of beef to be used. Bull meat was leaner and was preferred to the fattier meat of the cow. Also specified was the location of the meat on the animal (beef cheeks, brisket trim, etc.) and the type of casing employed. The ingredients were listed in proportional amounts or amounts per pound. The spices included garlic, paprika, and salt. Written out, the proprietary formula took up a page and a half of closely written text.

PR men might have attempted to make Ida over into the Colonel Sanders of Nathan's Famous, but she was happiest laboring behind the scenes. In the store's early years, she would post herself in the back kitchen, surrounded by a gaggle of sisters and friends. The whole group sat on wooden crates around the big bags of potatoes and onions, spending hours peeling and gossiping. The matriarchal atmosphere resembled a coffee klatch or a quilting bee. At these work sessions, Ida was always the headmistress, especially with her blazingly fast hands.

Said former Nathan's Famous manager Hy Brown: "If they would peel ten fifty-pound bags of onions in an hour, everybody would tell you that Ida could peel them in half an hour."

That particular matriarchal idyll came to an end with the installation of a water jet–powered peeling machine. But Ida continued to put in long hours at the store and still maintained her guarded, private persona.

"Ida worked her fingers to the bone in that place," testified Jack Dreitzer. Bill Handwerker, Ida's grandson, put it this way: "Everybody talks about Nathan Handwerker. I always say that it was both. My grandmother was right beside him during those twenty-hour days. That's important: it was not just him, it was both."

The woman behind the scenes occasionally stepped out front. A rare, memorable instance of Ida's hard-hitting public demeanor came when labor strife first hit Nathan's Famous in the summer of 1934. Union representatives attempted to organize the employees. They set up pickets in front of the store to agitate for shorter hours. The Handwerker family split along political lines. Among those protesting along Surf Avenue one day was Nathan's older brother, Israel, an occasional store employee.

Incensed by a family member's betrayal, Ida chased her brother-in-law off the picket line with a butcher knife.

The strike against Nathan's Famous was at least in part a product of the times, when large sectors of the American populace were radicalized by the economic injustices of the Depression. Both Ida and Nathan considered themselves Democrats, falling in with the prevailing Tammany Hall power structure. But they reacted to the union organizers with obstinate resistance.

The strike, the first of two major ones to hit Nathan's Famous, continued for weeks. Union agitators threw stink bombs into the store. They harassed those workers who crossed the picket line and tried to head off customers at the counters. Police escorted Handwerker family members to and from their homes. Coming during the hectic summer season, the strike threatened to thoroughly disrupt the business.

The mayor of New York City at that time, Fiorello La Guardia, stepped in to bring the warring sides together. He summoned the parties to his office at city hall in downtown Manhattan. Nathan faced off with the head of the Food Workers Industrial Union, the outfit that was attempting to organize the store's workers. The mayor, then only six months in office, acted as mediator.

At one point in the negotiations, Nathan turned to the union leader.

"Look, I don't have to go through this," he said. "I'll tell you what I'm going to do. If you don't stop this strike, I'm going to tear down the restaurant. I'll build a carousel on my corner. And I'll put horses on the carousel that don't eat and don't shit and don't strike."

La Guardia, at least, broke up laughing at the salty language. Eventually, Nathan prevailed. The Supreme Court of the State of

New York issued an injunction against the strikers, and the action fizzled out.

"By the summer of 1935 the strike wasn't on no more," recalled Jack Dreitzer. "How did it end? Nathan got his way. He did what he wanted with the union. He was a powerful man. He had a lot of power."

The Season

"At the end of the summer, we used to sit for days and days and count and roll change. That was our profit." Nathan's Famous, ready to serve.

EVERY BUSINESS ON Coney, including Nathan's Famous, lived and died by the summer season. The period actually extended far beyond the actual months of summer, embracing the thirty-five weeks from Lincoln's birthday in February to the early weeks of September. But the heart of the season stretched between what was then called Decoration Day—rechristened Memorial Day only in the 1950s—to Labor Day. Normally, there were fourteen weekends during this stretch. During lucky years, there could be fifteen.

No Nathan's Famous employee ever saw a leisure weekend in summer. Saturday and Sunday were the crunch days, when Coney flooded with visitors and the crowds stacked up outside the store. Then the job was seven days a week, twelve hours a day. In summer, the store was open twenty-four hours. The single day of the year when Nathan's Famous shut its doors: Yom Kippur.

The seaside resort town always played weather roulette. Nathan and every other businessman on Coney Island prayed for every single one of those fourteen or fifteen summer weekends to be hot and dry. Rainouts meant the crowds stayed away. A storm could blow away profits. Five or six rainy weekends out of the sacred fourteen meant ruin.

A carnival after Labor Day marked the season's end, as children started the school year and tourists remained at home. So the weeklong "Mardi Gras" celebration was largely a Coney-centric event. Employees and bosses alike celebrated a successful season or mourned a rained-out one. The whole resort town got swept up in a swirling street party. There were parades every night, with Nathan's Famous sponsoring several floats every year. The event culminated with a Saturday baby parade.

Then Coney shut itself down. The store was the sole business on the main drag that stayed open year round.

Throughout the twentieth century, Coney Island's popularity and vitality ebbed and flowed with the tide. For both Nathan's Famous and the wider resort town around it, the mid-1930s represented one kind of high-water mark. Before the explosive growth of the suburbs transformed the New York City urban matrix, before the 1939 World's Fair in Queens siphoned off visitors, before the war exploded and changed everything, Coney Island was on the upswing—popular, raucous, iconic, a symbol of American democracy.

Democracy, yes, but within limits. Areas of the beach were still segregated. The demographic pie was sliced pretty thin, too, with northern Italians accorded one zone, southern Italians another, and Sicilians gathering elsewhere. African Americans had their place beside the Steel Pier. The system was informal and not officially policed but carefully maintained nonetheless. In other cases, discrimination was official. Steeplechase Park invited African Americans in but denied them the use of its pool.

Coney Island's bathhouses were also strictly segregated, remembered former Nathan's Famous worker Hyman Silverglad. "If any black person wanted to go into any one of these very nice places, that had steam rooms, all kinds of athletic facilities, a huge Olympic pool, they said, 'No, this is a private club, we don't allow people to come in.' Two minutes later, a white person would come in and they would sell them a ticket."

New York City's population at that time hovered around seven million. A healthy percentage of that number, ranging as high as 18 percent, visited Coney Island during the hot weekend afternoons of summer. Some five hundred thousand of these sojourners, representing seventy million pounds of human flesh, crammed themselves onto the generous strip of seaside beach, fifty-seven acres of sand at high tide. Others resorted to the mammoth Municipal Baths or the area's celebrated commercial bathhouses.

"Every bathhouse, which today would be like a modern spa, had its ethnic flavor," said Silverglad. "Now take Ravenhall: basically Italian. Take Washington Baths: basically Jewish. Washington Annex: a lot of Asians there. Ocean Tide, Irish. Hahn's, Irish. Scoville's, Irish, upper-class Irish, if I may say so. McLochlin, Irish."

Seafarers could hear the dull roar of Coney Island's crowds, spielers, barkers, and touts a mile out into the Atlantic. Smells, too, wafted over the water. With offshore breezes, the residents of Sandy

Hook, New Jersey, six miles south across Lower New York Bay, reported the occasional odor of fried food and the sugary smell of cotton candy.

Eating was as much a pastime as ocean bathing. Small booths under the boardwalk offered easy access for swimmers and sunbathers to knishes, candied apples, corn on the cob. The scent of cooking onions came off the hamburger grill of the store.

During this period, the Coney Island of the imagination arose from a relatively limited rectangle of land, two and a quarter miles long and a thousand feet wide. Braced on all sides by residential districts, including Sea Gate to the west and Brighton Beach to the east, the amusement zone—the part of the island that comes to mind when the words "Coney Island" are pronounced—extended from the south side of Surf Avenue to the beach. Steeplechase Park marked one end of the zone, while Luna Park and Feltman's Ocean Pavilion marked the other.

Between the two ran the seven blocks of the Bowery, a narrow lane crowded with rides, games, penny arcades, sideshows, and food booths. The Bowery was also the realm of freaks: Spider Boy, Singing Lottie, and the Man with the Revolving Head, as well as the popular microcephalic "pinheads," Zippo and Pippo.

The sound of the ballyhoo—a sample spectacle that drew customers into the shows and attractions—punctuated the afternoons and evenings. Spielers called out their pitches, from a simple chant of "*Step* inside! *Step* inside!" to offers of "Three balls for a dime!"

Steeplechase Park, located to the southwest of Nathan's Famous, represented a fifteen-acre entity unto itself. The western entrance to the park, off the Bowery behind the store, featured the leering face that was the emblem of Coney Island and the promising words, "Steeplechase Funny Place." For an admission charge of fifty cents, fun-lovers gained access to all the park's attractions, including a

Ferris wheel, a roller coaster, and a five-acre pavilion. The latter was one of the wonders of Coney, with hardwood flooring and a soaring glass ceiling that shielded revelers from the elements.

Running along the park's perimeter was the Steeplechase ride, a pair of tracks with four horses on each, arranged eight abreast, two riders per mount. The race started atop a steep, twenty-two-foot rise, with the force of gravity plunging the riders forward. "Gaming the ride" meant maneuvering the mechanical beasts ahead of the competition, leaning forward on the downgrades, coming out ahead in the race.

Victors and losers alike exited from the tracks into the Insanitarium, a funhouse of intricate passageways, to be confronted by clowns, dwarves, or other tormentors, wicked figures intent on mischief. Armed with electric prods or paddles to be wielded against the unsuspecting, the figures pulled their pranks to amuse hordes of spectators—most of whom had just endured the same treatment. Jets of air blasted from concealed vents in the floor, blowing off hats, raising skirts, and delighting the leering onlookers. Other sections of floor abruptly dropped away beneath the feet of the hapless victims.

In 1938, at the tender age of eleven, Sidney Handwerker took a job at the store. "I worked in the kitchen. I knew everybody there, and everybody knew me." The boy was the son of Nathan's oldest brother, Israel. Sidney's father worked on and off at the store, and the family lived in the neighborhood, so it was only natural that he, too, would find a job with his uncle.

Sidney summons up idyllic memories of his life in those days. "Coney Island was a paradise. We'd get up in the morning and go to the beach when it was empty. It was wonderful. My father used to work at Nathan's. He'd work nights and come home in the early-morning hours, wake up all my brothers, and we'd all go out at seven o'clock in the morning, swimming on the beach when nobody was there. Then we'd all come home, and he would make us a wonderful breakfast of french fries—Nathan's style—and eggs. Afterward, we'd all go off on our own ways: some went to school, some went to work."

When he first got hired at his uncle Nathan's business, Sidney entered at the bottom of the store's pecking order. He worked in the kitchen, which was a different realm from the counter area, where the employees interacted with the public. His duties were limited, at first, to prep work on the two most popular offerings of Nathan's Famous—hot dogs and potato fries.

"I used to line up the frankfurters on boards so they could take them out on griddles. The frankfurters were not skinless. They were in natural casings, and they came on strings. I had to cut them apart."

Sidney also opened the sacks of potatoes and fed the spuds into an electric peeler. There was an art to the process, and the boss was watching. Nathan would come around on quality control.

"Make sure you don't peel too much!" Nathan would say. "Don't take off too much!"

When Sidney worked peeling onions, he put the onion peels into a garbage bag and the peeled onions into a bucket. Nathan would come by and perform a quick test, simply by lifting the bag of discarded onion peels.

"If I was taking too much onion off the onion, the bag would be heavier than if there were very thin onion peels." Nathan could judge by the weight of the bag if the work was being done properly.

The potato peeler might have gone electric, but there was an ancient hand-cranked device to give the crinkle-cut fries their shape. For years, six days a week in summer and on weekends during the school year, Sidney Handwerker worked the crank. "You put a potato in a machine, and then you went back and forth, and the cut pieces fell into a pot of water."

Sidney ascended up the staff hierarchy to become one of the store's potato men. The crinkle-cut fries went through the same two-step process as the traditional French recipe for *pommes frites*. The potatoes were blanched in oil once, reserved for later use when the rush came, and then finished off in a bubbling-hot deep fryer just before they were served.

"We had to precook the french fries to be finished when it got busy," Sidney recalled. "The potatoes came out in water. I would scoop out a wire basketful of potatoes, drain off the water, and then lower the baskets into round cooking pots. When they were almost cooked through, we had shelves and used to stack them up. And then, when I wanted to finish them, there was, in the front, the pots with very hot oils. I used to fry them so they were crispy and serve them to the public."

During this period, the facilities at the store gradually modernized. "I remember when we got our first electric glass washer in the kitchen, to wash the glasses and sterilize them," Sidney said. "That was a big, big occasion."

Incredible as it seems from the perspective of today's disposable culture, the beverages at Nathan's were served in glasses. The root beer came in heavy mugs, and all the drink glasses were targets for souvenir hunters. Whenever the employees saw a customer abscond with one, the chase would be on.

"We used to run out and grab them," remembered Jack Dreitzer. "We'd see who could catch the most glasses during the day. In those days, the root beer glasses cost forty-five cents apiece. We never let anybody steal glasses."

Drink preparation had come a long way from the days of Nathan's traditional hand-squeezed lemonade recipe. Nathan developed his own syrups. For the store's popular orangeade, he purchased fresh oranges and had them squeezed with the pulp left in. To the extracted juice, he added citric acid and brown and white sugars. The store's other drink offerings were mixed with custom-made syrups, one for flavor and one for color. Drinks were always the menu items with the biggest profit margins.

"I made the drinks," Sidney recalled. "Orange, pineapple, and grape. I used to mix it in a big pail. Out in the front where the drinks were served, we had big glass coolers."

The countermen would call out their needs to the kitchen workers. "They used to yell, 'Orange out!' or whatever. I would take the pail, mix in some color, mix in some flavor, fill it with water. The big glass coolers had a little button—push it to fill up the glasses. We put ice in the glass coolers so it looked cold. And it *was* cold. In the summer, there was always a long line for the drinks."

Sidney's first counter job—"My first time outside"—was at the drink station. Every drink was a nickel except for beer, which sold for ten cents and was the only alcohol Nathan offered. In all its years in existence, the store never had a full bar. In addition to the fruit flavors, there was also root beer for five cents. "In a mug, very creamy root beer; it was all foam."

The counter employees learned to work every job out front before settling into one. "Finally my station became roast beef, barbecue, and chow mein," Sidney recalled. "I was the fastest and the best."

Every ingredient had to be of the highest quality: the barbecue was made from pork butt, the roast beef from top round. Again, although Nathan's was known for the frankfurter, other menu items had their passionate fans. After he retired, Sidney would still field occasional requests from nostalgic friends, asking him to re-create the store's barbecue sandwich or, especially, the chow mein concoction.

"Who ever heard of chow mein on a bun?" Sidney asked. "But it was very popular." The creation of the sandwich was usually credited to Sinta, the store's legendary longtime head cook.

"The chow mein sandwich was built with thin fried noodles, Chinese raw noodles, which we used to fry in the potato fryer. I'd take a bun, crease it in the middle, then put in a handful of noodles and spread chow mein on top of them. There were bottles of soy sauce on the counter. Ten cents for the sandwich. People loved it."

When the innovative concoction was advertised on a placard hanging above the counter, Sinta rebelled. He didn't like the grinning, pigtailed "Chinaman" caricature painted on the sign. Nathan immediately apologized and had the offending placard taken down.

Another popular steam table item, roast beef, was thinly sliced and placed on a bun, which was then dipped in gravy and served. The barbecue sandwich featured thin slices of pork, onions, and relish, topped with a tomato sauce. None of the sandwiches could rival the frankfurter and hamburger in popularity, but they sold well enough to stay on the menu for decades.

For camaraderie and to cut the tension of a long, exhausting workday, the countermen occasionally took up singing in unison. Sidney Handwerker recalled one song that had all the employees joining in. "Hamburgers and onions and chicken chow mein, roast beef and barbecue and a schooner of beer, all hot, a nickel, a nickel, a nickel only." Nathan's signature line, "Give 'em and let 'em eat," became the refrain that the whole staff sang together, sounding like "The Song of the Volga Boatmen."

The countermen also indulged in a secret code to communicate among themselves. To call out "Eighty-six!" alerted fellow workers that a good-looking customer had approached the counter.

"If you said 'Ninety-three,'" said Hy Brown, "that meant you wanted a cop nearby. There was somebody either annoying people, panhandling, or pickpocketing, and you could see it from the counter."

Sidney Handwerker rose from kitchen help to steam-table man and, eventually, to manager. As a loyal member of the Nathan's Famous family, he was rewarded with a living wage, $125 a week, and a $1,000 bonus at the end of the summer. In present-day terms, that remuneration works out to be something like $85,000 a year with a $13,000 bonus.

There was a crude rule of thumb that many Coney businesses employed to determine their profit margin. The paper bills were immediately brought down to the bank. Those deposits represented funds used for overhead. Coins, on the other hand, were kept uncounted, stored in boxes, in recycled wooden root beer barrels, or in large metal custard cans.

"We deposited only the bills because we didn't have time to count the change," Sidney said, recalling a time when he had left Nathan's to work at Willy's, another Coney Island food stand. "At the end of the summer, at the end of the season, we used to sit for days and days and count and roll change. That was our profit for the season. That was your life. You waited for the season."

He tells the tragic story of his sister, Rosie, who had the misfortune of getting pregnant at the wrong time of the year. "You can't be pregnant during the season. You have to work. So Rosie

tried to abort herself. She was twenty-four years old. She hemor-
rhaged and died at Coney Island Hospital."

The season. A jealous god and a harsh mistress. World events
loomed on the horizon that would make the demands of the
business even more extreme.

———

Like a lot of first-generation immigrants, Ida and Nathan yearned
to give their children opportunities they themselves had not had.
As Leah, Murray, and Sol grew up during the '20s and '30s, the
family found itself with enough disposable income to be considered
well to do.

Summertime camp was a constant. During the rest of the
year, Ida arranged for such amenities as piano lessons, museum
visits, and concert tickets. Murray especially embraced these cultural opportunities, becoming a polished amateur pianist.

If Murray was his father's son and the designated heir apparent, Ida's youngest child was always his mother's darling. A shy,
sensitive boy, the introvert to Murray's extrovert, Sol was a fussy
eater like many younger children.

"I never saw my father cook at home," Sol recalled. "My mother
was in control of our kitchen. She did all the cooking. She used to
make things that I liked, sometimes much to the chagrin of my
sister and brother. She may have favored me in the kinds of food
she prepared. I was particular in what I ate. There were certain
things I didn't like that I wouldn't eat. Certain things I loved she
would be happy to make."

Perhaps recalling his own impoverished childhood and repris-
ing his early role as household provider, Nathan often brought home

steaks from the store. He made sure the family diet included a lot of meat. Ida fixed Sol special meals, including the lamb chops he loved. A special favorite of the picky eater was spaghetti made with ketchup and onions. Ida cosseted him with morning servings of bananas and cream.

The science of birth order and its effects on personality remains in dispute. The general rule of thumb is that older kids tend toward conservatism while younger children exhibit rebellious streaks. Such a dynamic certainly played out in the Handwerker family.

"One thing I remember about Sol, he always had something political for you to sign: ban the bomb or something," said his cousin Sidney. "He was always a socialist."

Sol would say later that his adult political leanings were taught to him as a boy by his brother. "I adored Murray when I was much younger," he said. As was the case with many people, Murray's political convictions would move to the right as he aged. His little brother would remain an adamant progressive. Their diverging viewpoints would cause trouble later on.

The Handwerker family displayed the gender bias of a traditional Jewish household. The sons were pushed to the forefront and encouraged to interact with the wider world. The oldest child, Leah, grew to adulthood during the precise time that her parents spent most of the time in the store. While Sol had opportunities to accompany their father and mother on what would eventually become annual visits to Florida, Leah was never invited along, presumably because of school obligations.

The imbalance engendered a certain level of bitterness in the spirited daughter of the family. Leah grew up feeling that she wasn't sufficiently loved. Once, when Leah entered the hospital with a serious condition, her father came to visit her.

"I didn't know I liked you so much," said Nathan to his ailing daughter.

Leah recalled her reaction. *Like? What about love?* Her nephew Steve Handwerker described Leah as not being especially sympathetic about the enormous amounts of time that Nathan and Ida spent at the store.

"The boys were more understanding. Murray, my father, was more understanding of that. And certainly Leah wasn't. I remember she was very angry, always blaming Grandma and Grandpa. And Grandma had a lot of guilt about that. They both had a lot of guilt about that."

Nathan freely admitted to the agonizing dilemma of the first-generation immigrant. "I just don't have the time," he said. "I feel badly about it, but I don't have the time to be with my kids. My children."

Later, as Leah grew into adulthood, there would be other injustices. Nathan and Ida ruled out a marriage to her "first love," believing the match to be inappropriate. Although she married later, she would never forgive her parents for their interference.

The high season on Coney Island remained a jealous god. During the glorious summers, when visitors flocked to the seaside in the millions, the Handwerker children were shipped the other way, to summer camps in the Pocono Mountains. They all loved the experience. Sol remembers his introduction to camp life when he was four years old.

"My mother and father brought me up to visit my sister and brother in Pennsylvania, at Camp Navajo. When time came to return home, I refused to go. I wanted to stay."

Remain behind he did. Nathan and Ida went back to their twelve- and fifteen-hour workdays in Brooklyn. Leah, Sol, and

Murray spent all their childhood summers at camp. It didn't seem like a particular hardship to the children.

"I loved camp," Sol remembered. "I was always looking forward to going back, and I enjoyed it when I did. I was good at sports and athletics. I was good at track and running. I liked everything about it. Baseball, basketball, handball. I just enjoyed it."

The family circle was forever becoming more and more extended. At one time, four of the brothers—Israel, Harry, Morris, and Nathan—all ran Coney Island businesses within blocks of each other. Phillip also had a candy store and a bar and grill. The sisters got into the act, too. Anna Singer ran a food stand and scooter ride located directly across Schweikerts Walk from Nathan's Famous, a sort of adjunct or branch of the store. The Schuchmans, Hyman and his wife, Lena—Nathan's sister—owned the Atlantis, a bar, eatery, and dance hall on the boardwalk where Frank Sinatra and other popular entertainers performed.

Although it might have seemed that Coney would go on forever, changes were happening that would transform the seaside resort town. The innocent fun-seekers of the midthirties were like swimmers in a tub whose plug had been pulled. They felt the underneath tug as the water began to drain but were having too much fun to realize the high times would soon come to an end. Historical forces acted upon the area that were beyond anyone's control. War was coming. America was shedding old ways and acquiring new ones. Few people grasped the full extent of the transformations ahead.

More than a few of those transformations came at the hands of a single man. In the halls of power, a figure had arisen who would threaten everything Coney Island was celebrated for, from the Bowery to Steeplechase, from Luna Park to Nathan's Famous. Master builder and political insider Robert Moses had little appreciation for the popular amusements that so many millions loved.

Son of a New Haven real estate speculator, Yale educated, Moses was often pictured posed in front of one of the scale models showing the various developments he championed. He gazed down at the miniature cityscapes like an all-knowing lord. The humans in those scale models would have been the size of ants, easily brushed aside.

The source of Moses's influence arose from force of personality, not from any mandate from voters. The only time he ran for office, as a Republican candidate in the 1934 race for New York governor, he lost by eight hundred thousand votes. His power was bureaucratic, not democratic.

Moses cast a cold eye on Coney Island, dismissing the whole affair as a low-class bauble that scarred the city's coastline—loud, garish, and louche. Confronted by the raucous reality of an amusement park, Moses was not amused. He had other plans for the place, radically different from the chaotic fun zone that was so fast, so cheap, and so out of control. Where others saw entertainment and enjoyment, Moses envisioned tidy parks and high-rise housing developments.

"Such beaches as the Rockaways and those on Long Island and Coney Island lend themselves to summer exploitation, to honkytonk catchpenny amusement resorts, shacks built without reference to health, sanitation, safety, and decent living," Moses said.

"Why did [the shoreline of New York] end up with so much government-financed housing?" asked Robert Caro, author of *The Power Broker: Robert Moses and the Fall of New York*. "Largely because Robert Moses wanted it there."

In 1934, Mayor La Guardia appointed Moses as commissioner for a new, reorganized citywide Department of Parks. Four years later, La Guardia transferred control of city beaches from the borough presidents to the Department of Parks. Coney Island thus acquired a new master. La Guardia's successor, Mayor William O'Dwyer, named Moses citywide "construction coordinator."

Robert Moses was a busy man. He had highways to plan, parks to develop, bridges to build. He couldn't act on his designs for Coney Island immediately. It would take a few years for him to get around to it, but he would eventually allow his heavy hand to pass across the landscape of the small spit of sand at the southern terminus of Brooklyn. When he did, the effects would be far reaching and ultimately catastrophic.

Nathan Handwerker and, in later years to a lesser degree, his son Murray would battle the power broker every step of the way. As it was, Coney Island in the years before the war stood poised on a precipice. The lights still shone like beacons, the barkers still barked, and the crowds still lined up outside Nathan's Famous. But looking east, toward Europe, a darkness gathered. Coney's midthirties high season was coming to a close.

The War

"Most of the business started at midnight. As soon as all
the lights went off all over the place, we got jammed."
Nathan's Famous during World War II.

IN THE SPRING of 1939 a sprawling, 1,200-acre exposition opened
on the site of a former swamp and garbage dump in Flushing,
Queens. Originally conceived as an economic boost for Depression-
ravaged New York City, the 1939 World's Fair would host forty-
four million visitors before it closed in October 1940. With a "Dawn
of Tomorrow" theme, the massive enterprise was supposed to
foster a progressive, optimistic atmosphere.

During the eighteen months the fair was open, world events
overtook the best-laid plans of its organizers. Citing "economic

reasons," Germany abandoned preparations for a colossal cannons-and-monuments pavilion, designed to showcase its imperial designs. Anti-Nazi opposition to the German presence at the fair had risen to fierce levels, and eventually, Hitler's government decided it would prefer to spend its money on tanks, not fair exhibits. But the Jewish Palestine Pavilion went ahead as planned, introducing and promoting the Zionist idea of a Jewish state.

Nathan's Famous was there, too. Nathan opened four outlets on the World's Fair grounds. Two of them braced the fair's famed Parachute Jump, later to become a fixture on Coney Island. The Nathan's Famous outlets were primarily drink stands that did not even feature the store's trademark hot dogs. The 1939 fair was one of the few times that Leah—then coming up on her nineteenth birthday—worked in the business.

Another of the Nathan's Famous booths was located in the six-acre Children's World area of the fair, near the Swan Ride and in the shadow of a small, very tame Ferris wheel. Working at this booth, busily making malteds, was a teenaged girl named Dorothy "Dottie" Frankel. At age seventeen, she was already Murray's longtime childhood sweetheart.

They had met in 1936, when she was fourteen and he was fifteen, while sharing an American history class at Abraham Lincoln High School on Ocean Parkway. Dottie was a Bronx girl whose family had only recently relocated to Brooklyn. Murray's opening line to his fourteen-year-old crush: "Are you interested in ballet?"

It just so happened that Dottie was. "How did you know?"

"I can tell by your legs," replied the budding Lothario.

"From the age of fourteen on," Dottie recalled, "it was really a romance."

Murray happened to have tickets to the Ballet Russe de

Monte Carlo, at that time one of the foremost ballet companies of the world.

"Would you be interested in going?" Murray asked.

"Of course," Dottie replied. He took her for a predate test run of sorts, on a walk down the boardwalk to the Tuxedo theater. The grand movie palace, on Ocean Parkway at Brighton Beach Avenue just north of the BMT subway line, was ornate, inexpensive, and jam-packed with activities.

"In those days, they used to have bingo plus movies and all sorts of other short features. And they gave away dishes. All for ten cents. On the back of my bingo card, I wrote, 'Nice boy,' with about seventeen exclamation marks."

Murray sealed the deal on his visit to Dottie's house to pick her up for the ballet. "We had a piano, and he sat down and played Chopin. Well, that did it. He invites me to the ballet, *and* he plays Chopin? What more could a girl want?"

But the course of true love did not run smooth.

"Right before the senior prom, Murray stopped seeing me," Dorothy remembered. "He didn't call or anything. Oh, I was flabbergasted." It turned out that her erstwhile boyfriend had a thrifty streak that prevented him from laying out the funds for a proper prom date. Dottie went to the dance with another boy.

"I accepted this other invitation not because I liked him—I really didn't—but because I wanted to show Murray, 'Ha-ha, who needs you?' Inside, I was devastated. And you know what? He wasn't even there! All of that was for naught. I mean, I went to the prom, but my heart wasn't in it."

Murray soon resurfaced with "a lovely letter" to Dorothy, and the two made up. In the letter, he quoted a truism of the day, attributed to automobile industrialist Henry Ford: "Never explain. Your enemies won't believe you, and your friends don't need it."

Later in life, Dorothy laughed over the memory. "That was his big explanation for why he vanished out of the blue!"

After that, the two were rarely apart. At first, Dorothy was blissfully unaware of what she was getting herself into. The fame of Nathan's Famous had not penetrated into the Frankel household. "I had never heard of Nathan's. First of all, my mother would never let us eat hot dogs or delicatessen. I think she thought it was poison. Even when I found out that his father was Nathan of Nathan's Famous, I was very unimpressed because I had never been there."

Eventually, Dorothy Frankel found her way into the Handwerker family fold. It was Murray who secured his young girlfriend the summer job at the World's Fair malted booth.

Among the visitors to the exhibition were King George VI and Queen Elizabeth of England, the first British monarchs to sojourn in the United States. Franklin Delano Roosevelt engineered the visit as part of his effort to cement relations between the two countries and to ease the grip of American isolationism. The trip was something of a PR effort. FDR knew war was looming in Europe, and he wanted his fellow citizens to see the royals as just plain folks, since he knew the United Kingdom would need its former colony's help in facing off with the Nazis.

In addition to the World's Fair, the king and queen visited a Civilian Conservation Corps camp, laid a wreath at the Tomb of the Unknown Soldier in Arlington—and trekked to Roosevelt's Hyde Park estate for a country picnic. It is a measure of the period that when FDR decided to serve the Windsors a downscale luncheon of hot dogs, the world let out a collective gasp. The June 11,

1939, picnic came to be nicknamed the "Hot Dog Summit," since it combined diplomacy with just-plain-folks democratic eats.

When the queen whispered a question to her hostess, Eleanor Roosevelt—"How do you eat this?"—was she referring to a Nathan's Famous frankfurter? She used a knife and fork, but when the king took his serving in hand and even asked for seconds, was he reacting to the quality of the bestselling hot dog in Coney Island? Was the frankfurter served at the summit from Nathan's?

That was the story that circulated in the picnic's aftermath. You can trace its genesis in the literature about the event. The Hot Dog Summit's frankfurter became a Nathan's Famous hot dog only after the fact. There is no evidence one way or another in reports from the time.

Given Nathan's in-tight relationship with Democratic leaders, he could conceivably have catered the event. It would be nice to think so. But again, as with Ida's secret spice recipe, a PR man's opportunistic imagination most likely was in play. His Majesty chowing down on Nathan's franks became an anecdote, taken up and repeated in histories of the summit and of Nathan's Famous. It's hard to keep a good story down. The *New York Times*, a.k.a. the paper of record, reports that it was a Smith's frank.

Even though the king's wiener probably wasn't from the store, the whole episode demonstrated the increasing identification of the hot dog with America's democratic ideals. The nationalistic icons of Mom and apple pie were joined by a sausage that emigrated to the United States from central Europe. And the astonishing popularity of Nathan's Famous and Coney Island contributed mightily to that populist association.

After it closed in fall 1940, the World's Fair turned into

something of a road show. More than a few of its attractions were carted off to Coney Island. Luna Park, then struggling, adopted so many of the exposition's rides and attractions that it earned the right to be officially called "New York World's Fair of 1941."

The famed Parachute Jump, defunct but still standing as a landmark today, was dismantled and taken from the World's Fair site in Flushing and reerected in its current place next to Coney Island's boardwalk, four hundred yards southwest of Nathan's Famous. (Even though it no longer drops thrill-seekers from its tower, the ride is recognized as "the Eiffel Tower of Brooklyn.")

Nathan himself participated in the wholesale transfer of the fair's infrastructure. From one of the pavilions, he got a bargain-basement deal on a collection of enormous walk-in refrigerators, gorgeous, overengineered wooden monsters that were heavily insulated.

"Those refrigerators are the best ones you can possibly get," Hy Brown said. "They retained the cold. They were compartmentalized. They could be refrigerated or used as freezers. He built the whole store around the freezers that he got from the World's Fair."

One of the behemoths was given over entirely to storage of frankfurters.

"We sold sixty thousand franks on a weekend," recalled Hy Brown. "We had that walk-in refrigerator, so, my goodness—it held tons and tons of frankfurters."

During this period in the late 1930s and early 1940s, the summer weekend tally—Friday night to Sunday—amounted to an incredible four tons of franks. The Nathan's Famous frankfurter counter had developed to the point it was doing the heaviest retail business in the entire world, when measured by revenue per square foot. All those humongous refrigerators were simply a necessary facet of doing business.

In keeping with his informal management style, Nathan occasionally repurposed the chilled spaces for private conferences
with employees. "If he ever didn't want to be overheard, he would
bring you into the refrigerator," said one longtime employee.
"And even then, he would whisper. You could see your breath. It
was crazy."

Sol was still living at home at the time. When the store was hit
by a second period of labor unrest, including another picket line,
Sol's support for the strikers caused some discontent on the part
of his parents. Dinner table conversation became fraught.

"I wouldn't say [Nathan] was mistreating workers," Sol said.
"He was tough on everybody, but he generally paid well. The fact
is, there was a strike, and it was hurting him, and he wasn't happy
with it. He couldn't have been very pleased that I would not cross
the picket line."

The second strike was a sign that the paths of the Handwerker sons might continue to diverge. Murray ignored the picket
line and continued to work at the store. His little brother balked.
Ominous clouds were piling up between them that would eventually develop into a full-fledged storm front.

Nathan couldn't hide from what was happening in the wider
world. The army recruitment *chappers* threatened to knock on his
door as they had when he was a young man in Galicia. Even though
he had fled across an ocean to avoid it, war searched Nathan out.
This time, it was coming not for him but for those near and dear.

———

Both Murray and Sol eventually served in the American armed
forces in World War II. Their time in uniform was largely benign,
but they each returned from service in Europe with transformed

outlooks, plans, and adult personalities. For Murray, especially, his posting overseas resulted in new tastes and attitudes that would have serious impact on the subsequent history of Nathan's Famous. But Sol also had experiences that shaped him forever.

The older son went first, drafted into the U.S. Army in 1942. Just before Murray left for overseas, he and Dorothy married. His new wife loved the Handwerker family, even though she had difficulty aligning her ways with theirs.

"I'm Russian," Dorothy said. "We're very warm and affectionate. We hug and kiss. I hugged and kissed Ida when she was around. And she would say to me, 'I love you, but I can't show my love the way you do.' Murray told me he didn't remember his parents ever hugging and kissing him. It wasn't lack of love. Ida was just not able to. First of all, she worked so damn hard when they were little that she probably didn't have the strength left over to give them hugs and kisses. She was worn out. But she certainly loved her children. She just didn't have time to be a mama."

Ida and Nathan saw their oldest son off and adopted his new wife into their family circle. It was a nail-biting time. Card-playing was always a great pastime among the Handwerker clan. Ida introduced Dorothy to the family's preferred game of gin rummy, teaching her so well that the student surpassed the teacher.

"You're cheating!" Ida would exclaim laughingly when Dorothy made gin time after time.

The trio bonded over cards and also over their shared concern for the fate of their boys in uniform, first Murray and then, in 1943, Sol, when he also entered the service.

The household kept the home fires burning. Nathan was beside himself with anxiety about his sons. For the first time in his life, he had difficulty applying himself at the store. He couldn't concentrate. "His time was mainly spent making packages [to send overseas], because it made him feel better to know he was doing something for his sons," Dorothy said. "During those years, he was really very, very distracted."

It was as though the forces of history were visiting their revenge upon Nathan. In 1912, he had slipped away from the slaughter that became World War I. But the bloody sequel—with some of the same forces slugging it out on some of the same battlefields—swept down on his life three decades later. He could run, but it turned out that he couldn't hide.

With German U-boats on the prowl in the waters off the eastern coastline of the United States, authorities considered Coney Island as the first line of homeland defense. The whole area became militarized. Civil defense authorities ordered the nighttime lights of the amusement parks extinguished in order to fox enemy plans for bombardment. On the west end of the island, at Sea Gate, the military installed a pair of immense circular gun batteries, the turrets made of concrete. The Coast Guard maintained a station in Manhattan Beach.

In the middle of all this, Nathan's Famous remained an oasis of normalcy. The government considered the store to be an American institution of sorts, central to the war effort as a symbol of everything the country held dear. Service personnel, the reasoning went, had to have at least a few landmarks of the good times before the war. They needed to remember what they were fighting for. A Nathan's hot dog was one of those things.

Thus Nathan's Famous was the single business in the neighborhood that was allowed to skirt curfew rules and remain open at night. The store had a comfortable, almost intimate relationship with the military. Many of the customers lined up were wearing uniforms, some of them fresh from a duty posting overseas and anxious for a nostalgic taste of home. Defense workers also had to have a place where they could get a quick bite. The local MPs (military police) and SPs (shore police) were on familiar terms with Joe Handwerker.

"I worked with the Coast Guard people; they had a base in Manhattan Beach," Joe recalled. "I had to teach them how to make french fries. They sent their chefs to me. They came down and watched what I was doing."

Air wardens permitted the store's lights to stay lit even in the midst of the blackout, after Joe Handwerker demonstrated to them that, when the sirens sounded, the whole display could be switched off with the flick of a switch.

"I showed them that we could be in complete darkness in sixty seconds," Joe said.

An issue arose during the blackouts with customers lighting cigarettes as they stood in line in front of the darkened counters, waiting for the all-clear.

"This was a big problem for the air wardens," Joe remembered. "So I set up a microphone, and I pleaded with the public, please not to light cigarettes until the alarm comes on that we're safe. And they were good."

When the nighttime curfew hit and the rest of the borough went dark, the city's human population reacted like moths. They gravitated to the nearest bright light. "We were busy all day long," remembered Joe. "But most of the business at that time started at midnight. As soon as all the lights went off all over the place, we got jammed."

Viewed from the air, the former electric fantasyland of night-time Coney Island became merely a dark smear upon the Brooklyn landscape, with only a single pinprick of light—Nathan's Famous.

The story of the store during these years centered around the rise of Joe Handwerker, who had steadily risen in the ranks of the business until he was the trusted second-in-command to Nathan himself. Their relationship became so tight that he could almost be considered Nathan's third son—or fourth son, if the store is to be counted as one.

Intensely loyal, not a great innovator but an individual who understood every facet of every front counter station, every kitchen procedure, and every supplier's order, Joe gave his uncle a great gift. With him in charge, Nathan could leave the store for days, even weeks or months, and return to find it still humming along smoothly. Joe allowed the man who never took time off to take time off.

"He never had a vacation," Joe said. "When I started to run the business, he started to take two weeks, two months, three months, and finally six months. When he came back, he found it better than he ever left."

After signing on to the store's labor force in November 1920 at age twelve, Joe thoroughly familiarized himself with the business. For a quarter of a century, he was king of the night shift, reigning over that prickly, unpredictable, but surprisingly lucrative time when Nathan's Famous was virtually the only game in town. In the wee hours, he battled boredom, drunks, thieving employees, and random nighttime craziness to keep the place running.

Joe usually sported a wide smile and a thin mustache. He had a ruddy complexion. He was, in the words of Steve Handwerker, "a kind of cherub of a guy." Nathan's Famous was Joe's first job and for decades his only one. It's a measure of how close he was to the boss that he and Nathan both moved into the same building, 1119 Ocean Parkway, their three-bedroom apartments literally one on top of the other.

Whenever Nathan wasn't in command at the store, Joe would step into the role. He would climb atop the Coca-Cola box behind the counter and monitor the situation, shouting encouragement at the workers just like the boss did, functioning as Nathan's Mini-Me.

In the course of his long service, Joe became adept at handling complaints. When a customer once objected to her drink having orange pulp in it, he was quick with an answer. "We got a new machine in there, ma'am," Joe told her. "That orange pulp is sterilized! It's perfect!"

The longtime night policy at the store was never to accept bills larger than twenty dollars. A group of customers came in one evening and put in a collective order for hot dogs and drinks that amounted to two dollars and change. They tried to pay with a fifty-dollar bill.

"I'm sorry," apologized Sidney Handwerker, working as a counterman that night. "We don't accept fifties. Nothing more than twenties."

A stocky, slightly inebriated gent in the group objected. "Look, that's American money. You'll take it, or you'll get nothing."

Other members of the group offered to pay with smaller bills, but the guy insisted.

Sidney summoned in his brother, Joe.

"What's the problem here?" the feisty night manager asked.

The big guy leaned over the counter. "You've got a fifty-dollar bill, and that's American. You'll take it."

"Okay," Joe responded, the soul of reason. "Just a minute."

The store always had a lot of change on hand. Joe came out with a canvas money sack heavy with rolled pennies.

"Take the fifty-dollar bill," he told Sidney. To the customer, he said, "You'll get change in pennies. That's American money, and you'll take it. If you're going to be a wise guy, I'll open every roll, and you'll get a loose fifty dollars."

That was that. The hulking customer shut his mouth, took back his big bill, and allowed others to pay with smaller ones. Chalk one up for the little guy.

Joe's relationship with his uncle and boss was oftentimes tumultuous. Nathan realized what a good worker he had in his nephew, but he never restrained himself from correcting Joe when something went wrong. Nathan could lose his temper about inappropriate staff scheduling, for example, or incorrect preparation of the food, improper storage, or poor cleanup. If he saw something, he'd say something, oftentimes to Joe.

The conversations would blow up into full-scale arguments. The two would sometimes rage at each other in full view of the public but more often would remove themselves to the store's upstairs office. There they would shake the rafters with top-volume Yiddish invectives. Manager Hy Brown once timed one of Nathan and Joe's shouting matches, clocking the exchange of screams, snarls, and yells at a full two hours.

"Everybody else would hide," remembered Brown.

"Everybody would be scared to death," added coworker Jay Cohen.

"You didn't want to be around," said Brown.

"Joe would have to walk away crying," said Nathan's grandson Steve Handwerker. "Grandpa would still be yelling at him from across the store. That was the typical once-a-month blowup."

Joe took on more and more responsibility, so there were more and more things for the two men to disagree over, more issues to shout about. Joe would almost always be the one to back down.

"Okay, Nathan, you're right," he would admit after the tiff cooled. "I'll do it differently."

Beginning in the late thirties, Joe was responsible for much of the store's purchasing. His boss relied on him. But whatever he did, whatever position he filled, Joe always had an authority figure looking over his shoulder. Nathan would double-check his work. It must have been maddening, but as volatile as the relationship was, it managed to endure.

In the New York area, the freshest ingredients came from the teeming central markets of Manhattan—the Gansevoort meat-packing district centered around West Fourteenth Street, and the Commission Market on Washington Street was for produce, located on what was then called the Lower West Side, before it became Tribeca. Joe would oversee the night shift and then journey into the city, checking the onions, examining the sides of beef himself, putting in a fourteen- or sometimes sixteen-hour workday.

"He enjoyed the politics of the purchasing," recalled Steve Handwerker. "He liked interacting with the vendors and being 'Joe from Nathan's.' He really enjoyed that part of it."

Wartime rationing and shortages made the purchasing job exponentially more difficult. Good beef was an especially sought-after commodity. It was only the mutual loyalty of Nathan and his suppliers that got the store through the war years. Nathan's Famous tried all sorts of strategies to stretch its supply of meat. The store shrunk the size of its servings, including dishing up a smaller frank.

"Then meat became very scarce to the point where we couldn't get enough product," Joe said. "So [Nathan] gave an order to only serve the servicemen, and only the servicemen in uniform. Civilians couldn't get served at certain hours. Then the servicemen got wise, and instead of buying two franks, they bought ten. They sold the extras. They paid a nickel, and they sold them for a quarter."

In response, the store had to limit even soldiers to two hot dogs apiece.

But with Nathan's Famous frankfurters selling for a quarter on the black market, the writing was on the wall. One high-profile casualty of the war was the celebrated nickel frankfurter. The price of meat became too high to sustain the price point. Nathan resisted as long as he possibly could, depending on sales volume to make up the difference. But it was a losing proposition.

"The frankfurters were seven to the pound, which was a pretty large frankfurter," recalled longtime manager Hy Brown. "As time went by, rather than raise the price, we would make the frankfurter a little smaller. We went to seven and a half to the pound. We'd try and keep the price as long as we could, because Nathan's theory was always to give the best for the least and trust that volume would cover everything else."

In terms of modern buying power, the nickels that customers were shoving across the counter were becoming worth less and less, the equivalent of today's eighty-seven cents in 1935, eighty-five cents in 1940, eighty-one cents in 1941, seventy-three cents in 1942, and down to sixty-six cents in 1945.

The business was beginning to resemble a Ponzi scheme, with increasing numbers of customers in one year making up for slimming profit margins from the year before. There was nothing for it. The nickel dog had to go.

Paul Berlly, the Hygrade Provision rep, was finally the one who tipped the scales. Nathan complained to him that the spiraling cost of meat was cutting into the store's profits. At the time, the store was going through a hundred and fifty barrels of franks per week, six hundred in each barrel. Hygrade was charging forty-five cents per eight count, which worked out to be more than five cents a frank. Nathan's Famous was actually losing money on its signature item, making up the difference on other menu offerings and especially on drink sales.

"So why don't you raise the price?" Berlly asked.

"Oh, we'll lose half the business."

"I'll tell you what, Nathan. Hygrade will back any amount of business that you lose. We'll make good. Understand?"

Nathan caved, but he was still upset about it. When the price rise went into effect, he reacted with a sort of embarrassed shame.

"He didn't want to face his old-time customers," recalled Hy Brown. "He didn't want for them to say, 'Ah, Nathan, now that you're getting rich, you're changing the price.'"

When the price of a dog got kicked up to seven cents in 1944, Nathan left town rather than face the music. He didn't show himself around the store for days. The seven-cent frankfurter was a major pain for the countermen, since they were forced to make change in pennies. But more than that, in Nathan's mind, it represented a kind of moral failing. In a quite literal demonstration as to how important Nathan's Famous was to the working class, the Communist Party USA organized a protest over the price hike.

Juggling price and size eventually got Joe in trouble from the wartime Office of Price Administration, which accused him, as the primary purchaser of the meat that went into the Nathan's Famous frankfurter, of market manipulation, a.k.a. price gouging. Facing the charges, a panicked Joe ordered a fresh sign painted with a revised set of prices.

"Five cents, small frankfurter," read the new, hastily assembled menu. "Seven cents, medium frankfurter; ten cents, large frankfurter." In reality, no separately sized franks existed. The whole scheme was a ruse to fend off the Office of Price Administration's allegations.

In whatever manner Joe maneuvered through his troubles, having a trusted second-in-command represented a great boon for Nathan during the war, when his gnawing worry over his sons distracted him from his usual hawk-like vigilance at work.

By the war's end, Nathan would be approaching his thirtieth year at the store, thirty years of vigilance and hard work, always on his feet, always watching, correcting, controlling. It wasn't that he was tired or ready to retire. He just wanted his boys to join him in the business, so the passing of the torch, when it came, could be done as smoothly as possible.

It didn't work out that way.

15

The Prodigal Sons Return

"And music, and dancing, with all the food you could possibly eat!" Murray *(left)* and Sol Handwerker in Europe, 1945.

FOR THE MAJORITY of 11.5 million men and women who served abroad during World War II, the experience represented an indelible and formative part of their lives. Murray and Sol were no different. They were both in the U.S. Army in Europe for over two years, and they both returned to the States changed men.

Murray spent a good portion of his service in France and came away as a confirmed Francophile, impressed with the people, the culture, and, most importantly for his future dealings with Nathan's Famous, the food.

The idea of cuisine—as opposed to eats—entered his personal makeup. He would forever afterward aspire to fine dining, white tablecloths, sit-down meals. The oldest Handwerker son's time in Europe worked to separate him from the basic "give 'em and let 'em eat" philosophy of his father. The developing friction did not express itself immediately, but it would soon act as a wedge that came between Murray and Nathan.

Sol's time with the U.S. Army could best be summed up by the fact that he spent a stretch of his time in Switzerland studying playwriting. He visited art museums. Although he did enter Dresden soon after the city was leveled by Allied bombing and was among the soldiers present at the April 25, 1945, meeting of the Russian and American armies in the city of Torgau on the Elbe River, he never saw actual battle.

This state of affairs is not so odd as it sounds. For the almost two million American soldiers in the European theater, the experience varied widely, from the bloody beaches of Normandy and the horrific winter conditions during the Battle of the Bulge to less dangerous service like Sol's.

Murray and Sol were quite literally brothers in arms. Incredibly enough, given the absolute chaos Europe was back then, they managed to meet up. Sol heard that his brother was nearby, found a car and driver, and sought Murray out. The two G.I.s had a short but emotional reunion amid the fog of war.

Murray had gone overseas first and returned first also. His parents greeted their all-grown-up boy like a conquering hero. "They were so enthralled," Dorothy remembered. She portrays Nathan as spreading the news throughout the Coney Island community.

"Thank God Murray's home," said the proud papa. "He's right here!"

Sol took a slightly different approach to his homecoming. One morning in 1946 the First Army headquarters phoned Nathan.

"The first American soldier to meet the Russians at the crossing of the Elbe has returned to the States," said the officer's voice on the other end of the line, an embellishment of the truth. "This G.I.'s first request was for a frank at Nathan's."

Could Mr. Handwerker possibly accommodate a heroic boy in uniform? Nathan didn't have to be asked twice. He quickly decorated the store with red-white-and-blue banners normally reserved for July 4th. He hired three musicians to provide patriotic songs in preparation for the G.I.'s arrival.

The soldier arrived with a public-relations officer and a photographer who posed him munching a Nathan's Famous frankfurter. Nathan came out of the store and pushed his way through the milling crowd, announcing "This frankfurter is on the house!"

His jaw dropped when he realized the G.I. was Sol, a wide grin on his face and a discharge emblem on his uniform. A miracle! And one that tested the cardiac systems of both parents.

Nathan was overjoyed. In celebration of the safe return of his sons, he commissioned a Sefer Torah at the local synagogue. The creation of a new holy scroll was an elaborate, highly prized, and expensive undertaking, a mitzvah that did great honor to Murray and Sol. The inauguration celebration, the Hachnasat Sefer Torah, is based on traditions that are at least three thousand years old. This one filled the streets around the store with dancing, singing, and feasting.

"The entire Coney Island was there," remembered family friend Claire Kamiel. "All the food that you could possibly eat was brought in by Nathan Handwerker. They walked with the scroll through the streets. And music, and dancing, with *all the food you could possibly eat!* Nobody was questioned. Only one thing: help yourself, enjoy! Nathan Handwerker!"

In the aftermath of the war's upheavals, displacements, and horrors, the mood in both the country at large and around Nathan's Famous centered on an overwhelming urge to return to some kind of normalcy. It was probably a vain hope. Monstrous revelations concerning the murder of six million victims in the Holocaust were beginning to filter over from Europe. Mushroom clouds hung above two cities in Japan. The world could never really be the same again.

But Nathan tried. His vision of normal was simple. He wanted his sons working at the store, continuing to learn the business, making themselves ready to take over when, in some unimaginable future, the founder would be ready to retire. At first, both veterans dutifully fell in line and took jobs under Nathan's watchful, hopeful eye. But they also indulged in other, grander plans, both entering college under the GI Bill.

Before the war, Murray had attended the University of Pennsylvania, but he returned to the States with other ideas. He enrolled at New York University and graduated with a degree in French. The boy who had so impressed his young girlfriend with a mastery of Chopin was essentially doubling down on his high-culture enthusiasms. How fluency in French might serve him at the store was a question largely left unasked. The father who had never spent a day in class (outside of a brief brush with Hebrew lessons) was probably too impressed with his son's college degree to voice any doubts.

"Nathan tried to teach his sons what he knew," said Jay Cohen. "I'm sure that he saw that some things they couldn't learn no matter what college they went to."

To some extent, Nathan himself was caught in the middle. To the old guard, he was a god, his way being the only way. He desperately wanted his sons in the business. But he wanted them there on his terms. The difference between the two camps cropped up constantly.

"Murray, you've got to be on the line," Nathan would tell his son. "You've got to be in the store."

"No, no, no," Murray would respond. "I have managers for that."

"Nathan was not an office person," said Jay Cohen. "As soon as lunchtime came around, he would be outside there, watching the potatoes and how they were cooked, how the frankfurters were cooked, and if this or that was served properly and so on and so forth."

That kind of vigilance was hugely responsible for the success of the store. But Murray and Sol could not bring themselves to follow their father's lead.

"The damned business was Nathan's life, and his family probably came second," Cohen said. "His children were not into the nitty-gritty of the business. Nathan was into the nitty-gritty. He was there behind the potato chopper. He saw to it that you understood what he wanted on a daily basis. But his sons were not into that. They were not into the nitty-gritty."

No one could challenge Murray's devotion to Nathan's Famous. His presence definitely relieved some pressure from his father. With the able Joe Handwerker installed as general manager and purchasing agent, and with his eldest son also taking larger responsibility for running the overall business, Nathan felt that he and Ida could at long last absent themselves from the store for extended periods. He didn't want to retire, and he still saw himself as very much in charge, but he did want to step back.

Nathan and Ida's winter sojourns in Florida at first lasted weeks and then stretched to months. They always returned for the season. Winter was a relatively slack time in Coney Island, anyway. There came to be a rhythm to the flow of power at the store. Nathan and Ida always thought it was their patriotic duty to vote. They would wait until after Election Day in November, then they would decamp, turning the business over to Joe and Murray. Months later, the couple would come back to take up their responsibilities during the busy summer rush.

"When Nathan was in Florida, Nathan's Famous was foremost on his mind," said Marsha Abramson. "There were calls from him and questions that had to be answered. When he came back to Coney Island in April, you felt his presence. Things started changing as soon as he came back."

Nathan was a "trust but verify" kind of person. Whenever he left the store for his Florida sojourns, he would always fully reassert himself upon his return.

"It wasn't a week in the spring when he got back [from vacation] that he changed every padlock in the building," recalled Jay Cohen. "That man must have gone through seven thousand padlocks in the years that I knew him, because that's how he operated."

Transitions were hard. The handover of authority was always a little difficult. Speaking of his father, Sol put it simply: "He couldn't not be in charge."

Even from Florida, the store was only a phone call away. Murray remembered a brutal winter day in December 1947, soon after he returned from the war. His father was on vacation and, as Murray phrased it, "the famous store was me." He and Dorothy lived on Twenty-Third Street between Avenues M and N at that time. Snow started to fall the day after Christmas and didn't stop until almost twenty-seven inches had piled up. Over his wife's objections, Murray pulled on his boots and set out for Nathan's Famous.

"You can't!" Dorothy wailed, about to be left behind with the couple's first child, Steve. "The snow is so thick on the roof, it's going to collapse. You can't leave me alone here!"

But neither snow nor rain nor heat nor gloom of night could stay Murray from his appointed job. "I walked four miles to get to the store from my house, down Ocean Parkway to Coney Island. Not a car was in the street. No cabs."

When he finally made it to Nathan's Famous, he found many of the employees marooned there, sleeping overnight because the subways were halted. That morning, the phone rang. Murray answered. It was Nathan, calling from Florida.

"What are you doing in the store?"

"I'm here," Murray said. "We're open."

"How did you get there?"

"I walked."

"You're crazy. There's fourteen inches of snow!"

"Twenty-seven," Murray corrected him.

A pause. "Did you do any business?" Nathan asked.

"Believe it or not, we sold 150 frankfurters already."

Murray felt responsible. With Nathan gone, he had to be there. But the store's clientele had to be there, too. Even in the decade's worst snowstorm, they heard the siren call of Nathan's franks. Murray went on to serve six thousand hot dogs that blizzard-bound day.

"People drove up and, so help me God, they didn't get out of the car," he remembered. "They drove on the sidewalk, parallel to the counter, opened up the window to the car and called out to us. 'Four frankfurters!' We handed the frankfurters directly over to them."

Murray was an able steward of his father's legacy and looked constantly to innovate. But the disagreements that arose between Nathan and Murray became a source of friction around the store during the postwar years.

A prime case in point came when Murray proposed adding seafood to the store's menu. His father instantly came out against the idea. He thought the move might turn the store's traditional customers away.

"You want to do seafood?" Nathan said. "People think our frankfurters are kosher. You're going to sell shrimp? They're gonna say, 'Wait a second.' You'll kill the business!"

"I never tell people it's kosher," Murray responded. "It's kosher-style."

"People will stop buying the hot dogs," Nathan said, thinking of his clientele of observant Jews. "They're not supposed to buy where there's nonkosher food."

"Don't worry about it, Pop. It's a new world. The people coming back from Europe, the soldiers, the thousands of soldiers, what did they eat in Italy? What did they eat in Germany and France? They weren't worried about kosher."

Round and round went the argument, Murray pushing, Nathan resisting. Finally, Nathan retreated from the field, taking a long winter vacation. "If you want to do it, then I'm going to go to Florida. Do it on your own. I want nothing to do with it."

With his father gone, Murray was free to do what he wanted. He installed his seafood counter, offering shrimp, fresh abalone, soft-shell crabs, lobster rolls, and a chowder made with fresh-shucked clams.

In terms of Jewish dietary strictures, many of the seafood

offerings were *trayf.* Murray took a calculated risk that customers would embrace the new menu items. After all, didn't pioneer
frankfurter man Charles Feltman start out selling clams?

In addition to the seafood counter, Murray also decided that
Nathan's Famous would be dragged into the contemporary age of
proper food service hygiene. Back at the dawn of time, Nathan had
installed original shelving made out of wood, a no-no in terms of
modern public health concerns, since wood could be a breeding
ground for germs.

"I came in early in the morning one day, and I went to the
counters in the kitchen," Murray recalled. "I saw a couple of
cockroaches, which just sickened me."

He confronted Sinta, the absolute ruler of the store's kitchen.
"How the hell can you work in here every day? How do you do
that?"

Sinta told him that the kitchen staff had to replace the cardboard lining on the shelves every week, it got so battered in the
ordinary course of doing business. Murray ripped the freshly laid
cardboard off and dumped it into a waste can.

"Strip the whole counter down," he ordered the cook.

"How are we going to work here?" Sinta asked.

"You're working in the other kitchen," Murray said, referring
to a secondary space at the back of the store. "You're doing a section at a time. I want everything stripped and thrown out."

Murray knew that wood was unacceptable for kitchen shelving and that the modern standard was sanitary stainless steel. "I
called my stainless-steel man, who became very wealthy because
of me. I told him to make measurements and that I wanted stainless-
steel shelves in the entire kitchen and in the entire refrigeration
section."

"Murray, I've got other customers," the man complained.

"No, no, I'm your only customer right now. You have to help me, because I have to change this whole kitchen. I don't want to see wood, and I don't want to see cardboard in the kitchen at all."

Out with the old wood, in with the new stainless. Murray had the ancient floor planking ripped out, too, and laid new concrete in the kitchens as well as along the counter spaces up front. The clock was ticking, since Nathan would soon be returning from his Florida retreat. When he did show up back at the store, he was confronted by the new world order.

Nathan said not a word. To receive a compliment from Pop was like pulling teeth, "well done" being an almost unheard of phrase around the store. Nathan believed that praise only rendered workers complacent. More than that, a good word might make them greedy.

"We had a little guy who was working on the counter," Jay Cohen recalled. "The guy was running around all over the place, really energetic. With a slip of the mouth, Nathan said 'good work' to the kid. The kid said, 'Hey, boss, how about a raise?' Nathan ran. He never once said good morning to that guy after that incident."

As Sol articulated it, referring to his father, "He was less inclined to compliment somebody on doing something well than to criticize someone for doing something wrong. He was not prone to complimenting people too much, especially his sons."

Giving a rueful laugh, Sol went on. "He took it for granted that they were going to do something good and that they should do something good. It was expected of them. But that seemed to be his old-school approach to personnel management."

It was all the more of a miracle, then, that Nathan extended an olive branch to his son when the seafood counter took off in a spectacular way, reeling in profits for the store.

"You had a good idea, Murray," Nathan said, finally giving credit where it was due, the terse compliment coming as if he were being charged by the word.

Nathan remained wary and slightly cynical about his son's penchant for innovation. There would be many more ideas emanating from Murray's young, ambitious, and very active brain. Some of them would be great, terrifically successful along the lines of the seafood menu or eminently necessary like modernizing the kitchen facilities.

Others would lead the business into difficulties.

When he returned from his military service, Sol went in a direction very different from his older brother.

"I was not particularly anxious to work [at Nathan's Famous] when I got out of the army. I went to NYU and then worked in a machine shop. I wanted to be on my own. I wanted to be independent. I felt [working at the store] was going to be a difficult thing, with my father and his personality and my brother and his personality. I was the odd man out."

If Murray came back from Europe with visions of French culture dancing in his head, Sol had proletarian dreams. He became a union shop steward at his new working-class factory job. He continued to be active in left-leaning causes, which in those days meant labor issues and peace initiatives.

The Cold War was ramping up, and the Iron Curtain was slamming down. The American right wing was busy whipping up anti-communist fervor. Almost overnight, the country found itself

In the Orwellian position of seeing its former Russian allies sud denly transformed and demonized as the enemy.

As the postwar era bled into the Eisenhower fifties, witch hunts of political radicals began in earnest. It was a bad time to be a card-carrying member of the Communist Party USA, which Sol had decided to become. This put him further at odds not only with Murray, whose politics increasingly veered toward moderation, but also with Nathan, the very prototype of a capitalist.

Nathan never forgot his poor upbringing and always arrayed himself on the side of the underdog. So he could be said to be at least partially responsible for Sol's leftward leanings. But Nathan was also leery of getting too directly involved in politics and chuckled at Sol's socialist passions.

In reaction to the proceedings of the House Un-American Activities Committee and the fiery demagoguery of Wisconsin senator Joseph McCarthy, Sol felt that he was vulnerable, and he briefly fled to California. He was probably too small a fish for the red-baiters to fry, but the mood of the country was dark and un-settled. Better safe than sorry. He soon returned to Brooklyn.

On a train ride from New York to Chicago for a Decoration Day peace rally in 1952, Sol found a seat next to a literal fellow traveler, a Brooklyn college student named Minnie Geller, who was headed to the same event. She and Sol had friends in common. Their romance kicked off on the trip, somewhere along the rail line in the vicinity of Cleveland.

"I remember being very impressed by his lips," Minnie recalled. "They were very luscious."

When the two returned home to New York, they began dating. Minnie knew the young Sol only as a union organizer and a machine shop lathe tool operator. He didn't tell her about his

Nathan's Famous connection until they had been seeing each other for months.

"I came from a working-class family," Minnie said. "I knew poverty. Maybe he was skeptical about anyone who might be interested in him for his background. But when he finally told me, I didn't recognize his dad's name. It really meant nothing to me."

Sol and Minnie made friends among his fellow workers at the machine shop. "We had a nice black couple that we used to go out with, to picnics with the guys from the shop. It was really, really nice." She laughed with the reminiscence. "Sol had a lot of commie friends."

Her parents, Chaim and Dora Geller, were simpatico with Sol's political views. "My parents were very pleased with the fact that he was a progressive person, fighting for good and just causes, which my parents liked very much. Sol's parents weren't progressive. But as long as Sol was, I guess that was good enough for my mom and dad. They liked that." Dorothy Frankel's parents were also committed leftists.

Sol finally introduced Minnie to Nathan and Ida at a dinner where he also proposed marriage, pulling her into the bathroom for privacy and presenting his sweetheart with what Minnie characterized as a "beautiful" wedding ring. "I guess he was shy or very bashful or whatever," Minnie recalled. "He didn't want anyone to be there except the two of us."

As befits a pair of freethinking iconoclasts, Minnie and Sol lived together before marriage, a relative rarity in those days. They also did not abide by gender-restrictive wedding traditions. They went together to pick out the bride's dress. They also arrived together at Casa del Rey, the banquet hall on Coney Island Avenue where the ceremony was to take place. It was Nathan and Ida who brought the tradition to the event, fattening up the guest list and underwriting the elaborate reception—not exactly a working-class affair.

Always, the store beckoned. When Minnie and Sol were about to have their first child, Nathan decided the proletariat experiment of the machine shop would have to end. He dispatched Murray as an emissary to lure Sol back to Nathan's Famous.

"Murray came to our apartment," Minnie recalled. "I believe I was pregnant with Nora at the time. He came with the request from Nathan that Sol return to work at the business. He was going to have a family, Murray said, and this was what he needed to do."

Murray added a sweetener to the deal. It is unclear if the suggestion came from Nathan and was only relayed by Sol's big brother. If Sol returned to work at the store, Murray said, he would have extra disposable income—funds that he could then donate to progressive causes, as both Murray and Nathan knew Sol would want to do. It would not be the first time that the wages of capitalism would be applied to further the goals of socialism.

Sol yielded. Working at his father's business would definitely be a lot more lucrative than slaving away at the machine shop or organizing labor meetings. He was going to have children to think of now.

In the midst of this, Murray performed a sort of rearguard action to protect his position at the store.

"He wanted a written commitment from our father," Sol said. "When my father was gone or couldn't run the business anymore, Murray wanted it in writing that he would run it, that he would be in charge, no questions asked. No threat from me. He wouldn't have to answer to me for anything. My father wasn't willing to do that—which was interesting, I thought, but he wasn't."

Murray believed because he brought Sol back into the business, that his brother owed it to him to follow his lead. "That was a source of conflict," said Marsha Abramson, who worked with both Murray and Sol on the business's PR.

Even without written assurances, by the time Sol came back to work at the store, Murray had a firm grip on the reins of power. He had been his father's second-in-command for five years and had settled into a management position. His innovation of bringing in a seafood menu was paying big dividends. On the other hand, Sol's years of independence had cemented his position as an outsider. He was having to play catch-up, and his big brother refused to help.

"He wasn't interested in helping me learn," Sol recalled. "Whenever I asked him about anything, he told me, 'Go out and learn the way I did, on your own.'"

The dismissal burned in Sol's mind. He would quote Murray's words again and again, to his wife and, later in life, to anyone who would listen. *Go out and learn the way I did, on your own.*

"I found that hard to understand," Sol said. "If I was in his position, I would have been happy to have somebody learn as much as they could and help relieve me of some of the pressures of running the business."

Marsha Abramson had a measured opinion about the different philosophies of the two men. Sol, she said, "was a very thoughtful, very analytic person. Before he would make a decision he wanted to know all the facts, the positives and the negatives. He would weigh them very carefully and he didn't rush into decisions."

Murray, on the other hand, "would move much faster. He was impatient, shall we say impulsive. If he wanted something done it had to be done immediately. There was a clash of personalities. Sol said, 'I want to know more about it before I make a decision.' Murray said, 'I am the older brother and if I say this, this is right.'"

Three years after his brother's successful expansion into

seafood, Sol proposed installing a delicatessen counter in the store. This also involved an expansion from the core menu items of franks and hamburgers. The deli offered sliced meat sandwiches of every kind, and it, too, proved very successful.

The location of the two counters, seafood and delicatessen, symbolized the growing estrangement of the brothers. Sol's deli opened onto Schweikerts Walk, facing west. Seafood was in the opposite corner of the store. The two new counters were located as far as they could be from each other, while still remaining within the confines of the same building.

"I was very unhappy," Sol recalled of this period. "It was difficult when I came home at night. I was upset by things that had occurred during the day, the things that Murray had said. I was affronted by many things, because he didn't understand that I wasn't a competitor. He saw me as a competitor. It was impossible."

Much of this was left unspoken at the time. Sol found it difficult to speak to his brother about the situation. When asked, Murray always declined to comment on family frictions.

"I never talked about our differences with Murray," Sol said. "There was never any discussion about it, never. He never brought it up. He never wanted to talk about it, so why was I interested in talking about it? I would only aggravate myself. So what's the point?"

Something had to give, and soon enough, it did. But it was Murray, not Sol, who would be the first one to leave Nathan's Famous. And he kicked himself out of the nest all on his own.

16

Glory Years

"Who marches into the dining room? There's Jackie Kennedy—Wow!" Nathan and Ida serve Governor Nelson Rockefeller *(center right)*.

IF THE LATE 1930s represented one heyday of Nathan's Famous, and the upheaval of wartime was something of a special case, then the 1950s marked a return of the store to peak form. The country yearned to get back to the good times of the prewar period. For a lot of people, a Nathan's Famous frankfurter held a nostalgic promise. Once again, customers lined up so deep outside the store that, as one counterman stated, "You could never see the sidewalk."

Few of those customers knew that Coney Island's demise was already being plotted by the city's power broker, Robert Moses. They didn't know anything about the mounting frictions between Murray and Sol. They spilled from the subway at the Stillman terminal, hit Nathan's Famous, went on the rides, enjoyed the beach, and then, on the rebound, hit Nathan's Famous once again. On the sunny, sand-in-your-shoes surface, all was serene and untroubled. After the horrors and upheavals of war, happy days were here again.

Feltman's closed in 1954. Nathan's Famous stood alone, having risen to the level of an American icon. It seemed that every Broadway and Hollywood star, every mayor, every gangster, VIP, socialite, and celebrity made the pilgrimage to the busy hot dog stand on Surf Avenue. Most of them ate like everyone else did, standing up.

The long list of celebrity customers told the story. Jimmy Durante, Cary Grant, Harry Belafonte, Danny Kaye, Sid Caesar, Buddy Hackett, Liza Minnelli, Robert Kennedy, Lucille Ball, Marilyn Monroe, Art Carney, Jerry Lewis, and many others all dined at Nathan's Famous at one point or another.

Occasionally, the big names resorted to the store's tiny dining room. Richard Traunstein, who served as a waiter there for many years, recalled a memorable visit. "Who marches into the dining room? There's Jackie Kennedy—wow!—in the schmutzy dining room of Nathan's, in the back, totally slumming it."

During this period, New York governor Nelson Rockefeller visited the store with a retinue of aides and photographers. He hobnobbed with Nathan and Ida and made sure the man in the street saw him, the oil company billionaire, as a man in the street just like them.

Rocky made a pronouncement that day: "No politician in New York can ever hope to be elected without being photographed eating a hot dog."

When the line got quoted later, Nathan's PR team of Max Rosey and Morty Matz made sure it contained an additional vital two words. "No politician in New York can ever hope to be elected without being photographed eating a *Nathan's Famous* hot dog." That's how Rocky's rule of thumb went down in history.

The shock troops who served as the store's countermen went a long way toward making the Nathan's Famous experience what it was. Joe Handwerker continued to run a very tight ship. During the high summer season, Nathan and Ida were there, just as in the pre-war days.

The boss demonstrated common-sense intelligence in his choice of employees. Many of them came to the store via unorthodox paths. Gerry Monetti was a case in point. Years before, in the thirties, Nathan had engaged in a price war with a nearby drink-and-hot-dog stand. Located a block away on Fifteenth Street and the Bowery, next to Steeplechase Park, the place went by the delightful off-rhyme name of Patsy's Tasties. Monetti was a manager there.

Kicking off the price war, Monetti matched Nathan's Famous by offering a five-cent frank. Nathan undercut him by offering a frankfurter and a drink for seven cents. Monetti responded with a six-cent frank-and-drink special.

"We kids were always waiting for bargains," reminisced onetime Coney Island street urchin Pat Auletta. "After all, it was our nickels and dimes, and we had to stretch them as far as we could. We knew this was taking place, and we knew that eventually we'd get a better bargain."

Finally, Nathan temporarily lowered his price to a nickel for a drink *and* a hot dog. Monetti was forced to throw in the towel.

Patsy's Tasties eventually went out of business, and Gerry Monetti came to work for Nathan.

He proved to be standout employee, a fixture on the fried-potato station. A heavyset guy with a large, Buddha-like belly, Monetti figures in the recollections of many people for his stripped-down working attire, no matter how cold it was and how bitter were the winds that blew in off the Coney Island Channel. The counters at the store featured open windows in every season.

"There was no heat in the kitchen," recalled the store's personnel director, Charles Schneck. "In the winter, managers used to come into the walk-in refrigerator to warm up."

None of that mattered to Monetti.

"He was very jovial and very loud, always yelling things out for the crowd to hear," Sol recalled about one his favorite employees. "He was the kind of guy that always used to fascinate me because in the wintertime, in the coldest days of the winter, he'd walk around with a T-shirt. He was not cold. His body held so much heat that he could stand it."

Sammy Fariello came to the store by a roundabout route similar to Monetti's. He didn't apply for a job with Nathan's Famous because he already had one. Before widespread refrigeration rendered the practice obsolete, he delivered bulk ice to the store for the big drink containers, hefting the blocks with heavy-duty tongs. Nathan must have liked something about the back of Fariello's neck, since he offered to take the deliveryman on. The iceman cometh.

Fariello proved to have the fastest hands of any counterman in the history of the business. He earned the top post in the store, the corner frankfurter griddle, where he could serve hungry hordes crowding in to the counter from both Schweikerts and Surf. He wielded a different kind of tongs now and could handle multiple franks at once, laying them into their buns in rapid-fire succession.

Customers could order four frankfurters, say, reach into their pockets or purses for the change, and by the time they produced the money, Fariello would already be there, extending the four franks in one hand and taking coins with the other. It was an amazing performance, more prestidigitation than food service.

"We had people who used to come by the store just to watch him," Sol recollected. "They'd stand there to see how quickly he served a hot dog."

One of the TV variety shows of the day filmed Sammy for the delight of its viewers. The producers clocked Fariello. It turned out he could dish up sixty frankfurters nestled into toasted rolls in sixty seconds—accepting payments and making change all the while. He maintained a steady pace for whole shifts, selling a hundred hot dogs every five minutes. At times, it was the customers who couldn't keep up with Sammy, instead of the other way around. Fariello's longtime fans knew enough to have money in hand by the time they made it through the crowd to his counter.

There were no regular lines during a classic Nathan's Famous crush. Customers simply pushed forward in a disorderly mob. Front countermen, such as Fariello and Monetti, became adept at dealing fairly with the crowds, never letting any one person believe he or she had been ignored.

The informal store practice was called "the sweep," beginning with one end of the station, taking care of one customer, moving to the left to take care of the next, continuing on to the other end of the station, at which point the counterman would reverse direction and take orders to the right. Back and forth it went, a nonstop barrage of food, delivered in a steady, machine-gun-style spread.

The tiny Nathan's Famous dining room off Schweikerts Walk represented a hidden world unto itself, a downscale diamond in the rough, just a place where a family might sit and eat. Most people didn't know it existed. There were about ten tables with metal, ice cream parlor–style chairs. Waiter Richard Traunstein laughed when he described it. "This was low-class dining, don't get me wrong. It was just as common as common could be."

The waiters there—among them Sol Gaber, Sol Siederman, Felix Vasquez, and Traunstein—stayed in the position for years, even decades. Originally required by city regulations when the store began to sell beer, the dining room endured long after it had served its original purpose. Nathan could have closed it, but he cared too much about the loyal employees working there.

Out front, the counters were more of a free-fire zone. The undeclared war between countermen and customers still occasionally flared up, just like the old days. The frenetic pace of service fostered a kind of impatient arrogance. Any misbehaving or wisecracking nimrod could cause the machine to slip a gear and was thus dealt with ruthlessly. Fights remained a not uncommon phenomenon. Rarely did they require police intervention, but at times they did.

"We had one drastic fight, where somebody was seriously injured," recalled Sidney Handwerker. "It was about three o'clock in the morning, and we were cleaning up. I was working on the steam table, scrubbing the pans for the next day and stacking them on top of the counter. Four or five guys—I don't know if they were drunks, but tough guys—started to pull the pans down and throw them into the gutter."

The toughs hadn't gotten the attention they thought they deserved. The sweep had somehow left them unswept.

Joe Handwerker came to Sidney's rescue. "I'll meet you outside," he suggested to the unruly customers. He tore into the street with two kitchen men backing him up. Everyone started swinging.

"Sidney," said Sammy Fariello pointedly, "your brother is in a fight."

Sidney took it as his cue to go over the counter. But his foot got stuck in a beverage tub on the way, and he wound up with a shoe full of grape drink. Meanwhile, Gerry Monetti dashed into the kitchen, retrieved a club-like tool used to push beef into the hamburger grinder, and dove into the fray.

The next morning, police officers showed up at Sidney's house. "You're under arrest."

They brought in the whole graveyard shift from the night before. The cops had checked the time cards at the store and took down the names of everybody who was working. One of the tough-guy customers had been clubbed senseless by Monetti's beef-stuffing tool.

"It was a good thing that the police were on our side" was Sidney's morning-after comment. The whole affair was smoothed over.

Except for his mystical check-the-back-of-the-neck routine, Nathan was an equal opportunity employer, long before the phrase was ever invented. All horses welcome, no prejudice in play. Sinta integrated the kitchen with fellow Chinese Americans. Tom Settle was an early African American hire. Both became trusted veterans at the store.

As early as the summer of 1947, a year before President Harry S. Truman desegregated the U.S. armed forces with his landmark Executive Order 9981, Nathan put a black man out front, interacting with the public. Derwood Jarrett became the Jackie Robinson of Nathan's Famous, the first African American to integrate the working side of this particular lunch counter.

The move caused a few problems with small-minded customers objecting to being served by an African American. Nathan
didn't care. He simply liked Jarrett and respected his work ethic.
It wasn't a political issue for him—the way it might have been
with Sol, say—just a question of simple practicality. But the final
effect was the same.

"There was no discrimination there," recalled Felix Vasquez,
a longtime store employee. "There was no discrimination whether
it was Jewish or black or Puerto Rican. You got people from all
over the world."

"We had a real United Nations around Nathan's," Jay Cohen
said. "All kinds, all types. If you could work, you had a place."

The old-time employees—Monetti, Jack Dreitzer, and Joe
Handwerker—and the favored newer hires—like Sinta and
Fariello—had a complex relationship with Murray and Sol. A
gulf separated them. Nathan's boys were the young princes, the
heirs apparent, the only ones who had a hope for equity in the
business. The best the others could receive were steady paychecks
and end-of-the-year bonuses.

Oddly enough, for all of Nathan's pronounced desire to have
his sons with him, at times he seemed to ally himself with his
hard-core workers. They were the ones who were cut out of the
same cloth as he was. They were the ones who put in the long hours
out front or in the kitchen.

Even at this late date, in the fifties, when he could have easily
eased off and assumed a purely managerial role, Nathan would
take on menial duties that usually fell to the lower-paid staff. He
always wanted to be, and wanted to be seen to be, an ordinary

worker, just one of the guys. The only employees Nathan unleashed his full tirades upon were Joe, Murray, and Sol. It was never a picnic being a Handwerker son at the store.

Manager Jay Cohen recalled an incident when Murray's style clashed with that of his father's. Nathan made it a habit to hang around in the kitchen early in the morning with a cup of coffee, shooting the breeze around with the inner circle of longtime employees. During this supposed downtime, he would be looking around, seeing what was in the refrigerators, checking the work assignments.

One morning, Murray and his African American driver swept by this group of old-timers. "He had a chauffeur that he used more like a personal servant," said Charles Schneck. "He liked the trappings of success."

The driver carried Murray's briefcase and wore a black coat and black hat. Murray hustled along behind him, heading for the store's second-floor office.

"Hiya, everybody!" the heir said before running upstairs.

After this display, one of the old-timers put a question to the boss. "Hey, Nathan, how come you don't have a chauffeur?"

Nathan's reply was instant. "Didn't have a rich father," he said in his usual clipped, deadpan way.

The group broke up laughing.

A division developed, largely unspoken but very real. Jack Dreitzer, Sinta, Joe Handwerker, and a core of other workers had been employed at the store for years, some of them for decades. They understood Nathan's ways. The business had been built on their backs, courtesy of their incredible work ethic.

Murray and to a lesser degree Sol represented a challenge to this group. Oftentimes they weren't present on the weekends, the busiest time. The sons came in with fresh ideas, different procedures, rewritten menus. The world war might have been over, but at Nathan's Famous, there arose a new conflict, a battle between the old and new.

Beyond modernizing the physical plant, Murray tried to bring the store's labor practices into the contemporary era, too. During the demanding summer season, none of the Nathan's Famous managers had the luxury of a day off. They worked twelve-hour days, seven-day weeks for the busy three months from Memorial Day to Labor Day. No extra pay for overtime, no weekends off.

"Dad, it's not right," Murray said to Nathan. "You can't have people working seven days. A man should have a day off, to be with his family and to take a break, go to the beach, go to the park, do what he wants."

"You think you can cover for them?" Nathan wanted to know.

"Yeah, the other people have to do their work for them on their days off."

Nathan shrugged. "You want to do that? Go ahead and do that."

Murray kicked off the new policy with one of the hardest-working employees in the store, Gerry Monetti, the star counterman on the fried potato station. "He didn't mind working seven days," Murray said. "He absolutely did not."

But like it or not, Monetti would simply be ordered to comply with the new regime. Murray called the man into his office. "Look, from now on, I'll give you a new work schedule. We'll give you a day off work."

"I don't want to take a day off," Monetti replied. He clearly considered the outlandish idea of taking a break during the season as some sort of punitive measure.

"It's unfair to your family," Murray said. "It's not fair to you, physically. You got to take a day off. I insist, and I'm the boss."

Monetti reluctantly agreed. His absence would be a real hardship for the business, since in addition to the fry station, he was the
all-around handyman for the store, a genius at repairing broken-
down machines. He lived in Bay Ridge, and he took a sort of
busman's holiday by bringing his whole family to the beach at
Coney Island. The next day, he didn't come in to work.

Monetti's wife called Murray. "Gerry's not coming in, because
he can't move, he's so sunburned. He went on the beach and got
burned. Seriously sunburned."

The store's Mr. Crinkle-Cut, its Mr. Fix-it, was out for a full
week.

"Where's Gerry?" Nathan wanted to know.

"He's not well," Murray replied. "He won't be in today."

"Why isn't he going to be here?"

Murray didn't want to be the bearer of the news, but he had to
do it. He told his father that his favorite employee had been burned
to a crisp.

Nathan shook his head, disgusted. "He took a day off, and he
went to the beach. Now you see what happens. Now you haven't
got him for the week. You haven't got him for ten days."

"His wife isn't happy, either," Murray added, baleful. He didn't
back down on his new day-off-for-managers policy. But from that
point on, he was careful to warn everyone about the perils of leisure.

Dorothy always said her husband missed his true calling, that
Murray fancied himself a public relations man. The heat of the sun
also disrupted another of Murray's innovations. In 1954, a group
of entrepreneurs purchased an enormous dead whale from a fish-
erman. Murray rented them a space behind the store to display
the carcass. The owners charged admission for a glimpse of the
beast. Murray believed the attraction would draw customers to
Nathan's Famous.

It didn't work out that way. In the heat of the summer, the carcass quickly began to rot. "It stunk up all of Coney Island," remembered Sidney Handwerker. The entrepreneurs quickly vanished, leaving Murray with a ton of dead whale on his hands. He had to pay to have it removed, with rumor having it that two Mafia soldiers were hired to do the job. The wise guys dragged the carcass out to sea and blew it up.

Murray also once suggested putting a glass tank of mustard on the roof, alongside the huge reservoir of corn oil. He thought the bright-yellow cylinder would attract the attention of passersby on Surf Avenue. Nathan shut him down with a question: "What if it breaks?"

Despite his setbacks, Murray doggedly continued his efforts to modernize. As a kid and as a teenager, he had spent long hours in the store's tiny counting room, putting coins into sleeves.

The miserable cubbyhole beneath the steps to the second floor was small, five feet by eight, and chronically underventilated. A single fan stirred the stale air. In four-hour, five-hour, or sometimes six-hour work sessions, Murray locked himself into the room and labored at the count, rolling quarters, dimes, nickels, even pennies.

Even to describe the process sounded wearisome. "You couldn't take the coins loose to the bank," Murray said. "Everything had to be packed. You spread out the coins—twenty, forty, sixty, eighty, using two fingers to separate out ten dollars of quarters or nickels, then put them in a paper tube, all by hand, no machines, not even a device to hold the tube. I had to seal one end, put them in, then fold it closed."

For some reason, the bulk of the work fell to Murray. His father might have considered it as a gesture of trust, but mistrust of other employees could have figured in, too. Also, perhaps unconsciously,

Nathan was hazing the young heir, putting him through the kind of labor that Nathan himself had endured for years.

Murray would also make the bank runs, making cash deposits. After a summer weekend, the amounts would rise to tens of thousands of dollars. "We didn't go to the bank every day at the same time. We'd vary it, two o'clock, three o'clock. So we never had a robbery."

Murray made it practice not to use obvious money bags or leather pouches. Instead, he would put the money in an innocent-looking brown paper bag or conceal it in a briefcase. Often he would take along the six-foot-two Tom Settle.

"With him, even a guy with a gun would never try anything. [Settle] always used to carry [the cash]. I didn't cargo. I had the car and pulled up to the alley beside the store and say, 'Tom, I'm ready to go.' We alerted the bank we were coming. We never had any problems, never."

Murray was becoming more and more active in the National Restaurant Association, a lobbying, educational, and advocacy group founded in 1919 and headquartered in Washington, D.C. One year soon after the war, he journeyed to an annual convention that the trade group held in Chicago. There, he glimpsed a vision of the future. The gleaming automatic coin-counting machines on display at the convention seemed an answer to his prayers, promising to help relieve him of his least favorite duty at the store.

Nathan initially balked at the idea. He hadn't even seen the machines, and he was already ruling them out. "Too expensive," he told his son. "The old way is good. You don't buy one, Murray."

"I'm not buying one, I'm just trying it out," Murray responded. "Promise me a two-week trial, and if it works, then I'll buy two machines." He had already proposed the test-period arrangement with the purveyor, agreeing to purchase only after they had proven effective.

"It'll never work," Nathan said, stubborn.

"Why?"

"You'll jam up the machines."

Murray had to admit his father made a valid point. The money that came in off the Nathan's Famous counter was filthy, contaminated by beach sand, fried-potato oil, frankfurter grease, and salt, if not mystery schmutz of unknown origin. Murray had to have the coins washed before they came into his cubbyhole office to be tallied.

Over Nathan's objections, Murray installed two machines in the counting room. The first machine separated the coins; the second packed them in the paper sleeves that he could take to the bank. Nathan was right. Sand, salt, and grease played hell with the fancy new devices. But thoroughly washing the coins first proved effective.

"We solved the problem, because cleaning the money was still much easier than doing it the old way," Murray said. The machines stayed, and Nathan's Famous took another small step into the brave new world of automation.

The machines represented something greater than a mechanical shortcut. They indicated Murray's enthusiastic participation in the National Restaurant Association, a group that promoted scientific applications to food service issues. As a general manager at the store, he was all about finding new solutions to old problems. He was a man of his time.

The fifties were a period of almost boundless faith in progress, science, and new technology. In furniture stores along Broadway in Manhattan, wooden boxes with glass windows displayed flickering images, the first hint of the television revolution to come. Cars became bigger, better, glossier. Nuclear war represented the dark side of progress, but even that looming shadow would be dissipated by such "scientific" measures as installation of fallout shelters and duck-and-cover training in schools.

Gripped by the same sense that a modern approach could resolve all issues, Murray sought help to update management practices at the store. But staffing wasn't a problem you could address with a machine.

You needed a consultant.

In 1954, Murray found one in the person of Dr. Victor Eimicke, president of V. W. Eimicke Associates. The two met through the supplier of paper goods at the store, Ted Pinska, who had employed Dr. Eimicke in his own business. The consultant's academic background was in psychology. He billed himself as an "industrial psychologist," or "business psychologist."

He and Murray hit it off right away. Their families became close, to the degree that the toddler daughter of Victor Eimicke and his wife, Maxine, took her first steps in Murray and Dorothy's home. The couples socialized together, with the two men spending hours discussing updates to the antiquated business practices of Nathan's Famous.

Dr. Eimicke had developed a management approach he called "the table of organization." He had used it before in consulting jobs with the insurance giant Blue Cross and a chain of grocery stores in Europe. Murray became determined that, under the good doctor's guidance, he would lift up the store by the scruff of its neck and shake some modern scientific sense into it.

Together, they worked up an alternative to Nathan's "I-look-at-the-back-of-the-neck" hiring philosophy, developing a rigorous program to test and train new managers. The recruitment process took a full year. Every step of the way was laid out in exhaustive detail. Potential candidates would submit to psychological evaluations and aptitude tests. Murray and Dr. Eimicke would also regularize the store's somewhat chaotic management structure, streamline the way the staff served customers, and change how work assignments were handled.

"Murray was just starting to get a handle on the new technique of the table of organization," recalled Maxine Eimicke. "Victor, my husband, helped enormously. At that time, Nathan's just had a bunch of fellows around the counter, everybody helping anyone that walked up. Nobody was in charge."

Flowcharts, organization, management training, and the scientific method would help smooth out the situation.

Nathan openly ridiculed the new methods. "Murray and his Dr. Eye-mick-keee," he'd say. Part of this reaction was the cynicism of a man who had put in over three decades developing management practices of his own—crude, unschooled, and instinctual, but ones that had served him in good stead as he built one of the most successful businesses of his time.

"Victor Eimicke was going to come in and train the managers. He'd organize things so that the managers followed the principles that he believed in," said Sol. "He ridiculed my father's method for a lot of it. Basically, I agreed with [Nathan]. I didn't have much use for Eimicke. I don't think he helped very much."

Nathan's impatience boiled over during the lunchtime rush one day. Murray and Dr. Eimicke were closeted in the store's upstairs office, working out their plans. As usual, Nathan was out front, perched atop his box next to the root beer barrel, surveying his domain. When he didn't see Murray on the job, he exploded. The thought that anyone could sit in an office and believe they could manage the activity in the front counters and the kitchens downstairs struck him as ludicrous.

He charged upstairs and confronted his son. "Why are you in this place doing almost nothing, when there's so much to be done downstairs?"

Ensconced behind a desk cluttered with their work, Murray and Dr. Eimicke stared at him, astonished by the sudden interruption. With a sweep of his hand, Nathan crashed the desktop full of papers and charts to the floor. He ordered his son to take his place at the front counters.

Dr. Eimicke, unused to such direct, almost violent reaction to his work, immediately grabbed his briefcase and beat a hasty retreat. "Vic was not a violent man," his wife said. "His policy was always to stay calm and talk things out."

When Eimicke arrived back at their Bronxville home that day, Maxine took one look at his face and asked him what had happened. "Well, I almost got fired," said the shell-shocked doctor. "Maybe I did and don't know it."

With the wisdom of hindsight, the consultant came to a belated understanding of Nathan's anger. "Looking back, it makes sense," he told his wife. "We should have broken off at the time, about eleven thirty or a quarter to twelve, going through the lunch hour, letting Murray be downstairs on the floor. Things downstairs weren't going right in [Nathan's] opinion, because there was a lunch-hour rush, and there were not enough servers to take care of the line. Nathan was upset about it. You know, that's money. That comes first."

"Those are the kind of things that even executives have to

learn," Maxine Eimicke commented. "You've got to learn by doing."

The storm passed. Dr. Eimicke wasn't fired, after all. Murray and he proceeded with their new table of organization methods. They took out blind ads in the New York newspapers that read, "Restaurant managers—$110 a week," without mentioning Nathan's Famous. In 1954, that was an attractive salary for restaurant work, equivalent to almost $1,000 in today's money.

Those who answered the ad received a letter in response, directing them to show up in the Grand Ballroom of the Hotel Astor in Times Square at a specific day. A thousand people assembled at the time appointed, all men. Dr. Eimicke went in front of the group and explained that a certain organization wanted to expand. He remained coy about which company it was, saying only it had $3 million in gross receipts—again, an impressive number at the time. Eimicke laid out the training program requirements and the battery of tests that candidates would face. Then he finally told the crowd that they would be interviewing for a job at Nathan's Famous on Coney Island.

"Those of you who are not interested in continuing may leave," Dr. Eimicke said.

A good portion of the crowd did. "All the chefs and cooks and gourmets got up and walked," recalled Hy Brown, who was there that day and was eventually hired through the new program. "To them, Nathan's was still a hot dog stand, and it was still Coney Island. It wasn't Broadway."

Dr. Eimicke allowed the uninterested to depart and the crowd to settle. "The rest of you will be given various aptitude tests over a period of time," he announced. "The group will be dwindling down to a select few. We will make our choices then."

The aptitude tests used various strategies to winnow out the pool of prospective managers. The questions were posed by psychologists seated on platforms, so that the experts would be elevated and could look down on the candidates.

When it came Jay Cohen's turn, the first questions were direct and challenging. "You have no restaurant experience at all. What do you know about a restaurant? What do you know about shrimp?"

"Listen, I'm a Jewish boy from New York," Cohen said. "I don't know anything about shrimp. I don't know anything about any shellfish because we never had it."

"Why do you think you could be a manager for us?"

"I have basic abilities in management," Cohen answered. "But not having any experience, I assume that you'll help train me to do what you want me to do. And if I learn what you want me to do, I'll do that. I won't know any other way, and I won't have any preconceived convictions."

The interviewers asked a final question. "Where would you like to be a year from now?"

"Sitting up there asking the questions that you're posing to people," Cohen responded.

The new initiative did result in some impressive hires, managers who would stay with Nathan's Famous for decades, including Cohen and Hy Brown. Other newcomers did not fit in. Charles Schneck, who signed on as the company's director of personnel in the 1960s, assessed the hiring program's successes and failures, including the complex battery of tests Dr. Eimicke instituted to gauge a prospect's suitability. Eventually he decided the process wasn't working.

"These tests don't do what they are supposed to do," Schneck told Murray. "I think we should change the tests or do away with them altogether."

"Let's give it a little more time," Murray said. But he finally saw the light, and stopped using Dr. Eimicke to test job applicants.

At the same time, the consultant had come to admire Nathan's native intelligence and canny business sense. Eimicke thought, for example, that Nathan's practice of reducing the size of his frankfurter rather than raising the price was a truly remarkable strategy.

"Victor thought that was genius, because no one could tell the difference," Maxine recalled. "The customer could not tell the difference in the size of the dog. It's in a bun! The size difference is very subtle. Vic thought that was fantastic."

Such a technique is called package downsizing or "shrinkflation." It's commonplace enough today, often employed in such varied products as coffee, candy bars, ice cream, even toilet paper and soap. Back then, it was novel. Dr. Eimicke gave credit where credit was due, describing Nathan as "the brightest guy with no education that I ever met."

The consultant served as a useful buffer between Nathan and his oldest son. Maxine Eimicke, who knew Murray well, said she believed he was "afraid" of his dad.

"Victor gave him more confidence," she said. "He was always there to back Murray up when he wanted to change things. Murray wouldn't stand up to his dad, which Victor would do, because Vic had nothing to lose."

No doubt there were things around the store that needed changing. But the whole Eimicke affair served to measure the gap between Murray's way of doing things and his father's. At best, Nathan only tolerated Dr. Eimicke's presence around the store.

He would come to grudgingly admit that some of the reforms served to optimize the flow of work. And he enjoyed teasing the consultant's twenty-nine-year-old wife.

"Your husband is so dumb," Nathan told Maxine, invoking the line repeatedly whenever he was in a playful mood. He was joking, to be sure, but it was a joke with a little sting in it.

Roadside Rest

"Times have changed. You've got to grow, and you've got to do different things." Oceanside, Nassau County, the first Nathan's Famous outlet outside Coney Island.

THE CITY OF New York Department of Parks commissioner Robert Moses would have been right at home as a bureaucrat in the Habsburg Empire. He exhibited the kind of heavy-handed, imperious attitudes that Nathan brushed up against as a youth in Galicia. Moses would have liked Dr. Eimicke, too. They shared a similar unshakable faith in the rightness of their approach, trusting themselves to guide the actions of the common folk. It was the kind of paternalistic, authoritarian viewpoint that ran through the postwar period like a virus.

Dr. Eimicke lacked what Moses had in spades: a poisonous, vengeful reaction to any and all opposition. It was his way or the highway—in fact, his way *was* the highway often enough, in that he developed the Belt, Grand Central, Cross Island, and Henry Hudson Parkways, among others. (The joke: if this Moses would have been the one who parted the Red Sea, it would have been with a stone-bridged parkway.) He leveled vicious attacks against his perceived enemies, slamming them both in the media and via bureaucratic channels.

Coney was the kind of sprawling, chaotic, untidy realm that an order-obsessed fanatic like Moses was born to hate. "His pathological dislike of the Coney Island amusement community was obvious," writes preeminent Coney Island commentator and historian Charles Denson, a longtime resident.

We don't have to take anyone else's word for it. In his 1937 master plan for the city's public beaches, *The Improvement of Coney Island, Rockaway and South Beaches,* Moses described the history of Coney as "sad," adding, "There is no use bemoaning the end of the old Coney Island fabled in song and story. The important thing is not to proceed in the mistaken belief that it can be revived." He came not to praise Coney but to bury it.

Square in the path of the Robert Moses juggernaut stood a little five-foot-three luncheonette man. Though Nathan had solid connections to the Democratic political elite of Brooklyn, he could not match Moses in clout. But he tried. To promote a hands-off "let Coney be Coney" philosophy, he used his own high standing in the community, plus Murray's inherited position as president of the Coney Island Chamber of Commerce.

Fire had long been Coney Island's accidental development strategy of choice. Flames leveled various parts of the resort town with stunning regularity: the fabled Elephant Hotel burned in

1896, followed by Steeplechase Park in 1907, Dreamland in 1911, and a widespread conflagration in 1932 that took out a huge section off Surf between Twenty-First and Twenty-Fifth Streets. Amid all these fiery assaults, Nathan's Famous managed to remain unscathed. Perhaps angels covered it up.

The Luna Park blaze in 1944 (actually two fires, separated by a few weeks) and another in 1946 managed to put the amusement park permanently out of its long-faded misery. The fires provided an opening for Moses. La Guardia named him chairman of the Mayor's Committee on Slum Clearance in 1949. Using Title I money from the federal Housing Act of 1949, he took control of the burned-out Luna Park site for residential development. Denson, in his book *Coney Island: Lost and Found,* judges that the Luna Park landgrab trimmed the resort town's amusement zone by a third.

Other Moses initiatives lopped off whole sections of beach by unilaterally straightening the boardwalk; they also moved the New York Aquarium from Castle Clinton in Manhattan to the old Dreamland site on West Eighth Street and chipped away at huge blocks of land using urban renewal, civil forfeiture, and eminent domain policies. The result was that Coney Island was squeezed from both the east and west, caught in a vise devised by Robert Moses.

"I didn't want to see Coney Island lose its entertainment features and amusement zone," Murray would later say in an interview with Denson, referring to the resort town's qualities that Moses had dismissed as being mere "summer exploitation."

"Moses was trying to get the zoning changed, to take over Coney Island like he did Jones Beach on Long Island," Murray said. "Moses wanted all the private industry out. He wanted to make everything south of Surf Avenue into a public beach. Moses wanted Coney Island for himself . . . That's why I fought him tooth and nail. He was against private industry, and he didn't want amusements. Little by little, he was trying to destroy Coney Island."

The Handwerkers, father and sons, were engaged in a losing battle. "Moses has shrunk the amusement center of Coney Island considerably," Nathan said publicly. "But never, and I mean never, will he shrink Nathan's frankfurters."

In hindsight, it is easy to trace how Moses's remaking of the area precipitated its decline. Rather than the safe and serene middle-class residential enclave that the parks commissioner envisioned, Coney Island tumbled into blight. His good intentions paved the way to a seaside hell. The process happened gradually. By the end, the transformations engineered by Robert Moses threatened to take Nathan's Famous down along with the rest of the neighborhood.

As Moses made war on the store and everything it stood for externally, internal forces were also ripping Nathan's Famous apart. In the battle between Sol and Murray over the future of the business, Nathan often found himself standing in the middle. If he had known the phrase, he would have been wailing the words of Rodney King: "Can't we all get along?"

"When Murray came home from the army," his wife, Dorothy, recalled, "Murray said to Nathan, 'You know I really feel that we can't just have one store. People are moving out to Long Island, out to the suburbs. All the vets are coming home. We should think of expanding.'"

Nathan refused to accept the whole concept. *I have one chair,* he would say, *what do I need with more? You can't sit your ass in*

*two chairs. Can I eat with two spoons? I have one car, why should I
have two or three?*

"Times have changed," Murray would respond. "You've got to
grow, and you've got to do different things."

"Nathan never wanted to expand at all," noted Jay Cohen.
"He only wanted to operate something that he could watch. Even
in the fifties, that man was in that store from seven, eight o'clock in
the morning until five or six o'clock in the evening. He saw every
delivery of food that came in. He checked it personally. He checked
every truck."

The argument over expansion continued for months, years.
Even in disagreeing with Murray, Nathan managed to express his
true motivation: love and concern for his sons. "Have one store," he
told them. "It's enough for all the families. You'll all earn a living."

The crux of the matter rested on more than just the simple
question of developing more stores. Sol and Murray differed fun-
damentally on how to expand. Murray had been exposed to a
whole range of worldly possibilities in France during the war, and
aspired to a more cultured existence than being the owner of "a hot
dog stand," as Dr. Eimicke referred to the store.

In the lunch rush pandemonium of Coney Island, Murray
would find himself envisioning a real, sit-down restaurant, less
frenetic than the store. Murray's dreams translated, in terms of
Nathan's Famous, to a quite specific approach to expansion:
larger restaurants, bigger menus, more formal dining.

In the opposite corner, wearing the white trunks . . . Sol, too,
thought Nathan's Famous should expand, in spite of his father's
resistance. But he wanted to take a path different from Murray's.
His vision was a chain of small stores with limited menus, each
modeled after the original at Coney Island, each based upon the

business model that had made Nathan's Famous so successful in the first place. Why futz with a winning formula? The highest-quality food, the fastest service, the most affordable prices. That was the way to go.

In other words, the McDonald's model. Although some might argue Ray Kroc stinted on that "highest-quality food" element, beginning in the midfifties, he would take the fundamental formula of Nathan's Famous and march on to global domination. He did it by repeating the same mantra that Nathan had lived by for decades.

"If I had a brick for every time I've repeated the phrase 'Quality, Service, Cleanliness, and Value,'" said Kroc, "I think I'd probably be able to bridge the Atlantic Ocean with them."

"In 1954, [Ray Kroc] visited a restaurant in San Bernardino, California," states the biography on the official McDonald's website. "There he found a small but successful restaurant run by brothers Dick and Mac McDonald, and was stunned by the effectiveness of their operation. They produced a limited menu, concentrating on just a few items—burgers, fries and beverages—which allowed them to focus on quality and quick service."

Small stores, small menu. This was, essentially, the same argument Sol advanced to his father and brother during precisely the same period, only at the opposite end of the country from San Bernardino. McDonald's Famous. It was, for all of its faults and compromises, a business strategy very much in tune with the times. Several factors, including car culture, women's entry into the workforce, and the increased tempo of life served to render fast food the wave of the future.

Back then, nothing looked so certain. Murray was peering into his crystal ball and seeing the same changes as Sol—the move to the suburbs, increased mobility, a growing demographic—but drawing different conclusions. To him, the changes to come meant people would want more choices, more formality, and a more settled restaurant experience.

"Opening gigantic stores, the way that Murray wanted to open them, took a tremendous investment," said longtime Nathan's Famous manager Hy Brown. "It was all stainless-steel equipment that wasn't movable. There was a big stainless-steel counter, and you couldn't do much with it after it was built, so you couldn't make changes."

"I opposed the idea of expanding based on building big stores," Sol recalled. "I thought we should build with small stores, more like a McDonald's today, more like a Burger King, with a more limited menu. We'd be able to control things better in terms of personnel and the products that we'd be serving."

The small-is-beautiful versus big-is-better debate wasn't the sole issue separating Murray and Sol. And it wasn't the only element contributing to tension at the store. Take two brothers with different outlooks, values, and personalities and then add in a strong-willed father with very distinct and determined ideas of his own, and there was little wonder that the atmosphere around Surf and Stillwell became increasingly fraught.

"Nathan would be very upset if [Sol and Murray] weren't there every day, because he expected them to be like him," recalled Jay Cohen. "It was very obvious to me that there was no way in hell that was going to happen. I never saw them last very long together. It was my estimation that they would never want to run that organization."

During this period, Nathan resurrected an old witticism from the past, one that he had tried out on Mayor La Guardia during the first strike at the store.

"I wish I had a merry-go-round," Nathan told the store's manager Hy Brown.

"Why?" responded Brown, willing to play the straight man.

"Because the carousel horses don't eat and don't shit and don't talk back to their father."

Nathan tied himself in knots trying to solve the problem of his warring sons. He might not have had the psychological acumen to deal with it. His experience with his own battling brothers proved the stubborn difficulties of sibling rivalry. He tried the strategy of giving his boys separate responsibilities, with Murray taking on the store operations and Sol handling purchasing, insurance, and marketing. But the effort didn't work. Literally and figuratively, the brothers kept stepping on each other's toes.

"I think it broke his heart, the fight between Murray and Sol," said Hygrade rep Paul Berlly. "He didn't understand. He thought the business was big enough to hold the two of them."

Desperate situations required desperate measures. Nathan briefly floated a larger, grander vision of Nathan's Famous, one that he thought could contain the ambitions of both his sons. He would move the store to the old Feltman's site and put it on a huge raised platform that ran from Surf Avenue to the sea. Underneath the platform would be space for parking.

Ida put the kibosh on the plan. At this point in their lives, she told her husband, they should be thinking about retirement, not embarking on grand building schemes. As usual, her opinion held sway with Nathan. The idea was shelved. But Ida and Nathan continued to have frequent discussions about what to do about the feud disrupting their family and their business.

Something had to give. One of the brothers had to leave. Any oddsmaker worth his salt would have put money on Sol, but it was Murray who jumped first.

The small Nassau County town of Oceanside was located fifteen miles to the east of Coney Island, past what was then called
Idlewild Airport but would later become JFK. A former clam-
digger's hamlet originally named Christian Hook, Oceanside in
the fifties was well on its way to turning into what every other
Long Island town around it was fast becoming—a bedroom community for commuters to New York City. It was of those budding
suburbs that Murray talked about whenever he argued changing
times meant Nathan's Famous had to expand.

The "dusty thoroughfare"—the description was from a *Newsday* report—of Long Beach Road ran north-south through Oceanside, linking the towns of the barrier island of Long Beach to
the larger municipality of Rockville Centre. Where Long Beach
Road crossed Windsor Parkway stood Roadside Rest, once a local landmark but by the midfifties just a large but fast-fading
restaurant.

Founded as a rural fruit and vegetable depot in 1921 by Leon
Shor, who would later run a chain of popular Long Island eateries
called Shor's, Roadside Rest developed into a thriving hot dog
stand, "one of the many imitators of Nathan's Famous," according
to a *Newsday* article.

Success led to expansion. In 1929, the Shor family built an
elaborate structure with Spanish architectural flavorings, oddly
out of place in its Long Island environs, probably the only outsize
Moorish villa this side of California. It occupied a full block, with
such amenities as seating for three thousand, a garden terrace, and
Kiddieland, a small amusement park on the grounds.

"The small place grew from hot dogs and hamburgers to the
heights of a well-known supper club," according to Morton Shor,
the son of the founder. "It featured the legendary big bands led by
Tommy Dorsey, Benny Goodman, Eddy Duchin, Lionel Hampton,

and others. There were nightly [radio] broadcasts of the bands' concerts and dancing under the stars."

Roadside Rest became, in other words, a hot dog stand on steroids. Exactly the place of Murray's dreams. "I wanted Oceanside," he recalled later. "Perfect deal. Seven acres. Seven! Beautiful business."

By 1956, when Murray first investigated taking it on, that "beautiful business" had hit the skids. The big bands weren't coming anymore, and the customers weren't, either. The fickle finger of public taste pointed elsewhere. Roadside Rest, its bleached stucco exterior stained and faded, was a white elephant. The sprawling restaurant had actually closed its doors.

Nathan begged off the whole project. "I want nothing to do with it," he said. "Absolutely nothing."

Murray and Dorothy proceeded with the project, anyway. They knew that he would have to escape from under Nathan's thumb somehow and that it was time to remove themselves from the toxic atmosphere of the Coney Island store. Murray would preserve his status as vice president of Nathan's Famous, but he would pursue his destiny elsewhere.

"I hocked everything we had," Murray said. "And at that time, my father did everything to discourage me to be successful. Everything!"

"Don't give him any help," Nathan advised his business contacts. "He's got to do what he's got to do on his own."

For three years, Murray valiantly tried to breathe life into a corpse—a corpse with wait service and white tablecloth dining. He served selected items from the Nathan's Famous menu, but expanded the choices with such full-bodied fare as turkey dinners and steaks. He threw a "Premier Champagne Carnival" to mark the opening of the summer season. A dance orchestra played on the terrace every Friday and Saturday night.

Roadside Rest was humongous, with two bars, a cocktail lounge, an ice cream corner, and an outdoor fast-service counter similar to the one at the Coney Island store. Murray gave grand new names to the multiple dining rooms. In the Old English Room ("Long Island's Most Unusual and Picturesque Dining Room"), he brought back marquee bands, hiring such well-known names as jazz great Gerry Mulligan.

On the grounds, the Kiddieland carousel continued to turn. Clowns and magicians came in to entertain the families. Murray even opened the stage to public school theatricals and local business promotions. He brought in manager Hy Brown to try to shore up the sagging operation.

Murray's Roadside Rest ("Now . . . Better Than Ever" read the motto) might have been someone's idea of destination dining, but it didn't click with Long Island residents. The truth can be read in newspaper ads for the place, which trace a series of increasingly desperate price drops ("A whole meal for only 99 cents!") to try to lure customers.

Nothing helped.

Meanwhile, back at the ranch . . . Sol experienced working under his father without the distracting presence of Murray. He instituted his own kind of innovations. One idea was to install closed-circuit TV cameras trained on the counters, so that Sol could monitor what was happening out front from the upstairs office.

It might have marked the corrosive effects of capitalism on the committed progressive, that Sol's reading of Orwell's *1984* hadn't stopped him from becoming a Big Brother himself. "You know, you're searching for new things to do," he said later. "So I thought of that."

Nathan just laughed at the idea but allowed it to proceed. Sol got his picture in *TV Guide,* along with a big article on the surveillance camera system, but the workers failed to appreciate it. Why would the boss need a camera when they had always done their jobs with such enthusiasm and passion? Sol took the cameras away.

"After a year or two, it really meant nothing," he admitted. "It accomplished nothing. Just sitting there watching, you don't see a hell of a lot on the televisions. You've got to be downstairs watching if you want to see something."

Another innovation of Sol's was more successful. Seeing workers struggle day after day with the small cellophane bags used for the store's crinkle-cut potato fries, he concluded that there had to be a better way. He came up with the "V-cup," a cone of paper that was much easier to fill. The delivery method had the added benefit of making a serving look bigger than it actually was, because the top end of the cone, piled high with fries, worked to trick the eye. The concept was something of a sleight of hand, odd for a confirmed socialist to come up with. But all was fair in sales and marketing.

Finally, in 1959, Sol's time as the only son at the Coney Island store came to end. Roadside Rest neared collapse. Nathan had a choice. He could allow Murray to go fully down the tubes. Or he could put an "I told you so" expression on his face and come to his son's rescue. Sol volunteered to be transferred to Oceanside.

"Nathan wanted Murray to come back to Coney Island," recalled Hy Brown. "Murray was not doing well in Oceanside. Too much property, too many things happening, too much going on.

He was getting into debt there. But the only way he would come back to Coney Island at that particular time was if he was in control. So Nathan sent Sol and Al Shalik out to Oceanside, but the condition was it had to become a Nathan's."

Sol had advocated for the change. Even then, he was forming a plan to get out of the Coney Island store. As Murray had Hy Brown as his chief aide, Sol had Al Shalik. The two camps performed a do-si-do, with Murray and Hy coming back to Coney Island and Sol and Al going to Oceanside.

"[Nathan] was very concerned that I would have less of an involvement with the Nathan's operation if I stayed involved with Oceanside," said Murray. "He came to me and wanted to know if I was willing to merge it into the Nathan's organization."

For the remainder of his life, Murray would stubbornly refuse to admit that his grand experiment had crashed and burned. The word "bankruptcy" never passed his lips. Others were not so discreet.

"Murray tried to build a large, regular restaurant and failed," Sol stated bluntly. "He was going bankrupt. [Nathan] saved him from that by buying him out and returning him to Coney Island."

This was Sol's truth, though it might have differed from Murray's. There can be no doubt of the fact that in 1959, Nathan purchased the former Roadside Rest. He reopened it as the first Nathan's Famous location outside of the original Coney Island store. Sol employed what by now was a tried-and-true public relations strategy. For the grand opening, the new outlet served free frankfurters all day.

Murray's failure had forced Nathan into an expansion he never wanted. The Oceanside disaster affected the business in other ways, too. The Long Beach Road restaurant was unionized, so when Nathan took it over, that also eventually resulted in the unionization of the Coney Island location. That in turn effectively meant the end of Nathan's informal employee benefits, including the year-end bonuses. Without him really doing anything, modernization was being done to Nathan. He didn't really consent to any of it, but suddenly he had union workers and another outlet.

Everything was changing. Robert Moses and his massive development projects transformed Coney Island to the degree that Nathan and other old-timers had difficulty comprehending the scope of the changes. Simply put, Moses was a killjoy. In 1953, he had pushed for rezoning that would "enable Coney Island to fit into the pattern envisioned for it as a largely residential seaside area." Coming to fruition throughout the fifties and sixties, his initiatives proved disastrous.

The beloved seaside resort town began a long slide into decline. Crime started to rise along with the public housing high-rises. Afraid for their safety, the beach crowds stopped coming. The store's customer base eroded, lured by more far-flung destinations, by trips in cars rather than by subway, as well as by the new habit of remaining at home to watch the marvelous novelty of television.

Increasingly, Nathan removed himself to Florida. His life took on an autumnal quality. "I wanted to die here," he said of the Coney Island store. "I didn't want to retire. Ever."

By the end of the fifties, Nathan was, in fact, a decade and a half from his death. Perhaps it's not really age that kills us but the world changing around us without our permission. The vacations in Florida stretched longer. Every return to the store felt more awkward, more foreign.

"He felt very bad about leaving," said Jay Cohen. "But he knew it was inevitable that he was going to leave."

Hy Brown concurred. "I think he got the idea that he wasn't wanted around there anymore. The expansion was a fact. It was going to go on, and Coney Island was going to have less attention paid to it because of that. The only one he could depend on in Coney Island was Joe Handwerker."

"Nathan had always worked so hard," said Dorothy Handwerker. "He really didn't want to see things change. He wanted it to remain status quo."

For Murray, having Ida and Nathan taper off their store schedules was not a punishment but a reward. His parents had worked long hours for so many long years. It was fitting that they would now be able to step back and enjoy the fruits of their labors.

Murray came into the store one day and found Ida hard at work in the kitchen peeling onions, as usual. He stopped her, taking the paring knife out of her hands.

"Ma, I want you to have a good life now," he said. "I'm going to help Dad. I don't want you to work anymore. You can retire. You can go."

Ida reacted, stunned. She immediately burst into tears. "You're throwing me out of the business?" she asked. "You don't need me anymore?"

"I need you," Murray responded. "I just don't need you at the store."

The son tried to reason with his mother. She and Nathan had a membership in a beach club at Brighton Beach. Murray told Ida to go there, relax, play cards with her friends. When pleading didn't stop her tears, he changed tactics.

"I don't want you in the store," he said. "You're only taking my place. If you're going to work, then I'm not going to work."

The standoff went on for a few weeks. Whenever Ida came

into the store, Murray made a show of getting up and leaving. "Oh, okay, you're here now? Fine, I can go home."

"Grandma was very upset," recalled Dorothy Handwerker. "She wanted to work. She didn't know what else to do. That was all she ever did. And we were so young and so stupid—we didn't realize she needed that. When Murray insisted that she not come into the store, he was being young and stupid. He thought he was being good to her. He thought he was helping her."

18

Snacktime

"I reached a point where I decided in my
own mind that I wanted to get out and start
my own business." A new opportunity on
Thirty-Fourth Street.

WHEN NATHAN PLACED Sol in charge of the Oceanside place, the
business stabilized and no longer threatened to be a drain on the
company's balance sheet. Putting Nathan's Famous on the sign
helped. Sol oversaw the bustling hot dog counter, eliminated the
waiter service, and managed to streamline operations in the dining rooms. But he had his eye on another prize. He liked the

independence that working at the Oceanside store gave him. Being out from under his father's thumb and his brother's gaze worked out well for him. He yearned to make the situation permanent.

"We became a Nathan's [at Oceanside], and then at a certain point, we achieved what we wanted there," Sol said. "Things were going well, but I reached a point where I decided in my own mind that I wanted to get out and start my own business. And that's when I started thinking about and developing the idea of Snack-time in New York and pursuing that."

In effect, Roadside Rest had been Murray's trial run, a test of his strategy of how to expand Nathan's Famous into more locations. Now it was Sol's turn. He formulated a plan to put into play his own ideas about the future of the restaurant business. His leadership of the Oceanside outlet served as excellent preparation for running a store by himself. In 1963, he took the leap.

Thirty-Fourth Street is one of Manhattan's main cross-street thoroughfares, marking the southern boundary of the Midtown business district. At Eighth Avenue, Thirty-Fourth slices past the James A. Farley Post Office Building, with a zip code of 10001 the city's main post office. In the midsixties, the area was the site of an enormous construction project. Opposite the general post office, taking up two entire city blocks, an entertainment and transportation hub rose from the rubble of the glorious old Pennsylvania Station. A new underground commuter station was being put in place with, built right on top of it, a new Madison Square Garden. If, for a high-volume business, location is everything, then Thirty-Fourth Street and Eighth Avenue was prime territory.

It was where Sol chose to strike. He was thirty-eight years old. Officially taking his leave from the Oceanside Nathan's Famous, he departed from the family business entirely. Instead, he would head up his own enterprise. He wanted to conduct a test case of his own, trying to determine if his small otoro expansion idea was a viable business strategy. Just to the east of the busy corner of Thirty-Fourth and Eighth, he would erect what was in effect a carbon copy of the Coney Island Nathan's Famous, emphasizing the same holy trinity that his father lived by: speed of service, quality of food, economy of price.

Sol called his new store Snacktime.

Having learned from his experience with Murray's Roadside Rest not to attempt to block the inevitable, Nathan gave at least a partial blessing to the move. He supplied Sol with a start-up loan of $250,000. He permitted him to advertise the fact that he was Nathan Handwerker's son and that he would be selling Nathan's Famous hot dogs in the new place. And he also got Murray to agree not to open any other Nathan's Famous outlet within eight blocks of the Snacktime location.

These were generous concessions, ones that had not been granted to Murray when he had set out on his own almost a decade before. Nathan was more flexible this time around. But he didn't have to be happy about it.

"[Nathan and Ida] didn't say much [about the new business]," Sol remembered. "It was too personal for them, the fact that I left his business, their business, so they weren't going to praise me for it. They wouldn't say something positive, because it was hurting them, the fact that I did that. They would have preferred I stayed and suffered."

Sol put a lot of consideration and money into designing a comfortable, clean, and attractive environment, down to the particular penny white tile he chose for the walls. It might have been possible to take the boy out of Nathan's Famous, but you couldn't take Nathan's Famous out of the boy. Snacktime imported many of the techniques, the policies, and the general double-time atmosphere from the Coney Island store. The only things missing were the screams of the roller-coaster riders and the beach sand.

"It was an interesting situation," Sol said. "Because many times, I had agreed with my father, against Murray, in terms of what Murray wanted to do or what he did. I had a very similar viewpoint with my father."

When Snacktime opened on September 17, 1963, Sol employed an old publicity trick that Nathan had used several times. He gave away free hot dogs all day, an estimated forty thousand total. The lines outside the new store stretched around the block, all the way to Macy's on Herald Square.

Sol also poached more than a few workers from his father. He hired Al Shalik as general manager of Snacktime. Shalik had been Sol's own longtime right-hand man at Coney Island, a hard-working manager whom he had also brought along when he transferred to Oceanside.

"I had worked for Nathan until 1963," Shalik said. "But when I was on Thirty-Fourth Street with Sol, we ran that place the way we were taught to run Nathan's at Coney Island."

Even those Coney Island workers who didn't follow Sol to Midtown approved of Snacktime when they stopped by. Hy Brown: "To build an operation with two doors, customers coming in one way and going out the other way, that was really good. Very good thought went into it. He had each station separate, the potatoes and the franks and the drinks. It worked very nice, very smooth."

Snacktime's grand opening brought father and sons together for a celebration, along with many of the other Handwerker relations. Murray and Dorothy were there, brimming with happiness. There didn't seem to be a trace of jealousy in the older brother's response to the new place. In effect, Sol's founding of Snacktime made it official. Murray's way was now cleared to become the unchallenged boss of Nathan's Famous. He was jubilant, wishing Sol well, but with an undeniable undertone of "good riddance."

As for Sol, he still nursed grudges from when he had worked with Murray on Coney Island. Especially galling was the high-handed way he felt the older son treated people, including Sol but other veteran employees, as well. "I would never forgive him," Sol said of Murray. "Never. He was very selfish and egotistical, and he had no feelings for the people."

Nathan and Ida had a more bittersweet reaction to the antagonism between their sons. They both realized that Snacktime's grand opening actually represented a sad ending, a signal that Nathan's dream of a family dynasty at the Coney Island store had finally died.

"The two brothers really could have made a go of the business, if they were willing to," said Jay Cohen. "If they could ever work out a way how to do this thing together. If they could, if they could, if they could. They couldn't."

It must have been very difficult for Murray to be the oldest son of Nathan Handwerker. It seems almost inevitable that he would overcompensate for his father's lack of praise by trying too hard to distinguish himself. Nathan was competitive with his sons, so it was not surprising that Murray was competitive with Sol.

The feuding between Sol and Murray repeated the history of bad blood between the Handwerker brothers of the generation before. Such psychologists as R. D. Laing believe human behaviors are handed down from generation to generation like heirlooms. Perhaps it was fated that Sol and Murray would not get along. But the end result was the permanent split that happened when the younger brother went out on his own and left the older brother in command of the business.

Nathan appeared surprised and a tad disgruntled when he recognized so many workers behind the Snacktime counters as former employees of Nathan's Famous. Sol's new place was, in fact, a Nathan's Famous in all but name. It also fit the common formula developed first by Nathan and later, independently, by Ray Kroc: limited menu, speedy service, dependable quality.

The humongous Snacktime sign towered over Thirty-Fourth Street, visible from the escalators of the new Madison Square Garden to fans heading up to the arena's Knicks or Rangers games. A companion neon sign was a true work of vernacular art, portraying a cartoon mascot man holding a hot dog and downing a soda, with the liquid visibly pouring into his belly as he drank.

The new enterprise was a rousing success. Snacktime grossed $1 million in its first twelve months of operation. Sol was able to pay back Nathan's $250,000 start-up loan a year after opening. More than that, Snacktime served to validate Sol's vision for small-store expansion. On a personal level, it freed the family's youngest child from the domination of his father and older brother.

Sol never worked for Nathan or under Murray again.

With his hand now firmly on the rudder of Nathan's Famous, Murray continued with his own expansion plans. In 1965, he opened an outlet at 2290 Central Avenue in Yonkers. In keeping with his bigger-is-better philosophy, and not having fully learned his lesson at Oceanside, the new place was a ten-thousand-square-foot colossus. As with Roadside Rest, Murray took over a struggling restaurant, Adventurer's Inn, an amusement-park-themed eatery that had just relocated from its former quarters in the Cross County Shopping Center.

Nathan's Famous Yonkers retained some of the features of Adventurer's Inn. "The Yonkers place had a tremendous game room," remembers Hy Brown. "It was on a big, tremendous parking lot, across the street from a Castro." A bakery in the basement churned out buns for the store's frankfurters and rye bread for the deli sandwiches. Nathan refused to submit to a franchise arrangement when opening new stores. He insisted that Murray buy the Adventurer's Inn site outright, and gave him money to do so.

The new store—technically, the first Nathan's Famous not located on Long Island—had a bumpy start. The game room was operated under a separate contract, as was the bakery. The managers of the restaurant came in via the new scientific training programs instituted by Murray and Dr. Eimicke. The results were mixed. In fact, it seemed that the overabundance of new management trainees had motivated the purchase of the Yonkers store, rather than the other way around. All those new employees needed a place to work.

"Murray forced the expansion," said Hy Brown. "When he bought Yonkers, I don't think he was ready to cope with the problems. [Dr. Eimicke] had brought people in and trained them, people who had their way of doing things, not Nathan's way."

The management difficulties were eventually smoothed out, in part by bringing experienced employees from Coney Island. After a rocky start, sales at the Yonkers location started to rise.

The success came at a crucial time. Murray was pushing a plan for the company to go public. To lure new investors for the initial Nathan's Famous stock offering, he could now point to three successful stores: Yonkers, Oceanside, and the Coney Island mother ship.

The stock sale, when it occurred in 1968, was hugely successful. Originally issued at $8 and opening at $14, a single share of Nathan's Famous soon hit $46. The stock then split two for one and headed even higher, reaching $42. The market cap for Nathan's Famous essentially meant that investors had valued the company at $145 million, the equivalent of $855 million in today's money.

Here was the payoff for all the decades of hard work and long hours. Everyone involved became wealthy, at least on paper. Nathan, Sol, Murray, and Leah each would end up with million-dollar stock holdings. When the stock peaked, Nathan was worth $40 million.

Veteran employees were given the chance to purchase shares at the initial public offering price. Joe Handwerker was granted shares and bought in heavily, winding up owning a full one percent of the outstanding stock. "He was a rich man," said his cousin Sidney, who also bought into the company. Murray laid down a rule that insiders from the business had to hold the stock for at least two years before unloading. That was okay. As the price continued to climb, no one considered getting out. The ride was too good, as exciting as a trip aboard the Cyclone.

Dr. Eimicke was one of those who benefited from the sale of shares in the company. He had pushed vigorously for the initial public offering and was granted generous stock options when it came. "Vic was one of the big, big promoters of the idea of going public," his wife, Maxine, recalled. "He had a lot of their stock."

The year of the IPO, Murray was elevated to president of Nathan's Famous, Inc. The rise in the company's share price made him look like a financial genius. Nathan remained as chairman of the board of directors but became increasingly less and less involved with the business.

There were a few doubters. "The day Nathan told me he was retiring, I sold my stock, I swear to God," said Jay Cohen. "Because the world knew it. The world knew that as long as Nathan was alive, as long as he was out there chomping on that cigar, the place was going to be well taken care of."

Murray wasn't finished yet. Flush with cash from the public offering, Murray secured a beachhead in Manhattan, taking over another fading restaurant, this one located at Broadway and Forty-Third Street in Times Square.

"They raised millions of dollars going public," recalled Marsha Abramson. "The money furnished lavish executive offices as well as the store on Forty-Third Street."

Again, Murray went massive. The former Toffenetti's had been called "the cathedral of restaurants" when it opened in 1940, a three-story, glass-fronted modern building with an escalator and an open, all-stainless-steel kitchen. Adding to the glamour of the place were lavish washrooms, air-conditioned telephone booths, ornate chandeliers, and walls covered in expansive surrealist murals. Calling itself "the Busiest Restaurant on the World's Busiest Corner," Toffenetti's featured seating for a thousand and a menu, as its motto proclaimed, "Famous for Ham and Sweets."

The sons of founder Dario Toffenetti sold out in 1968, and Murray leased the space from its new owners. With three floors to play with, he really went to town, creating a Nathan's Famous outlet on ground level, and a steakhouse and bar with formal dining on the lower floor.

"It was common knowledge among senior personnel that Murray always wanted to open a fancy restaurant," said Charles

Schneck. "He was very excited about getting the old Toffenetti's and turning that into a Nathan's. He just wouldn't listen to those who tried to talk him out of it."

Murray also leased new company headquarters one block away, in the brand-new One Astor Plaza office building on Forty-Fourth Street. The interiors there were particularly extravagant, with gold-plated bathroom fixtures, expensive wood paneling, and Persian carpets.

Part of the effort was for show, a shrewd move on Murray's part to portray the business as thriving. He could now invite potential investors to the Nathan's Famous offices, impressing them with the gorgeous surroundings and crossroads-of-the-world location. The executives hired by Dr. Eimicke felt right at home. Their salaries were in keeping with their environment.

On the main floor of the old Toffenetti's, Murray created what his PR guru Morty Matz called "a hot dog mecca." The new store debuted with all the hype that Matz and his partner, Max Rosey, could muster.

"Nathan was there, and of course he was the special interest of the press," Matz recalled. "He would tell his stories about how, as a young man, he used to buy a cake of soap for a nickel and stand in line in a public shower to bathe. Or how when he opened the original Nathan's in Coney Island, he would work for twenty-four hours on weekends—he would not sleep."

Despite these best efforts, the new outlet quickly proved to be a disaster. The Times Square Nathan's Famous did not do enough business to support the location's sky-high rent. The formal dining room and bar on the lower floor failed to attract a clientele.

"They found out the hard way that people don't come to a hot dog place to go downstairs to a steakhouse," noted Hy Brown. "The Forty-Third Street store was a complete abortion and money drain. Everybody associated with its construction was on the take. It was built wrong, it was overstaffed, everybody was stealing, security was five times what was needed. Oy vey, it was bad."

It was Oceanside all over again. Murray was forced to summon seasoned managers from the Coney Island store to right the listing ship. The bloated workforce of four hundred had to be trimmed in half. Once again, Murray needed help to pull himself back from the brink.

"To me, it was sad, how Murray ran the business and what he thought he had to do to make it successful," Sol said of his brother. "I was happiest when I left. I didn't have to deal with him anymore."

"Murray's ideas were always grandiose," said Hy Brown. "Oceanside and Times Square both ate money."

The blows just kept on coming. The National Labor Relations Board investigated the company and found its old-style personnel policies unfair and illegal. A third strike hit the company, effectively ending the "family business" ethos that had been put in place in Nathan's time.

All the changes served to break Nathan's heart. The Times Square expansion became a turning point. After visiting Murray's grand new corporate headquarters, the father could gauge precisely how out of step he was with his son's sensibility.

"Nathan hated, *hated* [the offices in] Times Square," said Hy Brown. "He didn't feel at home there. With the public [stock] offering, and with the expansion, it was like the business just wasn't his anymore. He didn't recognize it."

Murray's son Steve Handwerker, who spent time with his grandfather during this period, recalled Nathan's sentiments. "He was very leery of Times Square because he knew the city. He knew the politics involved in the city. He knew the lack of integrity that went on behind the scenes in a business like the Times Square store, with a bar and a restaurant. He didn't want to see his store develop into the complicated political situation that it became."

Out of deference to the family, Sol had never sold his Nathan's Famous stock, believing that if he did so, he would single-handedly trigger a fall in the share price. He became something of a gadfly at stockholder meetings. As a family member who held a substantial number of shares, he had standing to speak. He would rise to his feet during the open comment period and publicly challenge some of Murray's business decisions.

The feud between the brothers broke into the open. Sol did not try to hide his distaste for the direction Nathan's Famous had taken. He spoke out about the plush Times Square headquarters, criticizing the huge salaries enjoyed by the cadre of executives installed by Murray.

Nathan had set it up so that the Handwerker family retained ownership of the land and the building at the original Coney Island location. In 1968, Murray had arranged to have the family lease the store back to the publicly held company at very generous terms: a sixty-year lease with a low fixed annual rent. Nathan approved of the deal, believing along with Murray that the cheap rent would help the company's balance sheet, which in turn would keep the stock price high and therefore benefit all the Handwerkers.

Sol argued that the favorable lease wasn't just a sweetheart deal; it was essentially a steal. A renegotiation of the arrangement eventually included periodic cost-of-living rises in the rental rate. After the settlement, Murray and Dorothy went out to dinner with Sol and Minnie. Dorothy thanked Sol for helping to get the lease restructured. Murray said not a word.

19

Lion in Winter

"It was beautiful to see the love that Nathan had for his wife. That was a beautiful thing." Nathan and Ida in Florida, ca. 1960.

NATHAN AND IDA remained in Florida, out of the fray, only occasionally returning to New York.

During this twilight period of Nathan's professional life, a pair of high schoolers named Bob Levine and John Larosa hired on as summer help at the Oceanside Nathan's Famous. "We were out there one day, two high school kids doing a very menial job cleaning the parking lot, and this big Cadillac pulls in, and a guy in a suit got out," Levine remembered. "He took a broom, and he started sweeping."

Levine approached him. "Why do you want to help us do this?"

"I'm Nathan Handwerker," said the new volunteer. "I own this place."

"Wow! Nice to meet you."

Nathan spent an hour with the youths. Together, they swept the parking lot of the old Roadside Rest. Nathan spoke about the number of people who had gained experience working at the Coney Island store. He asked the boys where they went to school and how they were doing in their studies.

"He showed that he really gave a damn about us," Levine said.

The old man's words about the value of work stuck with Levine for the rest of his life. "He said that it doesn't matter what you're doing—do it right. Do it to the best of your ability, and you'll be rewarded for it."

Nathan was back where he wanted to be, back where he started, a man with a push broom engaging in the necessary task of keeping the premises of his business tidy. He had changed from the youngster in the Galician shtetl and from the person who had founded Nathan's Famous in 1916. After all, he had emerged from a Cadillac. But the world around him had changed more. It had moved on.

Nathan and Ida now led lives that divided into two sharply contrasting periods. Summers were the hectic high season that they had always known, and they put in long hours at the store. But beginning in the 1930s, they started spending time in Florida during Coney Island's slack winter period. The vacations were not extended at first, and they lasted weeks, not months. But the couple increased the length of their sojourns down south as they became familiar with the region and came to trust the store would not fall apart in their absence. They knew they could rely on such stalwarts as Joe Handwerker and Hy Brown to take care of the business.

"I'm going away for the winter," Nathan would tell them. "The store is yours, the store is for your employees, what you do with the store is what you get rewards for."

As she had when she'd introduced her brother to the joys of Coney Island, it had been Anna Singer who first brought Nathan and Ida to Florida. Anna had discovered the beautiful beaches of the Sunshine State in the early 1930s. Nathan and Ida visited several locales, from Sarasota to Miami's North Shore. In the 1950s, they built a three-bedroom home on Normandy Isle, in Miami Beach. The place was beautiful but by no means palatial, with terrazzo floors and two acres of land along the Intracoastal Waterway.

Florida was a godsend to the hardworking couple. Nathan became a different creature down south, unrecognizable as the stern, compulsive overseer of the store. In family snapshots, he sprawls in the sand, a huge grin on his face. He was clearly having a good time, earning a well-deserved respite from his eighteen-hour days at the store. His employees always typed their boss as a "workaholic." The word entered the language in 1947, probably helped along by the generational example of people like Nathan. The Florida photos represent a different portrait of the man, hard evidence that he was actually able to get away from it all.

"It was beautiful to see the love that Nathan had for his wife," recalled Marsha Abramson. "That was a beautiful thing. She was a very beautiful woman, with beautiful blue eyes. He would never let us forget that Ida worked right alongside him to build the business."

The couple had a serene, peaceful existence. Neither Nathan

nor Ida exerted themselves much. They didn't have a golf game. They liked to fish, visit the jai alai courts, play cards with friends and relatives. Ida enjoyed *The Jack LaLanne Show* and followed along with the exercises as she watched on TV. Sol and Leah would often bring their families over to celebrate Passover and Hanukkah. Leah moved down permanently in the early 1950s.

Nathan and Ida spent most of their time in the house on Normandy Isle but essentially remained Florida "bicoastals," shuttling back and forth between the Atlantic and the Gulf. Anna Singer had also introduced them to the Warm Mineral Springs area south of Sarasota. Local myth had it that the pools there represented the true Fountain of Youth searched for by Spanish explorer Ponce de León.

The Warm Mineral Springs spa invigorated the elderly Brooklyn refugees, and they bought an apartment in a nearby town to be close to the facilities. Nathan dressed the part. Wearing a white safari helmet and a tobacco-colored terry cloth robe, clutching a rubberized float, he'd set off for a soak.

Back at Normandy Isle, Nathan most enjoyed tending to the flowers and fruit trees on the property—bananas, oranges, grapefruit, and especially loquats. The evergreen shrub yielded fruit that was also called Chinese plums. He didn't forget his family and employees shivering back in New York, periodically bringing them boxes of oranges, lemons, and mangoes from sunny Florida.

The gifts flowed the other way, too. When Hy Brown vacationed in the neighborhood, he'd always stop by with a little something for the boss. "I went to their place often with fish," he remembered. "I caught it and brought it. They used to love fresh fish. It was a way of kissing ass, too." Brown talks about going to the Normandy Isle place for dinner and how hospitable they were, with Nathan barbecuing and Ida cooking.

Not only fish, but information passed between the Florida outpost and the Coney Island store. Nathan was always eager for reports. An informal jungle tom-tom network came into play, between Nathan, Murray, Sol, and several longtime Nathan's Famous employees.

"We always knew who we wanted to get what information," said Brown. "So we knew who to tell to make sure it went that way."

Have a message, a tidbit of information, or a comment for Nathan to hear? Tell Gerry Monetti. Hy Brown acted as Murray's guy, while Al Shalik served as proxy for Sol. A word dropped into the right ear always reached the intended target, even from the far remove of Miami Beach.

Like all doting grandparents, Nathan and Ida enjoyed having their grandchildren visit them. "They were very loving," remembered Sol's wife, Minnie. "Grandma would always be tickling the kids and have them sitting on her lap on the swivel chair. Grandpa would always take them out to the yard and peel the loquats and feed them. They were warm grandparents. They weren't the kind that would take their grandchildren to a museum or the beach or anything like that, but they were always there for them."

"He showed me every tree in the garden," Nathan's grandson Steve Handwerker reminisced about spending time at the Normandy Isle home. "How each different fruit and vegetable needed to be taken care of and when to pick the vegetables and when to water them and how to treat them. He was very, very attentive to all that, and he shared it with me."

His status as paterfamilias meant Nathan was allowed to pose questions about the future plans of his grandson. "Do you want to eventually go into the business?" he asked Steve during one of their early fruit-tree walks.

"No, not really, I don't," Steve replied after thinking it over.

"I want to work with countries. I want to be in international relations."

Nathan was shocked by the answer and took a minute to compose himself. "It's very good to be a professional," he said. "It's a good thing to do that."

What Nathan was always looking for—in his sons, and now in his grandchildren—was a version of his former self, the indefatigable, ambitious, and work-hungry young man who had founded Nathan's Famous. Apart from Joe Handwerker and, to some extent, his sons, he never found it within the family, certainly not in his grandchildren. A few of the longtime, hard-core employees fit the bill, people like Sammy Fariello, Gerry Monetti, Jay Cohen, Hy Brown, and Sinta. But they weren't kin.

"I was the stepson," said Cohen. "Pop used to call me the son he never had." He recalled Nathan coming into the store and asking him where Murray and Sol were. After working at Nathan's Famous for a quarter century, Cohen was let go when he opposed Murray's expansion plans.

Nathan, wholly untutored in business psychology, still managed to motivate his team of managers. Someone like Monetti devoted his energy to the store to an almost fanatical degree. He was constantly tinkering with the infrastructure, inventing new ways to approach common restaurant procedures. One problem with fryolators, for example, was that water from potatoes and other food items built up, mixed with the oil, and eventually contaminated it. Monetti created an ingenious grooved bottom in the deep fryer, linked to a nozzle that could separate and drain the water out.

"That extended the life of the oil, which was a tremendous money saver and a quality move that helped the product," Hy

Brown recalled. The Pitco Frialator company adopted the innovation as its own. Monetti was one of a few Nathan's Famous employees that proved their loyalty to the final degree—by dying at the store. After more than thirty years on the job, he collapsed one day and passed away from a heart attack. His coworkers laid his body out on a cold griddle. But the former Patsy's Tasties manager went the other diehards one better, reaching out from beyond the grave.

Hy Brown remembered the eerie incident on the day Monetti died. "The front countermen had called the police already. I went back into the office, and the tears started to come. I slammed my hand onto the desk. When I did that, an envelope fell off the shelf in front of me."

TO HY BROWN IN THE EVENT OF MY DEATH read the words handwritten on the front of the envelope. Inside was a list of all the projects Gerry Monetti thought needed to be done for the betterment of Nathan's Famous.

"There were old projects he was working on, who he had contacted," Brown remembered. "It was a comprehensive thing. He could write pages and pages on a subject. There it was in front of me. I read it and could not believe it. It was like an act of God."

Nathan had said that he wished to go as Monetti had, at work, on the job. With the old-timers either dropping in their tracks or retiring, he could have taken it as a sign to put his affairs in order. But he could never quite cut the umbilical cord linking him to the business he'd created. Throughout the sixties, when he and Ida were in their seventies, they still came back from Florida to work at the store for at least part of the season.

When another of the resort town's periodic fires ravaged the nearby Ravenhall Bathhouse on the night of April 28, 1963, just before the summer season began, Nathan's charitable impulses kicked in. He offered free food to firefighters and displaced residents. He took personal charge of the relief efforts.

"A lot of people there, all their clothes burned up," remembered Joe Handwerker. "We put out a sign to give the people shelter, and we gave them food. Mothers with children. We fed them, and we gave them cab fare to go home. Nathan never turned anybody down."

Ravenhall, next door to Steeplechase Park to the west of the store at Surf Avenue and Nineteenth Street, had been a Coney Island institution, opening in 1867 as a hotel. In the 1960s, the bathhouse represented a cherished holdover from the past. Its saltwater pool, with diving boards labeled "Jack," "King," "Queen," and "Ace" depending on their height, had survived when other bathhouses of the area closed one by one. Ravenhall encompassed a gym, handball courts, steam rooms, a dance floor, and a small private ocean beach.

When Ravenhall burned, it seemed one more nail in the coffin. Old Coney was passing from the scene. After the fire, Nathan became an outspoken advocate of rebuilding. He sat on Mayor John Lindsay's Seaside Advisory Board. Even though Coney Islanders widely fingered Lindsay as one of those destroying the resort town with redevelopment projects, the mayor reached out to his advisory board to ask what could be done for the resort town.

"What does Coney Island need most?" Lindsay asked.

Nathan was the first to answer. In the wake of the Ravenhall fire, he knew exactly what was needed and was going to tell truth to power.

"We need a place our visitors could take a bath."

Laughter from the other board members and the audience at the hearing. Lindsay laughed, too.

The Ravenhall bathhouse was never rebuilt.

The accumulation of such events finally moved Nathan to retire from the store he had nurtured and loved so long. The creation of the Yonkers branch of Nathan's Famous in 1965 was one marker. Nathan showed up to look around exactly once and never returned. The company going public in 1968 was another demarcation line, as was Murray's transfer of the company headquarters to Times Square in the same year.

Away from the store, away from his post atop the soda box next to the root beer barrel, Nathan lacked a vital, stimulating purpose. Nathan's Famous could have been called "Nathan's Lifeblood," and it would have been the truth. He was one of those men who do not take well to retirement. The essence of his existence dwindled.

"He was not happy, not really," Steve Handwerker said. "He did have his place, his Florida abode, but he was not happy. Whenever he went back to New York, he felt unwelcome in a certain way. He wanted to be more involved, until the day he died. He wanted to die in the store, actually. He said that to me more than once."

20

Endgame

"He wasn't blood or anything, but I respected him, I cared for him." Nathan's Famous employees line up as the funeral cortege passes by.

ON SUNDAY, MARCH 24, 1974, in the aftermath of a cardiac arrest he had suffered the day before, Nathan died at Saint Joseph's Hospital in Port Charlotte, Florida. He passed away near to his beloved Warm Mineral Springs, three months shy of his eighty-second birthday. A story circulated about the circumstances of the heart attack. Nathan had arrived at the Sarasota airport the day before to find there was no driver there to meet him. In frustration he hefted his two heavy suitcases himself and that's what precipitated the later attack.

Nathan Handwerker's death was big news, covered nationally in print and on TV. The body was flown back to New York, and a service was held on the following Tuesday at Riverside Memorial Chapel on Ocean Parkway, near Prospect Park. As a member of the Masons high up in the hierarchy of the fraternal order, Nathan was accorded the elaborate honors of Freemasonry at his memorial. Brooklyn political leaders and community figures crowded the ceremony.

The funeral cortege left the chapel and proceeded to Coney Island. As it drove past the store that morning, the employees lined up on the curb, hands over their hearts in a show of deference, more than a few of them with tears in their eyes.

"When the old man passed, his family was hurting, but his employees were hurting more," recalled employee Jimmy Bologna. "I mean, he wasn't blood or anything, but I knew him. I respected him. I cared for him."

After the procession had passed, the employees did what they believed Nathan would have wanted them to do. They opened the store for business and went back to selling hot dogs.

The Coney Island that Nathan's funeral procession passed through was no longer the same place it was when he had ruled the store. He had not been able halt the decline of the resort town that had nurtured him and that he nurtured in turn. The best he had been able to do was retreat to Florida, so as not to be present when ruin swept over Coney in consecutive waves.

If Nathan had lived, he would have no longer recognized the place. The store was still there, of course, but its neighbors had fallen all around it. In 1966, Fred C. Trump, Donald's father, a real estate developer and an enthusiastic demolisher of classic New York City landscapes, had held a celebration marking his $2.5 million takeover and destruction of Steeplechase Park.

Historian Charles Denson labeled Trump's event "bizarre," and even by Coney Island standards, the developer had gone totally over the top. Trump had sent out invitations and handed out bricks to those who showed up. Surrounded by bikini-wearing models, and evidently unaware of the biblical injunction regarding those without sin throwing stones, Trump himself had tossed the ceremonial first brick through a pane of the glorious glass windows of Steeplechase's Pavilion of Fun.

Two years later, in April 1968, something of a coup de grâce had occurred, when the unrest triggered by the assassination of Rev. Martin Luther King Jr. spilled over into Coney Island from other parts of Brooklyn. Denny Corines, owner of Denny's Ice Cream on Surf Avenue, later told the New York *Daily News* that he would "never forget" the night. The looters who broke into his store passed by the cash registers.

"They weren't interested in the money; they wanted the candy," Corines said. "They were just kids. They ran in, took the candy, and left." He reported that one teenager had reached into a 350-degree deep fryer to grab a funnel cake.

By the time Nathan Handwerker died, Coney Island had been reduced to half a wasteland. The amusement zone barely held on. Somehow Nathan's passing and the decline and fall of the resort town seemed to go hand in hand.

———

The sadness surrounding Nathan's death lingered. Sol took his family to the 1975 revival of Arthur Miller's *Death of a Salesman*, a searing production with George C. Scott in the lead role. Nathan's own passing was still fresh on the family's mind. Sol broke down in tears at the end of the play, the story of Willy Loman, a man whose next-door neighbor Charley articulated the home truth of his life: "The only thing you've got in this world is what you can sell."

Above and beyond all the other roles that Nathan took on—a son, husband, father, hard worker, entrepreneur, success story, tough boss, community leader, Freemason, philanthropist—perhaps the truest element of his character was that of a salesman. He started selling in his childhood, calling out "Hot knishes for sale!" in the streets of Galicia, did the same with lemonade on a street corner in Manhattan, and then reached his peak in a small store that he made big on Coney Island.

The public always wanted to believe that Nathan was a billionaire, or at least a multimillionaire. The years of toil had to have paid off big-time. People witnessed the crowds lined up twenty deep outside the store. Everyone assumed the founder of Nathan's Famous had amassed a huge fortune.

Americans increasingly subscribe to the jackpot mentality. The American dream used to be that if you worked hard, you would wind up with a little something. But by the late sixties, the dream had morphed into wanting it all.

The truth might be disappointing for anyone wishing to believe there was a pot of gold at the end of Nathan's rainbow. His wealth was, by modern hedge-fund manager standards, extremely modest. His estate totaled something less than $3 million. The billionaire ideal misses a fundamental truth about the way Nathan approached business and life.

Greed was not part of the equation. Slow and steady was the rule. It actually wasn't the nickel that made Nathan wealthy. It was the penny. He never took an exorbitant salary. In 1925, for example, according to his visa application, Nathan was making $75 a week in wages and had savings of $10,000. Twenty years later, in 1945, he listed $100,000 in total assets and earned an annual salary of $15,000. Even in terms of modern-day purchasing power ($1.26 million in assets, $200,000 in salary), this was not a bonanza.

Joe Handwerker found himself bitterly disappointed not to be listed as a beneficiary in Nathan's will. "When I worked for him, he buttered me, kept buttering me for fifty years, kissed me and hugged me. He loved me, and I'm his right-hand man, and he couldn't live without me. Everyone thinks he left me a million dollars. I didn't get five pennies [in Nathan's will], and that's what I'm a little upset about. I was his top man, right?"

Nathan's trusted manager fully expected to be taken care of when the last will and testament of his boss, uncle, and brother-in-law was read. Joe had retired in 1973 after fifty years at the store. At that time, Nathan presented him with a proverbial gold watch.

"Every time I look at it, I could cry," Joe said. "I don't even wear it. [Nathan] was only good to you when he could get something out of you, all right? He was two-faced, and I'm not ashamed to tell you. It's the truth."

Such sentiments were the exception to the rule. The overwhelming response to Nathan's death was one of fondness and respect. He was remembered as a tough boss but equally as a good man. A young Jimmy Bologna was one of the workers who cried as Nathan's funeral motorcade passed by the store.

"I don't care if you were sixteen or seventeen years old, like me, or you were a Sinta, who was sixty," Bologna said. "Everybody looked up to him. Everybody respected him. Not because he started with very little and made a success but because of how he treated people. How you treat people is how you're going to be remembered. Not because you sell a hundred million hot dogs. Anybody can sell a hundred million hot dogs in the course of time. But it's *how* you sold a hundred million hot dogs that's the way you're going to be remembered."

Of course, the person wounded most deeply by Nathan's death was Ida. "After Grandpa died, she just didn't want to go on," said her grandson Steve. "She had no connection to life anymore."

Steve recalls seeing his grandmother during this period in her apartment in North Miami. She wept a lot and tried to relieve her sadness by throwing herself into cooking, her favorite occupation. Obviously depressed, Ida gave Steve a bleak picture of her existence.

"You know," she said, "I have no reason to live, no reason to cook, now that Grandpa's gone."

Ida died of heart failure on the day before Christmas 1976, at age seventy-nine.

Wetson's, once a thriving fast-food chain, had fallen on hard times by the midseventies. Founded in 1959 by Herb Wetanson, the restaurants were slavish imitators of McDonald's. Wetanson had visited the same original San Bernardino McDonald's that influenced Ray Kroc. His stores served "Big W" hamburgers in imitation of Big Macs and displayed orange circles in imitation of golden arches.

At one time, the chain had seventy outlets scattered across Long Island and the New York metropolitan area, but that number had dwindled by 1975, when the Wetson's chain entered bankruptcy.

As he had several times before (Roadside Rest, Toffeneti's,

Adventurer's Inn), Murray swooped down upon a business that had already closed its doors. Nathan's Famous and Wetson's merged in 1975. At that time, the Wetson's chain was comprised of forty-three company-owned stores and ten franchised ones, so on paper, the merger must have looked like a good match.

It wasn't. Murray imported many executives from Wetson's, including Harold Norbitz and his son Wayne, a man who would eventually be named to lead the entire company. The acquisition marked the beginning of a downward spiral that left the combined businesses awash in red ink. Many of the Wetson's stores were failing and located in unsuitable locations. Instead of lifting Nathan's Famous up, the merger dragged it down.

Murray attempted to follow the same prescription he had disparaged when his brother first proposed it, opening small "Nathan's Juniors" with limited menus. In a fast-food marketplace crowded with McDonald's, Burger King, and Wendy's franchises, those didn't work either.

The failing Nathan's Famous outlets began to gain a seedy reputation. One of them, at Eighth Street and Sixth Avenue in Greenwich Village, was the target of a very public fight in the late seventies, when a local community board campaigned to have it closed down. New York City had hit a rough patch. Bankruptcy was a real possibility. These were the days of the famous headline FORD TO CITY: DROP DEAD! The city's financial problems filtered down to the streets in plagues of crime, homelessness, and drug use.

All this hit city businesses hard. Activists portrayed the Greenwich Village Nathan's Famous as a "shooting gallery" full of junkies and the "absolute dregs" of the neighborhood. Nathan, the neatnik and control freak, would have been appalled.

"Once, when I went in, the security guard served me my

drink," said Rita Lee, who sat on Community Board 2. "When I turned my back for a second and looked back, a dog was eating out of my plate."

"The community was not happy with us, and we were not happy with them," said Murray. "They said [the store] attracted the wrong people, and I couldn't convince them that it wasn't Nathan's fault."

The community board succeeded in kicking the place out of the neighborhood. But similar problems cropped up elsewhere. When families didn't come, the atmosphere of the empty stores turned sour. Part of the issue was the chain's prices, which had risen steadily from the post–World War II period onward.

The nickel dog was long gone. Nathan had pronounced his own eulogy over it in August 1970. "If hot dogs were still selling for five cents," he mused, "the country would be in bad shape." By the fifties, the price of a frank had gone up to fifteen cents, with drinks for a dime and crinkle-cut fries ten cents for a small cone cup and fifteen cents for a large one. During the sixties, those prices had doubled and then doubled again.

Oddly enough, for a business founded on a nickel hot dog, other fast-food outlets now undercut Nathan's Famous prices. A frank-fries-and-drink dinner for a family could cost five or even six dollars at the time, while at McDonald's or Wendy's, a meal could be had for three or four dollars. The lights on the Nathan's Famous landscape began to wink out, as twenty stores closed one after another, all in the vital New York metropolitan market.

The rise and fall of the chain during these years can be traced to the number of outlets that were operating. In 1974, there were eighteen. After the Wetson's merger in 1975, the number ballooned to fifty-three. Seven years later it had fallen back down to twenty-three.

Nathan's Famous found itself locked in a losing game of catch-up. In response to McDonald's popular Happy Meals, introduced in the summer of 1979, the chain debuted plastic hand puppets of its new mascot, Mr. Frankie, along with a "Happy Card" discount system and a free "Fun Book" for the kiddies. None of the measures found favor with a fickle public.

"We saw the handwriting on the wall, a little too late, I guess," Murray told the *New York Times* in 1981, in an article headlined NATHAN'S HUNT FOR AN UPTURN.

That year, the company posted a $1.6 million loss. The price of Nathan's Famous stock plummeted to a dollar a share. The million-dollar paper fortunes of the Handwerker clan had abruptly evaporated. The family still owned the Coney Island property and the store building itself, which Murray had leased to the company for a term of sixty years.

The specter of the nickel frankfurter continued to dog the company long after a series of steep price hikes. At the seventieth anniversary celebration of the Times Square Nathan's in 1986, Mayor Ed Koch jokingly complained about the demise of the five-cent hot dog.

Murray grabbed the microphone from the mayor. Nathan's would bring back the five-cent hot dog, he said, when the city brought back the five-cent subway ride. But more had changed with Nathan's Famous than higher prices. The decade of the eighties represented a trough from which the business barely emerged intact.

By then Sol's experiment with Snacktime had ended, at least partly a victim of the same changing realities that had hit Coney Island and the rest of the Nathan's Famous outlets so hard. He had opened another outlet and had advisers pressuring him to go national. But the rampant street crime of the period scared away

Snacktime's late-night customers. In 1977, tired of the daily grind, Sol decided he had had enough. He sold the stores and devoted himself to progressive politics, the true love of his life.

In 1984, Nathan's Famous, Inc. licensed Smithfield's, the giant pork producer and meat-packer, to make its all-beef frankfurters, to be sold under the store's brand for sale at supermarkets. The green-and-yellow logo eventually would be seen on grocery shelves throughout the country. It was all part of a Murray-led initiative to pry the company off the financial floor. Slowly, he began to right the listing ship. Sales increased, and the stock price rebounded somewhat. In 1987, Nathan's Famous, Inc. was sold for $22 million and taken private by Equicor Group, Ltd.

Two years later, the executives who led the buyout resigned. Stuart Benson and William Landberg took control in 1989. They hired Robert J. Sherman, a former Wall Street executive who had been with Prudential-Bache, to run the company. In 1990, Nathan's Famous, Inc. registered a $6.1 million loss, the largest in the company's history.

The board of directors dismissed Benson, Landberg, and Sherman, putting in place new management headed by former Wetson's executive Wayne Norbitz. The reorganized company survived a brush with Chapter 11 to become profitable once again. Management took Nathan's Famous back on the public stock exchange, offering shares on NASDAQ.

Murray had left the business in 1987, the year Equicor took Nathan's Famous private. He and Dorothy retired to Florida. Upon his death in May 2011, the *New York Times* hailed him in an obituary headline: MURRAY HANDWERKER, WHO MADE NATHAN'S MORE FAMOUS, DIES AT 89. His support for the Coney Island arts community, his achievements in creating popular gathering places in Oceanside and Yonkers, were also celebrated.

All of Murray's big-store behemoths fell, one after another. Bulldozers demolished the former Roadside Rest in June 1976. A condemnation proceeding that was part of a Forty-Second Street redevelopment project closed the Times Square restaurant in 1990, and eventually the towering Condé Nast building occupied the site. Nathan's Famous Yonkers, the old Adventurer's Inn, was the last to go, torn down in 2011. Another Nathan's will rise in its place, 3,500 square feet as opposed to the old 10,000-square-foot current restaurant, built in 1965.

"The menu will be the same [when it reopens], but the restaurant will be much smaller," said Nathan's Famous president and chief operating officer Wayne Norbitz. "Right now, that is a gigantic facility. The new one will be the size of a very large McDonald's."

Epilogue

An Old-Timer Shows Me the Way

"Where can you still get a good, old-fashioned frankfurter?"
Nathan and his grandson Lloyd Handwerker.

CONEY ISLAND IN the aftermath of a hot dog contest deflates like a party balloon.

At the 2015 Nathan's Famous International Hot Dog Eating Contest, a relative newcomer, twenty-three-year-old Matt "the Megatoad" Stonie, beats out perennial winner Joey "Jaws" Chestnut by downing sixty-two dogs to Joey's sixty. Just to put those numbers in perspective, a distant third contestant manages only thirty-five and a half.

For the occasion, Nathan's Famous president and COO Wayne Norbitz announces the company will donate one hundred thousand of its signature all-beef hot dogs to the Food Bank for New York City.

Looking around Coney Island that day, I sense a decline in the excitement about the contest. Maybe it's because the amazing Takeru Kobayashi isn't here, a champion who voluntarily absented himself six years ago over a squabble with the organizers. But perhaps there's a chance that the new Stonie-Chestnut rivalry will revitalize the event.

Nostalgia isn't what it used to be. I find it hard to let go of the idea that something real, something vital of the past was lost when my grandfather and people like him left the scene. The generational mythology goes something like this. We'll never see the likes of Nathan Handwerker again. The golden age has passed, replaced with corporate sponsors and televised binge-fests.

In the go-go atmosphere of the present day, my sentimental attachment to the way Nathan's Famous used to be seems irrelevant. People have always wished for "the good old days." Right now, immigrants all over America work just as hard as my grandfather ever did. The country has experienced incredible surges of innovation since the so-called Greatest Generation retired from the stage.

The Nathan's Famous is nowadays more of a licensing business. Consumers get to know the name from the supermarket, the movie theater, and the convenience store, from ball games and from the eating contest. Nathan's Famous now sells potato chips, mustard, and barbecue sauce, among other products.

There are several different types of Nathan's Famous frankfurters available at most grocery stores, including the "Coney Island Original," with natural casing, just like the old days. Simply in terms of satisfying the greatest number people with the most hot dogs, the modern, retooled, corporate-owned version of the Nathan's Famous frankfurter is the all-time winner.

Or at least a contender. With $71 million in 2014 sales, Nathan's Famous ranks as the fifth-most popular hot dog in America, behind four other brands: Vienna Beef, Kunzler & Company, Oscar Mayer, and Ball Park Franks.

Most of the franks consumed today—$700 million worth—are purchased at retail stores, not hot dog stands. The vast majority of frankfurters sold in the modern era have a standardized shape and appearance. They are almost always skinless, and thus, snap-less.

Some of the archival footage I used in my documentary film shows Nathan's Famous frankfurters in their glorious, Technicolor prime. The fat, glistening sausages rest in their buns, offering themselves up to that first juicy bite.

These marvels were the direct result of one man's will to excel, to be ever watchful, to devote himself to the proposition that quality can be gained and maintained only by ceaseless, unflagging effort. He insisted. He worked. He was always there. Compromise was the enemy. Laziness and the untoasted bun were sins.

Jiro Dreams of Sushi is another documentary film with a subject similar to my own—it's about a small restaurant, a rigorous master, and a father-son relationship. The Japanese philosophy of *shokunin kishitsu* ("spirit of the craft") is central to sushi chef Jiro Ono's success. The question posed by *shokunin kishitsu* is simple: How can we do the same thing day after day, year in and year out, with no loss of focus, no compromise on quality, no lessening of the energy that we bring to the task?

Sushi or frankfurters or filmmaking or writing or just plain old getting up in the morning, it doesn't much matter. How do we bring our best to it? How do we not, as the slang phrase goes, "sleep on life"?

My grandfather had a less fancy version of *shokunin kishitsu*: "Everything is common sense."

I remember going to the post-Nathan, corporate-run Nathan's Famous in Coney Island during the nineties, the old original store, now updated. With me were a couple of old-time employees, Hy Brown and Felix Vasquez. They noticed a change in the layout right away. Whereas in their day, the grills were up against the front counter and the cash registers were behind the server, now a row of cash registers faced toward the customers, and the grills were in back.

A subtle difference. The move was no doubt dictated by some efficiency expert schooled in time-motion studies, or perhaps board of health rules imposed with the thought that reaching directly over the food to serve the customers could be dangerous or unsanitary. But to me—and to Hy Brown and Felix Vasquez—the change symbolized a switch in philosophy. Money first, indicated the new arrangement. Food later.

Another change: The griddles were no longer heated by natural gas. Gone was the former method of increasing and decreasing the gas-fired flames to respond to demand. Electric griddles are much less easy to adjust. The cooks had only limited control over how cooked the franks were.

We sampled the fare. Hy Brown dug into an order of Nathan's Famous fried potatoes.

"Oh, my gosh. They are really not cooked enough," he said. "They should be browner and crisper. See, you can see the oil here and the oil on my fingers. That's a little too much oil. Either the oil's not hot enough or they didn't leave it in long enough."

"Nathan's turning in his grave," Felix added.

Does it matter? On both sides of us, customers crowded at the counters to place their orders. It wasn't the classic crush of the old-time Nathan's Famous, but the place was doing a steady business nonetheless. The modern Coney Island store racks up $8 million in annual sales. Who cared if the potatoes were sometimes not cut fresh at the store, that they were served soggy?

But there are voices crying in the wilderness. Complaints and laments on Internet message boards and online reviews: "In my day . . ."; "It used to be . . ."; "I remember . . ."

Maybe no one at the current-day Nathan's Famous notices. Or perhaps it is worth a few points of profit to the corporate owners—and the shareholders they are beholden to—that the workers do not heat the oil sufficiently or that they lessen the cooking time. Maybe it cuts a few pennies from the store's electric bill.

More likely, the expertise and attention to detail aren't there. Nathan-style vigilance is similar to the lost art of the medieval stone mason or the Italian Renaissance plasterer. *Shokunin kishitsu*? Spirit of the craft? What the hell is that?

Wandering among the weary thousands who showed up for the hot dog contest and are now trailing home, I run into a Coney Island old-timer, Joe Sciammetta, who worked the carnival rides and boardwalk during the sixties.

"I worked on the Tornado back in those days. I remember going to Nathan's there, the hot dog might've been, around thirty-five or fifty cents at that time?"

He gets more and more excited with each word.

"So I go to Sammy, I go, give me five hot dogs. The guy was quick. Before you know it you had five on the plate, the little cardboard plate, right? Mustard, everything on it, boom, he had the big tongs. You were in, you were out."

He shakes his head. "Now you go into Nathan's, I'm not gonna lie to you, it's not the same service. The quality of the hot dog ain't the same. I think it was a different grade hot dog. Something about that old grill, maybe, gave it the taste. The toasted bun, which they don't do anymore. That made it delicious."

He gestures toward the busy store on Surf Avenue.

"I can't even go there anymore. Even if there's two people ahead of me, it's like having twenty people ahead of me 'cause it takes forever. It's so frustrating. It's Nathan's, but it's not Nathan's."

"Okay, Joe," I say. "So where do you go these days for a hot dog? Where can you still get a good, old-fashioned frankfurter?"

"Oh, I can't go now, but I'll tell you how to get there."

He suggests a nearby Russian delicatessen. When I track down the place, sure enough, long linked strings of fat, beautiful frankfurters rest in a glass-fronted display case. The store has some of the franks cooking on an aluminum foil–covered grill.

I indicate the franks to the shop lady.

"Can I get one of those?"

"What do you want on it?" she asks,

"Just mustard, nothing else."

She prepares the hot dog and serves me. I've fallen into a sort of time travel daze and don't dare ask for an order of crinkle-cut fries, with the crispy bits still in the bottom of the cellophane bag.

"How much?"

"A nickel," she says.

I'm kidding. She doesn't say that. But the price is less than a Nathan's Famous dog today.

The smell of the frank is intoxicating. I don't want to break the spell, but finally I bite down.

Snap!

Acknowledgments

Three people deserve my very special thanks, and they all could not be more loved. To my dad, my role model, for his integrity, quiet strength, and rebellious spirit. To my mom, an extraordinary caregiver: I love you. And I love you, Leslie. You made this all possible. Thank you for your intelligence, creativity, and passion.

An especially huge thank-you to Hy Brown, still sharp as a tack at ninety-two. I can't thank him enough for his generosity and knowledge of all things Nathan's. Thanks to Jay Cohen, my grandfather's "stepson," for so much heartfelt insight into Nathan and Nathan's Famous; Jimmy Bologna, a survivor to the core and a treasure; Felix Vasquez, for his tremendous humanity and spunk; Richard Traunstein, who was equal parts hilarious and thoughtful; Sidney Handwerker, a smart, lovely man; Al Shalik, for his fantastic stories told in his inimitable style. Thanks to Joe Handwerker, who gave fifty years to Nathan's, you are deeply appreciated; to Murray and Dorothy Handwerker, for their great hospitality, time spent with me, and for their deep devotion to the business; and Steve Handwerker, for his many important insights into our grandparents and the business.

Thanks also to my sisters Nora and Lisa Handwerker; to Noah Delgado De Torres, Ilana Aide Handwerker, and Miguel Delgado De Torres; to Jacob and Rose Handwerker, Anna Singer, Sidney and Lorraine Handwerker, Lena and Hyman Schuchman, Jack and Leah Dreitzer, Max and Claire Kamiel, Bill Handwerker, Ken

Handwerker, Leah Sternshein, Lou Sternshein, David Sternshein, Alan Sternshein, Fran Basch, Russell and Ivan Basch, Hannah Sternshein, and to the entire extended Handwerker family; to my grandparents Chaim and Dora Geller and the entire Geller family; the entire Siegel family; and Jared DeFrancesco.

My gratitude also goes out to the great folks at Flatiron Books, including Colin Dickerman, James Melia, and Whitney Frick for the care and attention they brought to this project; to Gil Reavill, who conducted historical research and took hundreds of hours of interviews, then helped to weave them into stories and those stories into a book. To Paul Bresnick, my literary agent, who in very Nathan-like fashion made this whole book possible.

Thanks to the unbelievably generous workers: Maria Argano, Hyman Silverglad, Eddie Fuerst, Bob Levine, Johnny Poa, Izzy Rodriguez, Sol Seiderman, Sol Gaber, Frank Soto, Thomas Settle, Sinta Low, Leonard Markowitz, Marvin Lubeck, Paul Berlly, Jose Santiago, Sammy Fariello, Morty Matz, Max Rosey, Al Harris, Marsha and Marty Abramson.

On my documentary, for this book, and in other aspects, I am grateful for the participation of Madeleine Molyneaux, Russell Green, Heather Greene, Hanna Buck, Charlotte Farrel, Alex Bayer, Mandy Kordal, Angelo Corrao, Sean R. Smith, Dylan Puchala, Jeremiah Hawkins, Jeremiah Zagar, Frankie Marin, Sheri Manson, Rick Schnupp. To my good friends and the people of Coney Island: David Hellman, Hiroko Takeda, Margaret Cohen, Richard Cohen, Pegi Vail, Melvin Estrella, Terry Savage, Frank and Caroline Morris, Ergo Phizmiz, Paul Eli, Lenora Todaro, Josh Simons, Sonny Aronson, Amy Nicholson, Phil Buehler, Michael Schwartz, Caroline McCrory, Don Purple, Bea Sager, Harold Feinstein, Hal Ginsburg, Mike Zwerling, Pac Lab, Du Art, Maurice Schecter, Susan Hermuth, Nancy Arner, Jon and Christina Tucker,

Stan Fox, Zoe Beloff, Jay Singer, Matt Harvey, Matt Kennedy, Dewey Albert, Paul Georgoulakos, Gregory Bitetzakis, Johnny "Blackie" Casillo, Morris and Doris Sunshine, Larry Moyer, Nat Dubler, Larry Rocco, Joe Sciammetta, Jim McDonnell, Richard Egan, Charlie Denson, Dick Zigun, Rob Leddy, Tricia Vita, Michael Quinn, Roseanne Giordano-Semler, Al Lasher, Abe Feinstein, Stewart Kampel, Jimmy Prince, John Dorman of Phillips Candy, Mirela Iverac, Pat Auletta and family, Sylvia and David Barsion, Tom Volpe; thanks to all of the festival and theater programmers who supported my film; thanks to South Carolina University, Yad Vashem, New York Public Library Archives, the Mangels family, the Williams family, Tom's of Coney Island, the Vouderis family of Wonderwheel, and George Shea.

Author's Note

When I was ten years old, I asked my parents for a tape recorder so I could record my grandfather's stories. I had always loved listening to him speak about his childhood and his restaurant, Nathan's Famous of Coney Island. One day while my grandparents were visiting, I started recording my grandpa. He sat next to me on the edge of my bed. Fifteen minutes into the interview, my grandma Ida knocked on the door, calling him to eat. We never finished our talk.

Luckily, my cousin David Sternschein also interviewed our grandfather, and the recorded words of Nathan Handwerker represent an important historical document about a fascinating real-life figure. I was also lucky to be able to reach out to so many people who offered their recollections of Nathan Handwerker. They were his sons, grandsons, in-laws, other relatives, employees, patrons, as well as a few public figures. I would like to extend my gratitude once again to all those who cooperated in helping me chronicle my grandfather's life.

Interviews

Marsha Abramson (public relations for Nathan's Famous), Dewey Albert (founder of Astroland amusement park in Coney Island), Maria Argano (worker at Nathan's Famous), Pat Auletta (Coney Island businessman and longtime patron of Nathan's Famous), Paul Berlly (sales manager for Hygrade Provisions), James Bologna (longtime worker at Nathan's Famous), Hy Brown (former general manager of Nathan's Famous), Jay Cohen (former general manager of Nathan's Famous), John Doorman (formerly of Philip's Candy in Coney Island), Jack and Leah Dreitzer (longtime former worker at Nathan's Famous and his wife, sister of Ida Handwerker), Richard Eagan (cofounder of Coney Island Hysterical Society), Maxine Eimicke (wife of Victor Eimicke, consultant at Nathan's Famous), Aaron Eliach (accountant at Nathan's Famous), Stan Fox (Coney Island worker and longtime patron of Nathan's Famous), Ed Fuerst (former worker at Coney Island Nathan's Famous), Sol Gabor (former worker at Nathan's Famous), Luis Gargulio (longtime patron of Nathan's Famous), Hal Ginsberg (former worker at Nathan's Famous), Marty Greenfield, Dorothy "Dottie" Handwerker (wife of Murray Handwerker), Ida Handwerker (Nathan's wife and my grandmother), Joe Handwerker (Nathan Handwerker's nephew and right-hand man, former vice president of Nathan's Famous), Minnie Handwerker (my mother), Murray Handwerker (Nathan Handwerker's son and my uncle), Nathan Handwerker (my grandfather, founder and owner of Nathan's Famous), Phillip Handwerker (Nathan Handwerker's brother), Sam Handwerker (Joe Handwerker's son and a longtime former worker at Nathan's Famous), Sol Handwerker (Nathan Handwerker's son and my father), Steve Handwerker (Nathan Handwerker's grandson, Murray's son, and my cousin), Sidney Handwerker (Nathan Handwerker's nephew and former worker and manager at Nathan's Famous), Officer Jerod (policeman on the beat in Coney Island), Max and Claire Kamiel (good friends of Nathan and Ida Handwerker), Stewart Kampel (longtime patron of Nathan's Famous), Kenny Knudsen (longtime patron of Nathan's Famous), Ed Koch (former NYC mayor), Gary Lapow (longtime patron of Nathan's Famous), Albert Lasher (public relations for Nathan's Famous), Bob Levine (worked at Ocean-side Nathan's Famous), Herman Levinson (longtime patron of Nathan's Famous), Sol Litchman (longtime worker at Nathan's Famous), Bill Livert (worked with Murray at Nathan's Famous Oceanside/Roadside Rest), Marvin Lubeck (former worker at Na-than's Famous), John Manbeck (Brooklyn historian), Morty Matz (public relations), Larry Moyers (longtime patron of Nathan's Famous), Wayne Norbitz (present COO of Nathan's Famous), Johnny Poa (former worker at Nathan's Famous), Lou Posner (longtime patron of Nathan's Famous), Jimmy Prince (owner of Major's Meat Market on Coney Island), Izzy Rodriguez (longtime worker at Nathan's Famous), Charles Schneck (former head of per-sonnel at Nathan's Famous), Hyman and Lena Schuchman (brother-in-law and sister of Nathan Handwerker and co-owners of the Atlantis in Coney Island), Joe Sciammetta (former worker at Coney Island), Al Shalik (manager at Nathan's Famous and gen-eral manager at Snacktime), George Shea (public relations and host of Nathan's Famous hot dog contest), Sol Sidelman (former worker at Nathan's Famous), Hyman Silverglad (former worker at Nathan's Famous), Anna Singer (Nathan Handwerker's sister and Coney Island custard stand operator), Frank Soto (former general man-ager of Nathan's Famous), Doris and Morris Sunshine (longtime patrons of Nathan's Famous), Joel Thames (longtime patron of Nathan's Famous), Richard Traunstein (former worker in the din-ing room at Nathan's Famous), Felix Vasquez (former worker in dining room at Nathan's Famous), and Dick Zigun (founder of Coney Island USA).

Notes

Chapter 1: Narol

8   *"the poorest province in Europe"*: *God's Playground: A History of Poland: Volume II: 1795 to the Present*, by Norman Davies, Oxford University Press (2005), pp. 106–108.

9   *"kaptsonim"*: *The Golden Age Shtetl: A New History of Jewish Life in East Europe*, by Yohanan Petrovsky-Shtern, Princeton University Press (2014), p. 9.

10   *"The shadow of the Holocaust"*: *Shtetl: The Life and Death of a Small Town and the World of Polish Jews*, by Eva Hoffman, Houghton Mifflin (1997), p. 7.

Chapter 2: To America

26   SS Neckar, *one of four*: "S/S Neckar (2), Norddeutscher Lloyd," *Norway-Heritage: Hands Across the Sea*, http://bit.ly/1NEdlZX.

Chapter 3: Luncheonette Man

31   *Overall, only a small number*: *The Statue of Liberty*, by Anne Hempstead, Heinemann Publishers (2006), p. 20. See also History.com, "Nine Things You Didn't Know About Ellis Island," http://bit.ly/1R63aea.

31   *"the Plymouth Rock of its day"*: *American Civil Religion: What Americans Hold Sacred*, by Peter Gardella, Oxford University Press (2013), p. 210.

32   *Ellis Island was where the term: The New Joys of Yiddish: Completely Updated*, by Leo Rosten, edited by Lawrence Bush, Crown (2001), p. 177.

33   *40 percent of the people: Ancestry Magazine*, Vol. 18, No. 3 (May-Jun 2000), p. 43.

33   *a metropolis of five million: Summary of Vital Statistics, The City of New York: Population and Mortality*, Statistical Analysis and Reporting and Quality Improvement Units of the Bureau of Vital Statistics, NYC Health (2010), p. 4.

35   *And three quarters of the workers: Encyclopaedia Judaica*, Cecil Roth, ed., Macmillan Books (1972), "USA" vol. 15, pp. 1617–1618. Also see *Virtual Jewish Library*, http://bit.ly /1GFGHz4.

36   *the fact that employers "sweated" their workers: Lower East Side Tenement Museum*, "Sweatshops," http://bit.ly/1L7Gvg6.

36   *"shut in the qualmy rooms"*: Jacob Riis, quoted in *The Jewish East Side: 1881–1924*, Milton Hindus, ed., Transaction Publishers (1996), p. 100.

38   *"We place absolute confidence"*: Philip Franklin quoted in *Unsinkable: The Full Story*, by Daniel Allen Butler, Frontline Books (2011), p. 168.

39   *"The scene on Broadway was awful"*: Letter from Alexander McComb to his mother, reprinted in *Lost Voices from the Titanic: The Definitive Oral History*, by Nick Barratt, St. Martin's Press (2010), p. 211.

Chapter 4: The Tenth Ward

44   *money brought to America: The Immigrant Jew in America*, National Liberal Immigration League, New York City, 1907.

45   *the neighborhood had a population:* "The Tenement House

Exhibition of 1899," by Lawrence Veiller, in *Empire City: New York Through the Centuries*, Kenneth T. Jackson and David S. Dunbar, eds., Columbia University Press (2005), p. 421.

45 *"The rooms were damp, filthy, foul, and dark"*: cited in *A History of the Jews in America*, by Howard Morley Sachar, Vintage (1993), p. 142.

45 *Rent of a tenement apartment: Lower East Side Tenement Museum*, "Housing," http://bit.ly/1K6lLBp.

45 *Pushcarts were another common neighborhood livelihood:* Hidden New York: A Guide to Places That Matter, by Marci Reaven and Steven J. Zeitlin, Rivergate Books (2006), p. 167.

46 *A survey of a Manhattan magistrate's court: The Rise and Fall of the Jewish Gangster in America*, by Albert Fried, Columbia University Press (1994), p. 8.

48 *a literacy test:* "Immigration Bill Vetoed by Taft on Account of Its Literacy Test," *The Spokesman-Review*, Spokane, Washington, Feb. 15, 1913.

48 *news of the sinking for eighteen straight days: New York Times*, April 15, 1912, to May 2, 1912.

49 *"The remote cause":* Titanica: The Disaster of the Century in Poetry, Song, and Prose, by Steven Biel, W. W. Norton & Company (1998), p. 59.

51 *"For forty years, I've worked":* "The Tale of the Other Max Garfunkel," *Lost City*, Feb 28, 2012, http://bit.ly/1RtO9nq.

Chapter 5: Nickel Empire

57 *On a busy summer's day:* "How Coney Island Became the Unlikely Birthplace of Outdoor Dining," by Alex Swerdloff,

The Vice Channels: *Munchies*, June 30, 2015, http://bit.ly /1OZraC5.

59   *In 1908, Albany established regulations:* "Enforce Law, Hughes Says," *New York Times*, June 13, 1908, p. 3.

60   *Feuchtwanger supposedly handed out gloves: Fast Food: Roadside Restaurants in the Automobile Age*, by John A. Jakle and Keith A. Sculle, Johns Hopkins University Press (1999), p. 163.

60   *Stevens instructed his staff:* " 'Hot Dog,' This Company Says, After Being in Business Almost 100 Years," by Gail Collins, *Los Angeles Times*, January 15, 1985, http://lat.ms /1LzykfS.

60   *Smallish pork sausages: America in So Many Words*, by David K. Barnhart and Allan A. Metcalf, Houghton Mifflin (1997), p. 192.

60   *The first verified use of the term:* "Origin of the Term 'Hot Dog,' " by Barry A. Popik, Gerald Leonard Cohen, and David Shulman, G. Cohen (2004), http://bit.ly/1Pjkyh6.

61   *There he first fabricated an innovation: Coney Island: Food & Dining*, by Jeffrey Stanton (1997), http://bit.ly/1FXRf1z.

62   *Three years later, Feltman purchased:* Ibid.

62   *"the first Tyrolean yodelers":* "Charles Feltman Dead; Coney Island Pioneer Who Turned Sandy Wastes into Pleasure Ground," *New York Times*, Sept. 21, 1910, p. 9.

63   *"shore dinner":* "Coney Island: The Parachute Pavilion Competition," by Zoe Ryan and Jonathan Cohen-Litant, Princeton Architectural Press (2007), p. 16.

63   *With the advent of World War I: Coney Island: The People's Playground*, Mickael Immerso, Rutgers University Press (2002), p. 131.

64   *In 1913, forty-six collapsed: US Banking History: Civil War to World War II,* by Richard S. Grossman, EH.Net Encyclopedia, edited by Robert Whaples (2008), http://bit.ly /1OZi48s.

Chapter 6: The Store

66   *"It is blatant, it is cheap":* Quoted in "Coney Island: The Ups and Downs of America's First Amusement Park," a documentary film by Ric Burns and Lisa Ades, *American Experience,* enhanced transcript, http://to.pbs.org/1JSzjjP

66   *The good doctor labeled: Coney Island,* Immerso, p. 3.

68   *Every year, Feltman's served:* Ibid., p. 131.

69   *Coney Island became the most postcarded venue:* Quoted in "Coney Island," *American Experience.* See also Laura J. Hoffman, *Coney Island,* Arcadia Publishing (2014), p. 7.

Chapter 7: Ida

78   *Russia's celebrated June Advance:* "Steamrollered in Galicia: The Austro-Hungarian Army and the Brusilov Offensive, 1916," by J. Schindler, *War in History,* Vol. 10, No. 1 (2003), pp. 27–59.

79   *The navy erected a full-scale wooden mock-up:* "The Battle Ship in Union Square: Building the USS *Recruit* in the Heart of New York City," by Amanda Uren, *Mashable* (2015), http://on.mash.to/1OZixYq.

88   *Fifty to a hundred million victims:* "Updating the accounts: global mortality of the 1918–1920 'Spanish' influenza pandemic," by J. Mueller and M. P. Johnson, *Bulletin of the History of Medicine* (Spring 2002), pp.105–15. See also "1918 Influenza: the Mother of All Pandemics," by

Jeffrey K. Taubenberger and David M. Moren, Centers for Disease Control and Prevention (2006), http://1.usa.gov /1LzBCjh.

88   *"I saw hundreds of young stalwart men": The Enduring Vision: A History of the American People*, by Paul Boyer, Clifford Clark, Karen Halttunen, Joseph Kett, Neal Salisbury, Wadsworth (1995), p. 686.

88   *a record 869 New Yorkers died:* "Timeline: Influenza Across America in 1918," *American Experience: Influenza 1918*, http://to.pbs.org/1eAB1su.

Chapter 8: The Frank

93   *The filth, sludge, and scraps: The Jungle: The Uncensored Original Edition*, Upton Sinclair, Sharp Press (2003), pp. 81–82.

97   *Frankfurter consumption really took off:* "America in a Bun: A History of Hot Dogs," by Beth Kaiserman, *Highbrow Magazine*, July 10, 2013, http://bit.ly/1Zebz5o.

98   *"Mr. Slotkin's first loyalty":* New York Times, October 31, 1965, p. 87.

Chapter 11: The Count

137   *One of McKane's henchmen:* "K.F. Sutherland Killed by a Train," *New York Times*, May 21, 1910, p. 1.

Chapter 12: Growing Up Coney

151   *"baby hatcheries":* "The Incubated Babies of the Coney Island Boardwalk," by Michael Pollack, *New York Times*, August 2, 2015, p. B2.

160   *summer of 1934:* "50 Police Fight 1,000 in Coney Hot Dog Strike," *Brooklyn Daily Eagle*, June 11, 1934.

Chapter 13: The Season

165   *New York City's population at that time.* "Population of the
      100 Largest Urban Places: 1930," U.S. Bureau of the Census,
      June 15, 1998, http://1.usa.gov/1L7FdzE.

176   *Master builder and political insider Robert Moses:* "How
      the Coastline Became a Place to Put the Poor," by Jonathan
      Mahler, *New York Times*, Dec. 4, 2012, p. A29.

Chapter 14: The War

180   *Germany abandoned preparations: The 1939–1940 New
      York World's Fair,* by Bill Cotter, Arcadia Publishing (2009),
      p. 55. See also "Reich Withdraws from World's Fair," *New
      York Times,* April 27, 1938, pp. 1, 17.

180   *But the Jewish Palestine Pavilion: 1939–1940 New York
      World's Fair,* Cotter, p. 61. See also "Performing the State:
      The Jewish Palestine Pavilion at the New York World's Fair,
      1939/40," by Barbara Kirshenblatt-Gimblett in *The Art of Be-
      ing Jewish in Modern Times,* Barbara Kirshenblatt-Gimblett
      and Jonathan Karp, eds., University of Pennsylvania Press
      (2006), p. 98.

182   *Franklin Delano Roosevelt engineered the visit:* "King Tries
      Hot Dog and Asks for More," by Felix Belaire, Jr., *New York
      Times,* June 12, 1939, p. 1.

184   *"Eiffel Tower of Brooklyn": Coney Island: Lost and Found,* by
      Charles Denson, Ten Speed Press (2002), p. 123.

Chapter 17: Roadside Rest

235   *"I didn't want to see Coney Island lose":* Murray Handwerker
      interview quoted in Denson, *Coney Island,* p. 76.

236   *"Moses has shrunk":* "Nathan Handwerker Good Dog,"

by Jay Maeder, (New York) *Daily News*, March 31, 1999, http://nydn.us/1FTYGHb.

238   *"If I had a brick for every time"*: "The Ray Kroc Story," mcdonalds.com, http://bit.ly/1dqev3F.

241   *"one of the many imitators"*: "A Tribute to and Brief History of Our Own Nathan's Roadside Rest," by Howard B. Levy, *Our Little Town*, http://bit.ly/1NoLrko.

245   *"[Nathan] was very concerned"*: "Early History of Nathan's in Oceanside: An Exclusive Interview with Murray (Son of Nathan) Handwerker," by Howard B. Levy, *Our Little Town*, http://bit.ly/1GM5HKp.

246   *Robert Moses and his massive development projects*: Including 4,091 public housing units, 3,629 HUD-subsidized and Mitchell-Lama units, and over 1,000 Astella Development Corporation–built units. See "West of Nathan's: Planning Coney Island's Residential Community," by Oksana Mironova, *The Architectural League's Urban Omnibus: The Culture of Citymaking* (2014), http://bit.ly/1NH5xXf.

246   *"enable Coney Island to fit into the pattern"*: New York Times, April 3, 1953, p. 1.

Chapter 18: Snacktime

259   *The National Labor Relations Board investigated*: "Nathan's Found Guilty of Unfair Labor Activities," by Damon Stetson, *New York Times*, Nov. 5, 1970, p. 63.

Chapter 19: Lion in Winter

263   *entered the language in 1947*: Oxford English Dictionary, citing *Toronto Daily Star*, April 5, 1947, p. 6.

Chapter 20. Endgame

276   *Nathan's Famous and Wetson's merged in 1975:* "Nathan's
       Builds on Its Core Product, Hot Dogs," *New York Times*,
       April 6, 2003; the merger was finally completed in March,
       1978: "Wetson's-Nathan's Merger Set," *New York Times*,
       March 28, 1978.

Selected Reading

Baker, Kevin. *Dreamland.* New York, NY: Harper, 1999.

Cannato, Vincent J. *American Passage: The History of Ellis Island.* New York, NY: Harper, 2009.

Denson, Charles. *Coney Island: Lost and Found.* Berkeley, CA: Ten Speed Press, 2002.

———. *Wild Ride: A Coney Island Roller Coaster Family.* Berkeley, CA: Dreamland Press, 2007.

Epstein, Lawrence J. *At the Edge of a Dream: The Story of Jewish Immigrants on New York's Lower East Side, 1880–1920.* San Francisco, CA: Jossey-Bass, 2007.

Fangone, Jason. *Horsemen of the Esophagus: Competitive Eating and the Big Fat American Dream.* New York, NY: Crown, 2006.

Frank, Robin Jaffee, ed. *Coney Island: Visions of an American Dreamland, 1861–2008.* New Haven, CN: Yale University Press, 2015

Handwerker, Murray. *Nathan's Famous Hot Dog Cookbook.* New York, NY: Grosset & Dunlap, 1968.

Immerso, Michael. *Coney Island: The People's Playground.* New Brunswick, NJ: Rutgers University Press, 2002.

Jakle, John A., and Keith A. Sculle. *Fast Food: Roadside Restaurants in the Automobile Age.* Baltimore, MD: Johns Hopkins University Press, 1999.

Kasson, John F. *Amusing the Million: Coney Island at the Turn of the Century.* New York, NY: Hill and Wang, 1978.

Marianski, Stanley, Adam Marianski, and Miroslaw Gebarowski. *Polish Sausages: Authentic Recipes and Instructions.* Seminole, FL: Bookmagic, 2009.

Petrovsky-Shtern, Yohanan. *The Golden Age Shtetl: A New History of Jewish Life in East Europe.* Princeton, NJ: Princeton University Press, 2014.